YOUNG AMERICANS CHRISTIAN SCHOOL
1701 HONEY CREEK ROAD SE
CONYERS, GA 30013

BRITAIN AND THE CONGO
IN THE NINETEENTH CENTURY

Sir William Mackinnon   J. F. Hutton
                          H. M. Stanley

(Reproduced by kind permission of Rear-Admiral R. M. J. Hutton, R.N.)

BRITAIN AND THE CONGO
IN THE
NINETEENTH CENTURY

BY

ROGER ANSTEY

GREENWOOD PRESS, PUBLISHERS
WESTPORT, CONNECTICUT

Library of Congress Cataloging in Publication Data

Anstey, Roger.
   Britain and the Congo in the nineteenth century.

   Reprint. Originally published: Oxford [Oxfordshire] : Clarendon Press, 1962.
   Bibliography: p.
   Includes index.
   1. Zaire--History--To 1908. 2. British--Zaire--History--19th century. 3. Zaire--Relations--Great Britain. 4. Great Britain--Relations--Zaire. I. Title.
DT654.A57 1981   967.5'1   81-20224
ISBN 0-313-23366-7 (lib. bdg.)   AACR2

© Oxford University Press 1962.

This reprint has been authorized by the Oxford University Press.

Reprinted in 1981 by Greenwood Press,
A division of Congressional Information Service, Inc.
88 Post Road West, Westport, Connecticut 06881

Printed in the United States of America

10 9 8 7 6 5 4 3 2 1

TO
E. M. A.
AND TO THE MEMORY OF
J. F. A.

PREFACE

I AM anxious to acknowledge a number of debts of gratitude.

To the Librarians of the School of Oriental & African Studies, of University College, Ibadan, of the Durham Colleges, of Cambridge University, of the Institute of Historical Research, of the Bodleian, of Rhodes House, of the Scottish National Library and of the *Bibliothèque Royale*, Brussels and their staffs I should like to express deep appreciation of a variety of services and kindnesses. The officers and attendants of the Public Record Office and British Museum have been extremely helpful, whilst M.P-H. Desneux and the archive staff of the *Ministère des Affaires Etrangères*, Brussels greatly facilitated my research on a number of occasions. The Secretary of the Manchester Chamber of Commerce kindly allowed me to examine the relevant portions of the Chamber's records, whilst the late J. Arthur Hutton and in more recent days Rear-Admiral R. M. J. Hutton gave me all possible help in my inquiries about J. F. Hutton. Col. J. W. C. Kirk kindly permitted me to examine portions of his father's papers and the Chief Archivist of the Central African Archives arranged for a portion of the Johnston papers to be microfilmed and sent me (they are now in the possession of the Royal Commonwealth Society).

At an earlier stage of this work, the Senate of University College, Ibadan awarded me a sabbatical term. I also gratefully acknowledge a number of grants from the Durham Colleges Research Fund.

I owe a very great deal to the guidance of Dr. R. E. Robinson, the late Dr. E. C. Martin, and Professor K. O. Dike. Professor J. Stengers of the *Université Libre*, Brussels has given me immense help, both in discussion and in assisting me to find my way amongst the Belgian archives, and Dr. Roland Oliver, as well as giving much helpful advice, undertook the labour of reading the manuscript at two different stages of this work, made numerous most helpful comments, and, altogether, has given me invaluable guidance. It will be evident to the reader that the *Mackinnon Papers* have been of particular importance in the making of this book. The collection was located by the enterprise of Mrs. J. Hemphill (*née* de Kiewiet). To all of these and to my wife, who has greatly encouraged me and patiently endured a good deal, I express my profound thanks. The faults in this book are my own.

The Durham Colleges in the   ROGER ANSTEY
   University of Durham.
June 1961.

CONTENTS

	List of Plates and Maps	xi
	Acknowledgements	xii
	Some Abbreviations used in Footnotes	xiii
I.	Tuckey's Expedition	1
II.	The Assertion of British Paramountcy on the Lower Congo and adjoining Coast (1)	10
III.	The Assertion of British Paramountcy on the Lower Congo and adjoining Coast (2) The Diplomatic Background	37
IV.	The Beginnings of British Collaboration with Leopold of the Belgians	57
V.	The Evolution of Britain's new Congo Policy	84
VI.	The British Opposition to the Anglo-Portuguese Treaty	113
VII.	The Anglo-Portuguese Treaty—Stiffening of Terms, Signature and Abandonment	139
VIII.	British Recognition of the *Association Internationale du Congo*	168
IX.	The Congo Railway Concession	186
X.	Aftermath and Conclusions	210
	Bibliography	231
	Appendix A: The Anglo-Portuguese Treaty	241
	Appendix B: Memorandum of the Congo Railway Syndicate	247
	Appendix C: Extracts of letter from Stanley to Johnston, 23 July 1883	251
	Index	253

LIST OF PLATES AND MAPS

Sir William Mackinnon, J. F. Hutton, and
H. M. Stanley   *Frontispiece*

Captain Tuckey's voyage in Africa   *facing p.* 8

Map of the western portion of the River Congo
and adjoining coast   32

Hauling canoes round the Inkisi Falls   82

Map of Equatoria   212

ACKNOWLEDGEMENTS

For permission to make certain quotations, acknowledgements are due to: The Royal Commonwealth Society and Dr. S. E. Crowe (S. E. Crowe, *The Berlin West Africa Conference, 1884–5*); Longmans, Green & Co. Ltd. (C. Lloyd, *The Navy and the Slave Trade*; H. C. F. Bell, *Lord Palmerston*; Lord E. Fitzmaurice, *The Life of Lord Granville, 1815–1891*); The Navy Records Society (*Naval Miscellany, III*); Chatto and Windus Ltd. (Sir Harry Johnston, *The Story of My Life*); Messrs. Hodder & Stoughton and Messrs. A. P. Watt & Son (Lady G. Cecil, *The Life of Robert, Marquis of Salisbury*); Sampson Low, Marston & Co. Ltd. (H. M. Stanley, *Through the Dark Continent; The Congo and the Founding of Its Free State; In Darkest Africa*); The Cambridge University Press (*The Cambridge History of the British Empire, III*); John Murray (S. Gwynn and G. Tuckwell, *The Life of Sir Charles W. Dilke*); *Académie Royale des Sciences d'Outre-Mer*, Brussels (A. Roeykens, *Léopold II et la Conférence Géographique de Bruxelles, 1876;* Dr. R. Slade, 'L'Attitude des Missions Protestantes vis-à-vis des Puissances Européenes au Congo avant 1884', *Bulletin des Seances de l'I.R.C.B.*, XXV–1954–2; J. Stengers, 'Rapport sur le Dossier "Correspondence Léopold II—Strauch" ', *Bulletin*, XXIV–1953–4); The National Archives of Rhodesia and Nyasaland (*The Johnston Papers*); The Hutchinson Publishing Group (F. Hird, *H. M. Stanley, The Authorised Life*); Charles Dessart (Baron P. van Zuylen, *L'Echiquier Congolais*); The Bodley Head Ltd. (E. Smith, *The Life of Sir Joseph Banks*); La Renaissance du Livre (E. Banning, *Mémoires*); and Mrs. D. M. Stanley (H. M. Stanley, *Autobiography*).

I am most indebted to Rear-Admiral R. M. J. Hutton, C.B., C.B.E., D.S.O., R.N. (Retd.) for permission to reproduce the photograph which forms the frontispiece, and to the proprietors of the *Illustrated London News* for permission to include a page of their journal's 'Stanley in Africa' supplement of 6 February 1878.

SOME ABBREVIATIONS USED IN FOOTNOTES

A. & P.	Accounts and Papers.
Ad.	Admiralty.
A/S Papers	Anti-Slavery Society Papers.
B.M.S.	Baptist Missionary Society.
B.o.T.	Board of Trade.
C.H.B.E.	Cambridge History of the British Empire.
C.O.	Colonial Office.
D.D.F.	*Documents Diplomatiques Français*.
Encl.	Enclosure.
F.O.	Foreign Office.
M.P.	Mackinnon Papers.
M. des A.E.	*Ministère des Affaires Etrangères* (Brussels).
Manch. Ch. Comm.	Manchester Chamber of Commerce.
n.d.	no date.
P.R.O.	Public Record Office.
S.P.	State Papers.

CHAPTER I

TUCKEY'S EXPEDITION

Your reasoning is quite thrown away upon Lord Bathurst and myself for we fully coincide with you in opinion as to the advantage of making an expedition up the Zaire. . . . We are quite prepared to sanction a small expense for discovering the source.[1]

So wrote Henry Goulburn, Under-Secretary of State for War and the Colonies, to Sir John Barrow, Second Secretary to the Admiralty, in July 1815. The wording of this reply of Goulburn makes clear that the proposal for an expedition up the Zaire —'the river that swallows all others', the modern Congo— had originated in the Admiralty, whilst the fact that the note was a private reply to Barrow suggests that the idea may have come from Barrow himself. This is inherently likely, for Barrow was a keen amateur geographer and was later to be responsible for the formation of the Royal Geographical Society.[2] But the commissioning of an expedition is not sufficiently explained by Barrow's enthusiasm for discovery. The proposal for a Congo expedition had, in fact, been put forward as the complement of a project already agreed[3]—an expedition through Senegal to the Upper Niger to trace the river's course beyond the Bussa rapids, where Mungo Park had met his end, and to discover its outlet. The belief that that outlet would prove to be the Nile had by this time been largely abandoned, but it was possible for respectable geographers to hold to one of three theories—that the Niger emptied itself into a great swamp in the heart of Africa, that it reached the sea in the Gulf of Guinea (the existence of the Delta was of course known, but it had so far proved impracticable to penetrate inland from the coast), or that it would prove to be identical with the Congo. The basis of this last theory was simply that the Niger was clearly a considerable river, that the Congo, by the evidence of the width of its estuary and flow of water at its mouth— 'thinking even to swallow the ocean', as Purchas had put it

[1] *Ad.1/2617*, Goulburn to Barrow, 28 July 1815, Private.
[2] *Dictionary of National Biography*, I, 1225-7.
[3] *Ad.1/2617*, Goulburn to Barrow, 28 July 1815, Private.

—was no less so, and that it was thought that a short distance from the coast the Congo turned decisively to the northward. Park himself held this third view and the influence of his considerable authority was thus conferred upon it.[1] Of more immediate significance, the arguments in favour of the identity of the Congo and Niger had recently been expounded in a popular journal and this had apparently been responsible for a revival of interest in that particular solution of the Niger problem.[2] It was this revival of interest which Barrow took up and sought to make effective by his proposal for a Congo expedition.

In origin, therefore, the proposed Congo expedition was a part of the Niger quest. That quest had begun with the foundation of the African Association in 1788[3] and, through this body, was linked to the wave of exploration and expansion which marked the beginnings of the Second British Empire. Best known of the episodes which marked the foundation of that empire are the three voyages of Captain Cook. Discovery and scientific observation were integral to these voyages but were not their only purpose. As the additional secret instructions for Cook's first voyage put it:

> ... the making discoveries of countries hitherto unknown, and the attaining a knowledge of distant parts which though formerly discovered have yet been but imperfectly explored, will redound greatly to the honour of this nation as a Maritime Power, as well as to the dignity of the Crown of Great Britain, and may tend greatly to the advancement of the trade and navigation thereof.[4]

In considering the origin of the Second British Empire as a whole, it is indeed a determination to extend British commerce by various means—and with a minimum of territorial responsibility—that is the primary motive at work. The reaching out for the Celebes, Cochin China and the China trade, the search for *Terra Australis Incognita* and the interest in the Falkland Islands as a key to the Pacific, the acquisition of the Cape as a

---

[1] For geographical information see especially J. N. L. Baker, *A History of Geographical Discovery and Exploration*, 2nd ed. (London, 1948), 302–6.
[2] *Narrative of an Expedition to explore the River Zaire* ... edited anonymously, but probably by Sir John Barrow (London, 1818), xvi–xvii.
[3] Baker, op. cit., 302–3. *Cambridge History of the British Empire*, II (Cambridge, 1940), 616–17.
[4] Additional Secret Instructions for Cook's first voyage, 30 July 1768, published in *Naval Miscellany* (London, The Navy Records Society, 1927), III, 347.

staging point on the traditional route to the riches of India and the East, all tell the same story.[1] The aims of the African Association were not exclusively commercial as were, say, those of the East India Company in its desire to open out the China trade. But the advancement of British trade was an important object of the Association, and both the Association and the British Government, when the latter assumed responsibility for the Niger quest, had as their major aim the development of trade with the peoples of the Niger basin.[2]

As foreshadowed in Goulburn's private note, official authorization of a Congo expedition was soon forthcoming,[3] and, as might be expected, the nature and general tenor of the instructions issued to its commander, Captain James K. Tuckey, R.N., make it clear that something more than geographical discovery for its own sake was envisaged, although, of course, accurate geographical knowledge was an important object. Tuckey's fundamental task was to assist in substantiating or disproving the hypothesis of the identity of the Niger and the Congo—ideally by following the latter's course until he met the expedition of Captain Peddie and Lieutenant Campbell which was to follow the course of the Upper Niger downstream. He was therefore instructed to give preference to the main channel as long as it flowed from between the north and the north-east. If and when this should prove no longer possible, in order that valuable geographical knowledge might still be gained, he was to ascend a supposed eastern or south-eastern branch which, if it proved to be navigable, would probably constitute the most important discovery of the expedition, for

---

[1] The section on the origins of the Second British Empire is based on Vincent T. Harlow, *The Founding of the Second British Empire, 1763–1793* (London, 1952), I, 1–145, 172.

[2] See especially the summary of Park's memorandum to the Secretary for War and the Colonies on the subject of his last expedition made by E. Smith in his *The Life of Sir Joseph Banks* (London, 1911), 150. Its aims are given as:

The extension of British Commerce and the enlargement of our Geographical Knowledge.

The investigation of the nature of the countries passed through, especially with regard to their natural productions and the establishment of possible trade routes.

The articles of merchandise and their relative value, and the extent to which the habits of the natives would bear upon traffic.

The study of Natural History, and correct records of latitude and longitude; together with a survey of the Niger, and of the Settlements thereon, and their inhabitants.

[3] *Ad.1/4234*, War and the Colonies to Admiralty, 2 Aug. 1815.

it would open 'a convenient communication through a fine country from the Southern Atlantic to the proximity of the Indian or Eastern Ocean; and with the once opulent kingdoms of Melinda, Zanzibar, etc.' Of tertiary importance was an alleged southern branch.

At every stage Tuckey was to make detailed observations. The river must be charted and

> the general appearance of the country, its surface, soil, animals, vegetables and minerals; everything that relates to the population; the peculiar manners, customs, language, government, and domestic economy of the various tribes

described in detail. The climate and topography of the river were to claim his attention as well as

> the vegetables, and particularly those that are applicable to any useful purposes, whether in medicine, dyeing, carpentry, etc., scented or ornamented woods adapted for cabinet work, and household furniture; and more particularly such woods as may appear to be useful in ship-building; hard woods fit for tree nails, block sheaves, etc. . . . A circumstantial account of such articles, if any, as might be advantageously imported into Great Britain . . . and [of] those which would be required by the natives in exchange for them

should be prepared. Tuckey was also ordered to inquire closely into the nature and organization of the slave trade, and especially that with Europeans, an instruction which reflects that humanitarian element in the British approach to tropical Africa which had first found expression in the foundation of Sierra Leone as a settlement for liberated slaves in 1787, which had partially inspired the foundation of the African Association in 1788, and which had found its most notable manifestation in the prohibition of the slave trade to British subjects in 1807. Tuckey was instructed to report on 'the state of slavery' among the native peoples, and on slave trading, more especially

> whether wars are carried on for the purpose of making slaves: how their prisoners are treated; how disposed of; and every possible information that can be collected, as to the manner and extent to which the slave trade is conducted with Europeans: who those Europeans are; where residing: how their agents are employed; what the articles of barter are; in what manner the slaves are brought down to the coast, etc.[1]

[1] *Ad.1/2617* and *Narrative*, xxxi–xlii, Memorandum of an Instruction to Captain Tuckey, n.d.

To assist Tuckey, three scientists accompanied the expedition—Professor Smith, a botanist and geologist, Mr. Tudor, an anatomist, and Mr. Cranch, styled 'Collector of Objects of Natural History'. They were to report upon phenomena in their various disciplines and both assist Tuckey in the compilation of his journal, and provide more detailed accounts of their own. Amongst the more curious instructions to the scientists was the sylleptic injunction to the anatomist closely to examine the hippopotamus and 'preserve in spirits and if possible in triplicate, the organ of hearing of this animal'.[1]

In view of its nautical character, the organization of the expedition was entrusted to the Admiralty. The Lords Commissioners, doubtless because of Barrow's enthusiasm, went to work surprisingly quickly. The most noteworthy feature of the preparations was the decision to construct, especially for the expedition, a steam vessel—the first ever to be built for the Royal Navy. The suggestion came from Sir Joseph Banks, former President of the Royal Society, eminent scientist of his day and patron of explorers (he had actually accompanied Cook on his first voyage and had been one of those responsible for the foundation of the African Association).[2] Barrow had asked him to recommend a good naturalist to accompany the expedition and it was in his reply that Banks suggested the use of a steamboat. One of the Rennie family of engineers (either John Rennie, senior, or his eldest son, George) and Messrs. Boulton and Watt were consulted but reported that they considered it impracticable to build one suitable for the Congo.[3] But Banks had now become enthused with the idea and would not drop it.

'Is it conceivable', he wrote, 'that a rich and powerful nation, undertaking to explore the swiftest river in the world by ascending the stream, and having newly discovered a method of stemming the currents of rivers, should neglect to use this discovery as a public measure, when individuals find it profitable to avail themselves of it in their private concerns?'[4]

Largely, it seems, because of the perseverance of a man of such reputation, the proposal was accepted,[5] and Boulton and

---

[1] *Narrative*, xxxviii–xlii. *Ad.1/2617*, Instructions to Mr. Tudor, 7 Feb. 1816.
[2] *D.N.B.*, I, 1049–53. *C.H.B.E.*, II, 616.   [3] Smith, op. cit., 278.
[4] Quoted in Smith, op. cit., 278–9.   [5] Smith, op. cit., 279.

Watt, despite their earlier adverse opinion, undertook to provide the engine. The construction both of the vessel, which was built on the general lines of, and rigged as, a sloop and named the *Congo*,[1] and of the engine proceeded rapidly, Tuckey reporting in mid-October 1815 that the 'steam engine apparatus' was ready for fitting.[2] But the sea trials in January were disappointing, $5\frac{1}{2}$ knots proving the maximum speed at which the 24 h.p. engine could drive the vessel. Moreover the doubtful benefit of steam propulsion was secured only at the cost of giving up one-third of the *Congo*'s length to the engine. Boulton and Watt, doubtless wishing that they had stuck to their original refusal, were now anxious to redeem their reputation, whilst the failure of their engine brought forward 'a shoal of projectors, every one ready with his infallible remedy'. But both Mr. Seppings, the Surveyor of the Navy, and Tuckey recommended that the engine be removed. No doubt naval conservatism played a part in determining this attitude, but Tuckey can hardly be criticized for not wishing to burden himself with what might well remain a white elephant. Moreover modifications to the engine would involve delay at a time when other preparations were well advanced, and Tuckey himself was particularly influenced by the conviction that the *Congo* would be a good sailer, and by the testimony of a merchant captain that he had several times ascended the Congo to a distance of 140 miles with the aid of a reliable sea-breeze. The upshot was the removal of the engine.[3]

A troopship, the *Dorothy*, was appointed to accompany the *Congo* and was to be used not to carry men, but additional stores. The *Congo* itself carried a number of boats for the ascent of the river beyond the cataracts which were understood to exist.[4] Eventually on 25 February 1816 the two vessels left Deptford and beat down the Channel to Falmouth. On 19 March Falmouth dropped astern and the two vessels headed for the coast of Africa. Their combined complement was some sixty men.[5]

[1] *Ad.3/186*, Minute, anon., 13 Sept. 1815.
[2] *Ad.1/2616*, Tuckey to Barrow, 19 Oct., 1815.
[3] *Ad.1/2617*, Seppings to Barrow, 20 Jan. 1816. 'Journal of an Expedition to the River Zaire'. *Ad.1/4234*, Barrow, Minute, 18 Sept. 1815, on War and the Colonies to Admiralty, 2 Aug. 1815. *Narrative*, xxiv–xxvi.
[4] *Narrative*, xxviii.
[5] *Ad.1/2617*, Journal. *Narrative*, xxix–xxx, 5, 8.

The expedition reached the mouth of the river it was to explore early in July.¹ Europe was not entirely ignorant of the Lower Congo. Portugal, after all, had had a lively contact with the Kingdom of the Congo between the late fifteenth and early seventeenth centuries, and Diego Cam had penetrated to the first of the cataracts in 1484 or 1485. But no Portuguese is known to have reached the upper river, and such information as the early Portuguese may have gleaned had not been recorded or, if recorded, had either perished or had not been made known.² Of most use to Tuckey, for it proved to be tolerably accurate, was a chart of a considerable portion of the lower river constructed by a contemporary, Maxwell, a sea-captain turned geographer, on a visit to the Congo. Moreover he was able to locate the cataracts at a point some fifty or sixty miles beyond his farthest penetration, on the information of native slave dealers who also told him that the Congo was as broad 600 miles from the sea as it was in its lower reaches.³ Two frigates, the *Amelia* and *Thais*, had visited the river as recently as 1814 but they had only penetrated some fifty miles upstream and their captains had apparently not recorded any particularly valuable information, save to draw attention to the strength of the current and to warn against the danger of large floating islands, themselves evidence of the river's force. These islands, said one of the captains 'with the trees still erect and the whole wafting to the motion of the sea, rushed far into the ocean', forming, he weightily observed, 'a novel prospect even to persons accustomed to the phenomena of the waters'.⁴

The ascent of the Congo began. The *Dorothy*, being of relatively deep draught, was left at the Congo mouth whilst Tuckey, in the sloop, pushed cautiously upstream, reaching Boma on 27 July. This he found to be a resort of European slave ships on their periodic visits to the river, and, very infrequently, of merchant vessels also. Moreover, Liverpool ships had formerly taken on small amounts of raw cotton there. It was also the seat of the chief who was clearly the most important authority on the lower river, and with him Tuckey had a somewhat

---

¹ *Ad.1/2617*, Journal. *Narrative*, 73.
² For a brief elaboration of the early Portuguese contact see pp. 40–41 below.
³ *Narrative*, xiii–xiv.   ⁴ *Narrative*, xiii.

inconclusive interview. Tuckey's account of it throws an interesting light on his own conception of the expedition's purpose. In explaining to the chief the purpose of the expedition as it affected him, Tuckey clearly put his own gloss on that purpose but there is no reason to suppose an intention to deceive, especially as his account is to be found in his official report. It reads:

'the King of England, being equally good as he was powerful, and having, as they already had heard, conquered all his enemies, and made peace in all Europe, he now sent his ships to all parts of the world, to do good to the people, and to see what they wanted, and what they had to exchange; that for this purpose I was going up the river, and that, on my return to England, English trading vessels would bring them the objects necessary to them, and also teach them to build houses, and make cloth', etc.

'These benevolent intentions', Tuckey continued, 'were however far beyond their comprehension, and as little could they be made to understand that curiosity was also one of the motives of our visit.'[1]

Navigation of a vessel the size of the *Congo* now became increasingly difficult and nine days later, and only a little above Boma, the sloop was moored and left in the care of a portion of its ship's company, whilst Tuckey, with the scientists and the remainder, continued in the boats brought for the purpose. On 10 August Tuckey called on the Chief of Nokki, which place he found to have been a former resort of European slave traders (Tuckey does not indicate why they had ceased to frequent it). Shortly afterwards the proximity of the Yellala Falls obliged the party to leave their boats and attempt to round this obstacle by land. The journey thus far—some 145 miles—had been relatively easy and the party remained in good health. But the overland journey proved physically arduous, whilst frustrating delays were caused by recalcitrant porters and, when the Falls had been surmounted, by lazy paddlers and an insufficiency of canoes. Above all, when the comparative health of the river had been exchanged for the landward passage round the Falls, fever set in and affected many of the party, including Tuckey himself. At the beginning of September his journal became disjointed and on the 9th he was compelled to turn back. The party reached the *Congo* a week later and the sloop rejoined the *Dorothy* on the 18th. By

[1] *Ad.1/2617*, Journal. *Narrative*, 102–3.

Reproduced from the *Narrative of an Expedition to explore the River Zaire* ... (London, 1818)

that time death had taken a severe toll. Tuckey himself, two of his officers, the three scientists and eleven others succumbed to an undiagnosed fever. The circumstances of its contraction and diffusion suggest, however, that it may have been yellow fever rather than malaria and that it was caught originally by contact with the riverain peoples, themselves enjoying a high degree of immunity from its effects, but who none the less were carriers of the disease.[1]

Through no fault of Tuckey's, but rather because of inadequate resources and the ravages of fever, the expedition (like its Upper Niger counterpart) was scarcely a success. Tuckey seems only to have reached a point about 200 miles from the Congo mouth—where, with a certain insularity, he observed that 'the scenery was beautiful and not inferior to any on the banks of the Thames'.[2] The immediate result of the expedition was to confirm delusion, for Tuckey's report that at his farthest point the river flowed from a northerly direction, was taken as tending to confirm that the Niger and Congo were one. This hypothesis was of course destroyed by Lander in 1830 when he traced the course of the Niger to the sea, but as far as the Congo itself was concerned, the fearful mortality of Tuckey's expedition ensured that for another sixty years the upper reaches would have no acquaintance with European commerce, customs, or religion, whilst on the lower river the slave trader would continue his depredations for almost another half-century.

[1] *Ad.1/2617*, Journal. *Narrative*, xliii–xlvi, 113–225.
[2] *Ad.1/2617*, Journal. *Narrative*, 342.

CHAPTER II

THE ASSERTION OF BRITISH PARAMOUNTCY ON THE LOWER CONGO AND ADJOINING COAST (I)

WITH the failure of Tuckey's expedition, official British interest in the Congo region was dead for a quarter of a century. Thereafter interest in the lower river and the adjoining coast revived as the Navy turned its attention to this last great stronghold of the transatlantic slave trade. Partially independent of this revival of official interest, but significantly linked to it, was the growth of British commerce, first, and in a small way, on the coast, subsequently, and of increasing importance, on the lower river. The result was a real, if informal paramountcy.

Men-of-war were the first substantial British influence to appear on the Congo coast. It was as cruisers in search of slave ships that they initially came, but although the campaign against the Atlantic slave trade had begun at the end of the Napoleonic wars, it was not until the forties that it extended to the Congo coast. Through the third and fourth decades of the century, when the Congo coast was the responsibility of the Cape of Good Hope Station, there is hardly a mention in the reports of the Commander-in-Chief even of visits by vessels under his command, let alone of operations against the slave trade.[1] Indeed, of ninety seizures of slavers by ships of the station between October 1834 and March 1838 only one took place anywhere near the Congo—the capture of a Spanish brig in Ambriz roads.[2] It is significant of a still prevailing official ignorance of the region that as late as 1845, in a minute on the ascent some thirty miles up the Congo of a vessel belonging to Horsfall & Son, a Liverpool firm, a Foreign Office official could write, 'we hear very little of slave trade on the Congo, and yet from the report of the merchant captain here quoted . . . it is evidently carried on to a great extent'.[3] This neglect was partly, no doubt, a consequence of the station's

[1] *Ad.1/67–86 passim*, C.-in-C. Cape of Good Hope to Admiralty, 1815–39.
[2] *FO84/262*, List of captures, Sub-Encl. in Ad. to F.O., 22 May 1838.
[3] *FO84/609*, Minute, n.d., unsigned, on Ad. to F.O., 19 Apr. 1845, and Encls.

other commitments, notably (whilst Napoleon still lived) the watch on St. Helena, the demands on its attention of the southeast coast of Africa and Madagascar and, during the thirties, when the Cape and West Africa stations were combined, the more intensive slave trade of the Bight of Benin. But it was also due to the fact that in this period treaty restrictions, or the absence of a treaty, made impossible effective anti-slavery operations against the three nations most vigorously engaged in the slave trade of the Congo region—Spain, Portugal and Brazil. A number of factors led to a change from the late thirties onwards. From 1835 effective measures could be taken against Spanish, and from 1839 against Portuguese slavers;[1] in 1840 the Congo coast became the responsibility of a separate West Africa station which, having anti-slavery operations as its principal *raison d'être*, was likely to be the more forceful in the execution of them; again, during the 1840's, the strength of the West Africa squadron increased considerably, jumping from 13 to 21 ships between 1843 and 1844, reaching 30 in 1847 and usually remaining over 20 right up to the ending of the Atlantic slave trade in the mid-sixties,[2] thus permitting a greater concentration in the southern sector; finally, the centre of the trade moved to the Congo region in the early forties or possibly a little earlier, the trade being well on the way to extinction north of the Equator by mid-century.[3]

Tactics, enthusiasm, success—all varied, but for over twenty-five years British warships were constantly on the coast. Sometimes they cruised out of sight of land: more frequently, especially in later days, they kept close to the shore, blockading for weeks at a time notorious points of slave embarkation and pre-eminently the Congo mouth. Much of this work was wearisome and unhealthy but was enlivened by periodic excitement and sudden success, bearing with it the promise of prize money. Thus in 1857 Commander Hunt of the steam sloop *Alecto*, as the climax of a successful patrol, captured a slaver and liberated 603 slaves, reporting the chase to his Commodore in these graphic terms.

[1] See pp. 37-38 below.
[2] C. Lloyd, *The Navy and the Slave Trade* (London, 1949), 281-3.
[3] See especially *FO84/442*, Bishop to Foote, 29 July 1842, Encl. in Ad. to F.O., 24 Nov. 1842; *FO84/616*, Jamieson to Nicolls, 25 Mar. 1845, Encl. in Nicolls to F.O., 17 Apr. 1845; Lloyd, op. cit., 115.

Sir,

In my report of the capture of the *Clara B. Williams* I mentioned that I proceeded to the Congo to land the prisoners [a reference to the common practice of landing the crews of captured slavers on the coast and leaving them to take their chance].

On arriving at Shark's Point [at the mouth of the Congo] and learning that the prisoners landed there are ill used and plundered of everything, for humanity's sake I determined to proceed to Medora Creek for despatch and then send them to Punta da Lenha in our pinnace and cutter which would thus land them in a safe place and enable me to complete water, clean ship's bottom, and obtain information at the same time.

I anchored at Medora Creek at 12.30 p.m. of the 29 October, and the boats returned at 7 p.m. of the 30th having ascertained that the brigantine *Windward* and barque *N. G. Lewis* were preparing to ship slaves and that the slave dealers imagined the *Alecto* was in want of coals and would have to go to Loanda for them. I hoisted in my pinnace that evening, steamed on lowest grade out of the River at 8.30 p.m. of the night of the 30th and on rounding Point Padron steered to the southward to deceive their lookouts, at 4.30 of the 31st I banked up fires and made sail to topsails, wind S.E., steering to reach a position where I expected to meet the above named vessels.

At 2.50 p.m. of 2nd instant a sail was reported a little on the lee bow coming out from the land on port tack close hauled, I then shortened and furled all sail, drew forward fires and went on in chase. The stranger was soon made out to be the *Windward*. At 4.30 set fore and aft sails, 5.30 set topsails and 7 ft. sails, shewed our colours and fired a blank gun. Found chase was leaving us fast and shewing no colours, at 6 p.m. fired a shot ahead of her, ceased firing, shot falling short, the wind fresh with considerable motion.

During the night I had considerable difficulty by reason of the moon being hid partly by clouds to keep sight of chase, as the wind rose or fell so we neared or distanced each other during the night. I kept the few hands I had left in the ship (5 prize crews being away) at Quarters, in case the chase should suddenly alter course. At 2.40 stranger kept away the wind falling a little, and consequently we closed him sufficiently to bring him within range. At 3 fired two shots at stranger, on which he hove to. On boarding her she was found to have on board a cargo of upwards of 600 slaves in very good condition. The person we supposed to be the Master declined to produce any colours or papers, observing that the cargo was quite sufficient for us. I therefore seized her as a vessel engaged in the slave trade, not entitled to the protection of the flag of any state or nation. He calls his vessel the *Lucia* but there is not a doubt of her being the *Windward*. She is 177 tons American measurement.

Having put a Petty Officer and some seamen and kroomen [locally engaged Africans] in charge, I have kept company with her, standing under sail to the S.E., fires banked, in hopes of meeting the barque, which, should I meet her, will be the last vessel we know of now on the Coast for slave purposes. Should I not see her by the evening of the 5th inst. I shall proceed in company with the prize to St. Helena, as I have no officers to put in her, the only remaining officers in the ship at present being the Master, and two Warrant Officers who are on the sick list, and being myself so unwell at times as to be obliged to give a petty officer charge of the ship. Taking all this into consideration and the suffering I might entail on so large a number of slaves confined in so small a vessel by any further delay on the Coast, and the uncertainty of obtaining any assistance at Loanda as there was no coal there by last report, and being by long chase upwards of 4 degrees to the westward of Point Padron with only [illegible] tons of coal left, I have felt compelled to come to this decision. . . .

Jas. Hunt,
Commander.[1]

In a postscript to this episode Hunt reported that 149 of the 603 liberated slaves died before they were landed.[2]

Hunt's chase was successful. It might well not have been. Indeed, the cruisers of the anti-slavery squadron, especially whilst sail reigned undisputed, were frequently outstripped by fast sailing slavers. Why, then, was direct action not taken against the coastal depots of the European slave dealers, a policy which would have had the incidental effect of considerably increasing British political influence on the coast? At the very beginning of the campaign against the Congo slave trade, just this was done. In 1842, under Palmerston's inspiration, Commander Matson gave a convincing demonstration of the Navy's ability to strike heavy and effective blows against the coastal centres of the trade when he sent ashore both at Cabinda and Ambriz a landing party from the vessels under his command and forcibly liberated a total of 1,314 slaves.[3] But even before this highly effective action had been taken, the Whig ministry had been forced out of office by successful opposition to its proposal to increase revenue by equalizing the sugar duties. Since the proposal had, in its turn, been evoked largely by the expense of an expanded Navy, it is hardly surprising that the new ministry, and its Foreign Secretary,

[1] *FO84/1068*, Hunt to Wise, 5 Nov. 1857, Copy, Encl. in Ad. to F.O., 12 Jan. 1858.
[2] *FO84/1068*, Hunt to Ad., 21 Nov. 1857, Encl. in Ad. to F.O., 12 Jan. 1858.
[3] *FO84/551*, Foote to Ad., 31 May 1842, Copy, Encl. in Ad. to F.O., 23 Nov. 1844. Lloyd, op. cit., 96. R. J. Gavin, *Palmerston's Policy towards East and West Africa 1830–1865* (Cambridge, Ph.D. thesis, 1958), 138–40.

Aberdeen, were not enamoured of a policy which involved heavy naval expenditure.[1] Enthusiasm for the anti-slavery crusade was also dulled by the failure of the 1842 Niger expedition,[2] whilst at the same time the reference to the Queen's Advocate of a test case concerning the destruction of slave barracoons led to the ruling that

> the blockading of rivers, landing and destroying buildings, and carrying off persons held in slavery in countries with which Great Britain is not at war, cannot be considered as sanctioned by the law of nations, or by provisions of any existing treaties.[3]

Naval officers were therefore warned against destroying slave factories unless empowered to do so by a treaty previously concluded with the chief on whose soil the factory lay. At the same time they were enjoined to take care not to destroy merchandise and property pertaining to legitimate trade, and carefully to distinguish between blockading points of slave embarkation, and a stretch of coastline as a whole and in every respect.[4] The use of force against slave trading establishments as a general policy therefore ceased, coercion of this type being used only occasionally and where naval officers had secured treaties granting the necessary powers in a penalty clause. On the Congo coast, indeed, no use seems to have been made of this right of coercion, where it existed.

In 1861, under the sponsorship of two of the most vigorous opponents of the slave trade, Palmerston and Russell, who were now in office, an attempt was made to revive the policy of direct action against slave trading tribes. The notorious points of slave embarkation on the Congo estuary and adjoining coast were to be watched, a close blockade being instituted, and it was proposed that force be used against chiefs who refused to stop participating in the slave trade. This militant policy was part of a wider scheme which was to include similar measures against Dahomey,[5] the only considerable centre of the slave trade north of the Line now remaining, and of a piece with the acquisition of Lagos in that same year. Nothing came of this scheme—it foundered on the

---

[1] Gavin, op. cit., 143–5. [2] Ibid., 141–3. [3] Quoted in Lloyd, op. cit., 97.
[4] *FO84/436*, F.O. to Ad., 20 May 1842 and 29 Oct. 1842, Drafts. Lloyd, op. cit., 97–98.
[5] *FO84/1149*, F.O. to Ad., 21 Aug. 1861, Draft.

conservatism of the Admiralty[1]—save in that Commodore Wilmot, who had conceived it, shortly afterwards succeeded to the command of the naval squadron and in 1863-5 directed the blockade of the Congo which, in conjunction with the right of search of American vessels, belatedly accorded to the Navy by the Treaty of Washington of 1862, brought the Congo slave trade to an end.

The first purpose of the British naval squadron was to stop the slave trade. But even action directed solely against this trade, provided it was effective action, necessarily opened the way for legitimate trade. Nor was this the full extent of the Navy's encouragement of licit commerce; the squadron had as a conscious, related role the promotion of British commerce. This is clearly shown in the terms of the instructions by which Palmerston revived a treaty-making policy in 1846.

Our naval officers . . . should sweep along the whole African Coast from end to end, West and East, . . . and use such means of persuasion as belong naturally to a strong naval force to persuade the chiefs of any part of the Coast from whence slave trade is or can be carried on to sign and conclude . . . treaties for Commerce and against slave trade. . . .[2]

The terms of the treaties, of which eleven were concluded in the Congo region between 1848 and 1877, themselves abundantly demonstrate the dual task of the Navy. The first part of the text provided for the abolition of the export slave trade and granted to Great Britain the right of enforcement: but also included in the treaties were clauses securing freedom of trade and most favoured nation treatment for British subjects. In its standard form the text ran—

The subjects of the Queen of England may always trade freely with the people of ———, in every article they may wish to buy or sell . . . and the Chief(s) of ——— pledge themselves to show no favour and give no privilege to the ships and traders of other countries which they do not show to those of England.

[1] *FO84/1192*, Russell, Memo., 2 Apr. 1862. *FO84/1207*, Wylde, Memo., 19 Mar. 1863 on Ad. to F.O., 16 Mar. 1863. For this project see also various dispatches and minutes in the vols. cited, and in *FO84/1150, 1160, 1182, 1186*.

[2] *FO84/702*, Palmerston, Minute, 9 Aug. 1846. For the personal conviction of Palmerston (who was the most influential framer of African policy over the period 1830-65) that the slave trade must be stamped out in order to make possible the development of legitimate commerce and, in particular, to enable Africa to become a large-scale supplier of cotton, see Gavin, op. cit., 20, 24, 128-9, 171, 229-31.

In addition, the later treaties contained two articles providing for the crushing of piracy[1] which had become a serious threat to lawful trade by the early sixties. The twin role of the Navy is again asserted in a minute of Russell of 1861:

> Commodore Edmonstone should use the force at his command to protect those chiefs and tribes who have given up the slave trade [and, by implication, who have commenced legitimate trade or who are ready to do so]. He should blockade the ports of those chiefs who continue to drive the trade.[2]

On a coast where there was no strong central authority and where the fragmented tribes had been conditioned to lawlessness by their rivalries and by participation in slave hunting, attacks on the property of British—as of other—merchants were occasionally made. When this happened, the agent of the company concerned would try to obtain the help of the captain of any warship with which he could get in touch. Thus in 1849 Hatton & Cookson's factory at Ambriz was set on fire and some £2,600 worth of property destroyed. Hannah, the agent, then requested Commander Tudor of H.M.S. *Firefly* to intervene. This officer was able to obtain an indemnity for the destroyed property from the king and chiefs of Ambriz by threatening to stop the trade by naval blockade.[3] Nor was this the only occasion on which naval power was used to a similar end and with similar effect. [On the other hand there is no record of the Navy using coercion in the Congo region to enforce the collection of debts owing to British merchants. Indeed, whilst naval officers, by their standing orders, were required 'to give such countenance and protection to... British commerce as may ... be requisite', they were specifically warned against using force to secure the recovery of debts.]

In the closing years of the slave trade, and particularly after its ending, naval power was used to support legitimate commerce in a yet more positive way. The lawlessness fostered by the slave trade was now commonly diverted into piracy, in the form of the plunder of trading vessels as they sought to penetrate up the river. In 1861 a schooner belonging to Tobin &

---

[1] *A. & P.*, 1883, C3531, xlviii, 87–100.
[2] *FO84/1150*, Russell, Minute, 20(?) Dec. 1861 on Ad. to F.O., 14 Dec. 1861 and Encls.
[3] *FO84/825*, ?.d. to F.O., 31 May 1850 and Encls.

Son, a Liverpool firm, ran aground at Shark's Point, near the Congo mouth, and was attacked. Retribution came in the form of the destruction of the two adjacent native towns, together with numerous canoes, by H.M.S. *Arrogant* and H.M.S. *Wrangler*.[1] Two years later the warlike Mossilongi (or, perhaps, Misorongo) tribe, which had come to blows with Tobin's agent at Punta da Lenha, was left in peace but only because, as a result of subsequent investigation by naval officers, the agent himself was found to have been partially responsible for the episode.[2]

In 1865, however, the *Sverige*, belonging to Hatton & Cookson, another Liverpool house, was plundered by a piratical tribe living on the south bank, and Wilmot, who in 1863 had accepted a subordinate's recommendation of a cautious policy, now took strong action. After several ships of the squadron had been mustered, some nineteen 'towns' on the banks of the river were destroyed by fire and much loss of life was inflicted.[3] In the following year a certain Manuel Vacca, probably a mulatto, who was held to be responsible for the *Sverige* affair, was caught and subsequently kept in detention on Ascension Island,[4] whereupon tranquillity prevailed for some three years. But 1869 saw the beginning of another series of attacks on British trading vessels—and on one occasion, at least, on a foreigner—which resulted in minor punitive measures being taken by the naval squadron on five separate occasions in the next three years.[5] Vacca had been released by the beginning of 1873[6] and in January 1875, with three other notorious pirates, led an attack, in the Lower Congo, on the British schooner *Geraldine*. The ship was pillaged and four kroomen, who were members of her crew, killed.[7]

[1] *FO84/1150*, Ad. to F.O., 13 Nov. 1861 and Encls.
[2] *FO84/1208*, Comdr. Hoskins to Comm. Wilmot, 5 June 1869, Encl. in Ad. to F.O., 24 July 1869.
[3] *FO84/1253*, Wilmot to Ad., 7 June 1865, Encl. in Ad. to F.O., 4 Aug. 1865.
[4] *FO84/1267*, Ad. to F.O., 12 Apr. 1866 and Encls. *FO84/1268*, Wylde, Minute, 13 July 1866.
[5] *FO84/1310*, Ad. to F.O., 31 Mar. 1869 and Encls. *FO84/1327*, Comm. Dowell to Ad., 30 Apr. 1870 and Encls. Encls. in Ad. to F.O., 20 June 1870. *FO84/1329*, Dowell to Ad., 18 Nov. 1870 and Encls. Encls. in Ad. to F.O., 21 Dec. 1870. *FO84/1345*, Ad. to F.O., 23 Mar. 1871 and Encls. *FO84/1358*, Ad. to F.O., 6 June 1872 and Encls.
[6] *FO84/1380*, Ad. to F.O., 13 June 1873.
[7] *FO63/1029*, Hopkins (Loanda) to F.O., 13 Feb. 1875, No. 4. *FO84/1420*, Hewett to Ad., 18 Sept. 1875, Encl. in Ad. to F.O., 2 Nov. 1875.

Commodore Hewett, inquiring into the affair soon afterwards, got no satisfaction and learned, moreover, that the Lower Congo was in such a condition that trading vessels had to be heavily armed, whilst excessive payments could be extorted from merchants with impunity. In this situation Hewett, rather as Wilmot had done ten years before, resolved on a punitive expedition by the whole of his force as soon as it could be mustered.[1] By the end of August seven warships were collected at the mouth of the Congo.[2] The European merchants were then advised to move their goods in outlying factories to a place of safety. This done, in the following three weeks a series of attacks was made on towns and villages believed to be implicated in piracy. As a result, two chiefs of note and several of their people were killed and the pirates, in the opinion of Hopkins, the Loanda consul, who accompanied the expedition, taught a thorough lesson.[3]

British consular authority in the Congo region was scarcely even ancillary to the power of the naval squadron. No permanent official representative of any kind resided anywhere in the area until the appointment in 1843 of two slave trade commissioners to the Anglo-Portuguese Court of Mixed Commission, established in that year at Loanda in accordance with the Anglo-Portuguese treaty for the suppression of the slave trade, signed the previous year. The duties of these were, however, purely judicial and confined to cases which came before the court. Their political influence on the coast north of Angola was nil—though they performed a service of some value by retailing to the Foreign Office information about it. For a long time the vice-consul at Loanda, an appointment first made in 1844, was similarly ineffective since for many years the occupant of this post was also the clerk to the British commissioners, and clerical duties appear to have occupied most of his time. In any case Angola was the limit of the Loanda consul's area until 1873 when it was extended to Black Point, which is situated at about 4° 50′ south latitude (in response to the suggestion of both Consul Hartley and the

---

[1] *FO63/1029*, Hopkins to F.O., 26 Mar. 1875, No. 5.
[2] *FO63/1029*, Hopkins to F.O., 28 Aug. 1875, No. 20.
[3] *FO63/1029*, Hopkins to F.O., 27 Sept. 1875, No. 24. For this episode see also *FO84/1419*, Ad. to F.O., 6 May 1875 and Encls. and *FO84/1420*, Ad. to F.O., 2 Nov. 1875 and Encls.

Senior Naval Officer on the Station).[1] Consequently it was not until the mid-seventies that the Loanda consul paid appreciable attention to the Congo and adjoining coast. Even then the number of his visits was limited by the relatively few opportunities for taking passage in H.M. ships, whilst frequent changes in the tenure of the post, owing to death or invaliding home, prevented any one man establishing a personal ascendancy. Moreover, the (by the mid-nineteenth century) fragmented Congo tribes were as bricks without straw compared with the city-states of the Niger Delta and did not therefore offer the same opportunity for informal empire building.

The British political position on the Congo coast rested, then, on naval power. From the 1840's, when significant naval activity began, until the mid-sixties, when the transatlantic slave trade ended, anti-slavery operations were the principal concern of the squadron. But it has been noticed that right from the beginning the Navy had the related task of promoting legitimate commerce and it continued to carry out this second role in the years after 1865. The question now to be considered is that of the effect of the exercise of naval power on the growth of licit trade, and the nature and organization of that trade.

An appreciable legitimate commerce in the Congo region was slow to establish itself. Significant licit trade on the Congo itself originated as an extension of the operations of the British factories lying on the coast between the river mouth and Angola—indeed, the lower river and the coastline to the north and south constituted an economic entity right up to the creation of the Congo Free State in 1885 and the accompanying territorial changes resulting from the Berlin West Africa Conference. (This entity approximated to the coastal territory, geographically defined as bounded by the parallels 5° 12′ and 8° south latitude, which as will be seen, was the subject of prolonged dispute with Portugal from mid-century onwards, and of the principal clauses in the abortive Anglo-Portuguese treaty of 1884.)

From a negligible quantity in 1807 the British trade with the river and adjoining coastline grew to about £2,000,000

[1] *FO84/1008*, Hartley to F.O., 7 Jan. 1873. F.O. to Hartley, 19 Apr. 1873, Draft.

sterling by 1884,[1] and by the close of the period this Congo trade was comparable with the British trade on the Niger.

An incipient legitimate trade with the Congo River had begun—and ended—by the time of Tuckey's expedition. This was in raw cotton which was loaded in small amounts by Liverpool ships on the Lower Congo.[2] On the coast, British commercial houses appear to have existed at Ambriz, just beyond the northern boundary of Angola, at least as early as 1790.[3] But these were doubtless slave trading establishments which, if they made the attempt, were not conspicuously successful in adapting themselves to the licit trade which, after 1807, was the only one open to British subjects. Nor are these failures surprising, for the more lucrative slave trade was still vigorously carried on by foreigners on the Congo and adjoining coast, and, indeed, with increasing vigour in measure as the pressure of the British anti-slavery squadron was increasingly felt between Senegal and the Bight of Biafra in the years after about 1820.

Despite the long shadow cast by the slave trade, the Liverpool house of Tobin & Son, itself a former slave trading firm, began to trade at Ambriz in the early 1820's.[4] Its business on the Congo coast—the main centre of its activity was the Niger Delta—must for some years have been small. In 1831 a naval officer engaged in anti-slavery work reported that trade other than commerce in slaves was 'quite trifling' and that a small British schooner he had met with at Ambriz (probably Tobin's) had been there for five months and had not disposed of half her cargo.[5] Four years later, in 1835, Lieutenant Mercer of

[1] At no time before the foundation of the Congo Free State in 1885 were official Board of Trade returns for the British Congo trade published, the Board's published tables containing no smaller division than 'The Western coast of Africa not particularly designated'. In 1884, however, the Board made an estimate of the direct British Congo trade for the information of the Foreign Office, but at the same time expressed doubts as to its accuracy (see p. 33 and f.n. 1 below). The only alternative sources of information are the estimates made from time to time by the Loanda Commissioners or Consul and by merchants interested in the trade.
[2] See p. 7 above.
[3] *FO 84/2254*, Hertslet, Memo., 27 July 1892, on Liverpool Chamber of Commerce to F.O., 19 July 1892.
[4] *FO 84/977*, Tobin & Son to F.O., 17 Aug. 1855, Encl. in T. B. Horsfall to Ad.(?), 17 Aug. 1855. K. O. Dike, *Trade and Politics in the Niger Delta, 1830–1885* (Oxford, 1956), 49–50.
[5] *FO 84/126*, Comdr. Harrison to Comm. Hayes, 23 Sept. 1831, Copy, Encl. in Hayes to Ad., 4 Oct. 1831.

H.M.S. *Charybdis* found only one British vessel at Ambriz (though he also remarked an American brig engaged in legitimate trade) and none anywhere else south of the Gaboon River. The numerous other ships encountered were all slavers.[1]

Something of an improvement came in the later thirties and forties. The development of trade in ivory, gum, and malachite (copper ore) initiated a limited prosperity which, by 1845, had attracted two more Liverpool firms—C. Horsfall & Son and Hatton & Cookson, possibly followed soon afterwards by Bibbens & Blagden—to Ambriz.[2] The malachite deposits were some miles inland from Ambriz but the ivory and gum were obtained from a variety of points along the coast to the northward. At these points branch factories were set up including, by 1850, two as far up as Loango, somewhat above latitude 5° 12' south. The ivory, gum and malachite were purchased with trade goods the nature of which scarcely varied throughout the period; they consisted of textiles—chiefly cotton piece goods and blankets—old uniforms, muskets and powder, variegated hardware—rods, padlocks, etc.—and spirits.[3] Cotton goods predominated and were mostly of poor quality. Writing in 1884, Sir Joseph Lee, himself a Manchester merchant, was most disparaging.

The goods sent to the Congo are the greatest rubbish manufactured in this country. The Congo merchants get them specially made for the market. The cheapness is obtained in two ways. 1. Paying English workpeople starving prices for their labour. 2. The adulteration of the goods sent. A cloth which cost the merchant 1d. per yard is made to have the appearance of a cloth double the value by filling it with China Clay and other weight giving substances.[4]

Whilst what Lee said was doubtless true, the adulteration which he condemned was common in the textile industry, and cloth of comparable quality was commonly sold on the home

---

[1] *FO84/208*, Lt. Mercer to Adm. Campbell, 6 Sept. 1835, Sub-Encl. in Ad. to F.O., 29 Jan. 1836.
[2] *FO84/569*, Commercial Agents, Ambriz to Gabriel (Loanda), 21 Oct. 1845, Encl. in Gabriel to F.O., 2 Nov. 1845, Separate. *FO84/977*, Bibbens & Blagden to F.O., 4 Dec. 1855. Tobin & Son and Horsfall & Son went into partnership as far as trade with the Niger Delta was concerned, but either restricted the merger to that particular trade, or traded under separate names in the Congo region.
[3] *A. & P.*, 1875, C1132, lxxv (Report by Consul Hopkins on the Trade, Commerce, Navigation, etc., comprised within the northern limits of Angola and Black Point, including the River Congo), 243.
[4] *FO84/1810*, Encl. in Lee to F.O., 23 Mar. 1884.

market at the time. Cheap gin, brandy and rum were the next most important items. Emanating from Germany and Holland they were handled in large quantities by British merchants.

Most of the trade appears to have been carried on by barter, and, to look ahead, by the seventies quite a sophisticated form of barter had developed, its essential element being a generally accepted standard of value, the 'long', in which the value of both produce and trade goods was measured. Trader and African would agree on a price of so many 'longs' for the produce offered. The agreed price was written on a 'book', or piece of paper, and taken to the store where goods were given out to the value of the 'longs' agreed. Six yards of ordinary cotton cloth commonly equalled one 'long' whereas a keg of powder might equal two or more.[1]

From the merchant's point of view, the organization of the trade was in one sense simplicity itself. In the absence of large political units anywhere on the Lower Congo and adjoining coast, with the qualified exception of the Boma district, all that was required to begin trade were 'dashes', or presents, to the local chief or chiefs. How African society in the region organized itself for commerce is somewhat obscure. It would appear that the dealings of the European houses were with a variety of African middlemen, but that the congeries of petty tribes in this region, being so much less integrated than the city-state society of the Niger Delta which Professor Dike has described, produced no really substantial merchants.[2] On the other hand, some of the Upper Congo tribes, certainly by the late seventies, and quite possibly well before, had evolved a means of trading along hundreds of miles of the river, which involved commercial organization on a larger scale, and which was not reproduced on the coast or lower river.[3]

A portion of the British trade was conducted on a cash basis. This was a section of the trade which survived into the middle years of the century at least and which can only be termed legitimate trade in a euphemistic sense. The Liverpool (and American) houses at Ambriz, says Monteiro, sometime a merchant on the coast, sold 'for hard cash, Manchester and other goods to the slave dealers from Cuba and the Brazils,

---

[1] J. Monteiro, *Angola and the River Congo* (London, 1875), I, 106–8.
[2] Dike, op. cit., *passim*.   [3] See pp. 29–30 below.

with which goods the slaves from the interior were all bought by barter from the natives'.[1]

A British scheme of the mid-fifties for the direct exploitation of the malachite deposits on a relatively large scale was frustrated by the Portuguese occupation of Ambriz in 1856, the imposition of differential duties, and the steps which the Portuguese Colonial Government subsequently took to concentrate the ore trade on that port.[2] As a result of the occupation, Hatton & Cookson and Tobin & Son moved their establishments to Kinsembo, a few miles to the north,[3] and Ambriz became decreasingly important to British trade. Horsfall & Son had already withdrawn from the area, probably in 1850 or 1851.[4]

The Portuguese occupation of Ambriz marks the close of the first phase of the British commercial connexion with the Congo region in the period of legitimate trade. Only fragmentary figures as to its value exist. In 1850 the annual British imports at Ambriz, through which most of the general trade with Europe probably passed, were estimated at £30,000 annually, and exports at between £50,000 and £60,000, but this estimate specifically excluded most of the malachite since this was mainly shipped not from Ambriz but from the neighbouring port of Ambrizette.[5] Thus assuming British merchants to have been the principal shippers of this mineral, the value of the malachite exports, which in 1854-5 was said to be £50,000,[6] must also be allowed for. By this date, also, groundnuts and palm oil had been added to the list of Ambriz exports.[7] But for all this, and although worth while to the handful of companies concerned in it, the British commerce with Ambriz and the coast to the northward in 1855 could subsequently be described by the Manchester Chamber of Commerce as 'of small importance'.[8]

[1] Monteiro, op. cit., I, 152. See also *FO84/826*, Comm. Fanshawe to Ad., 10 Apr. 1850, Encl. in Ad. to F.O., 18 June 1850.
[2] *FO84/977*, Bibbens & Blagden to F.O., 4 Dec. 1855. *FO63/1113*, Liverpool African Association to F.O., 10 Nov. 1856.
[3] *FO63/1114*, Comm. Wise to Adm. Grey, 19 May 1858, Encl. in Ad. to F.O., 5 Aug. 1858.
[4] *FO84/865*, Fanshawe to Ad., 29 Apr. 1851, Encl. in Ad. to F.O. 26 June 1851.
[5] *FO84/792*, Gabriel to F.O., 5 Aug. 1850.
[6] *FO84/977*, Bibbens & Blagden to F.O., 4 Dec. 1855.
[7] Ibid.
[8] *FO84/1809*, Statement of Manchester Chamber of Commerce, 5 Mar. 1884, Encl. in March. Ch. of Comm. to F.O., 6 Mar. 1884.

In this early period of the British trade with the Congo region the merchants owed to naval support only limited assistance against native tribes, even after the early 1840's when men-of-war were present on the coast in some numbers. The hazards of a trade carried on in this independent fashion had been demonstrated both by the fact that Portugal had been able to occupy, and, in effect, to drive the British merchants out of their emporium at Ambriz, and by an earlier episode. In 1844 or 1845 one of Horsfall's ships had tried to penetrate up the Congo. It had ascended the river to a distance of some thirty miles but had been prevented from going further partly, it is true, by adverse currents but mainly by the threats of the Portuguese and Spanish slave dealers established near that point, at Punta da Lenha.[1] This was clearly a portent for the future and, indeed, in the second period of the British Congo trade the development of a secure commerce on the Congo itself depended not only on the Navy making particular exertions against the slave trade of the river, but on naval action against the piracy which succeeded it.

There was certainly an economic inducement to try to open up the Congo. On the adjoining coast, as has been seen, a trade in palm oil had sprung up. From the mid-forties onwards there was a steadily rising European demand for palm oil (elsewhere on the West African coast the palm oil trade was already of major importance) and the Lower Congo offered access to a larger catchment area. Thus in 1853 or 1854, Tobin & Son, followed shortly afterwards by Hatton & Cookson, established a factory on the river.[2] In 1856 some £28,000 worth of oil was exported but it is significant that this was a year in which the vigilance of British cruisers at the Congo mouth brought the slave trade almost to a stand.[3] In the following year the export of palm oil dropped sharply, apparently because the nuts were used to feed slaves awaiting shipment,[4] and because of the fillip given to the slave trade by the activities of the Cuban slave dealers, the effects of which were accentuated by the

---

[1] *FO84/609*, Col. Nicolls to Ad., 18 Apr. 1845, Encl. in Ad. to F.O., 19 Apr. 1845.
[2] *FO84/977*, Tobin & Son to F.O., 17 Aug. 1855, Encl. in T. B. Horsfall, M.P. to F.O., 17 Aug. 1855. *FO84/985*, Loanda Commissioners to F.O., 16 Feb. 1856, No. 14. *FO84/1013*, Gabriel to F.O., 11 Feb. 1857, No. 11.
[3] *FO84/1075*, Gabriel to F.O., 15 Apr. 1859, No. 17.
[4] *FO84/1043*, Gabriel to F.O., 25 Feb. 1858, No. 18.

competition of the agents of an officially sponsored French 'Emigration' scheme (whereby Africans were 'indentured' to service in the French sugar colonies).[1] In 1858 although the slave trade continued brisk, there was a recovery to £18,000[2] and in 1859 the prospects of the river trade were sufficiently attractive for the Dutch house of Kerdyk & Pincoffs to build a factory at Punta da Lenha.[3] But the slave traders, despite the increasing hazards of their job, were still very active on the river[4]—indeed, they appear to have moved their headquarters to Punta da Lenha following the Portuguese occupation of Ambriz in 1855.[5] As well as witnessing the continuation of the slave trade it has been seen that the early 1860's saw outbreaks of piracy—outbreaks which were encouraged by the European slave dealers. The punitive expedition of 1861 in the Shark's Point region seems to have had at best only local success and, if the export slave trade was now being slowly strangled by an ever more effective blockade of the river mouth, conditions for trading vessels on the river were still uncertain. At any rate, in varying combination the uncertain peace of the river, together with the superior attractions of a not yet extinct slave trade and of the French 'Emigration' scheme precluded for a time the further development of legitimate trade on the river.[6] At the end of 1861 Commodore Edmonstone reported the obstacles to be such that Hatton & Cookson were understood to be about to close their factory on the river,[7] whilst a year later he stated that legitimate trade was inconsiderable.[8] Again, in 1863, only one lawful trading vessel, a Dutchman, appeared on

[1] For details of the scheme see *FO84/1069*, Comm. Wise to Ad., 19 July 1858, Encl. in Ad. to F.O., 9 Sept. 1858.
[2] *FO84/1075*, Gabriel to F.O., 15 Apr. 1859, No. 17.
[3] *FO84/1099*, Extract, Comm. Wise to Ad., 18 May 1859, Encl. in Ad. to F.O., 23 July 1859. See also *FO84/1104*, Gabriel to F.O., 25 Feb. 1860, No. 17.
[4] *FO84/1104*, Gabriel to F.O., 25 Feb. 1860, No. 17.
[5] *FO84/1009*, Extract from journal of Comdr. Need, H.M.S. *Linnet*, Encl. in Ad. to F.O., 20 May 1856. *FO84/1150*, Edmonstone to Keppel, 24 Mar. 1861, Encl. in Ad. to F.O., 1 Oct. 1861.
[6] *FO84/1183*, Edmonstone to Adm. Walker, 7 Nov. 1861 and Meecham to Edmonstone, 13 Nov. 1861, Encls. in Ad. to F.O., 6 Jan. 1862. *FO84/1207*, Edmonstone to Walker, 22 Oct. 1862, Encl. in Ad. to F.O., 23 Jan. 1863. Walker to Ad., 20 Feb. 1863, Encl. in Ad. to F.O., 14 Mar. 1863. *FO84/1209*, Wilmot to Walker, 3 Oct. 1863, Copy, Encl. in Ad. to F.O., 24 Nov. 1863. *FO84/1228*, Wilmot to Ad., 31 Dec. 1863, Encl. in Ad. to F.O., 29 Apr. 1864.
[7] *FO84/1183*, Edmonstone to Walker, 7 Nov. 1861, Encl. in Ad. to F.O., 6 Jan. 1862.
[8] *FO84/1207*, Edmonstone to Walker, 22 Oct. 1862, Encl. in Ad. to F.O., 23 Jan. 1863.

the river during the whole of the year.[1] It was only when the Washington Treaty of 1862—which denied to slave traders the protection, albeit equivocal, of the United States flag—and a stringent naval blockade virtually stopped the export trade after March 1863,[2] and only when a measure of law and order had been restored to the river by Commodore Wilmot's large-scale punitive expedition of 1865 that legitimate trade began again to increase.[3]

The coast had hardly been affected by piracy and, latterly, as a result of the main slave dealers moving their headquarters to Punta da Lenha, only to a limited extent by the slave trade. Thus from 1861, at least, naval officers can regularly bear witness to an increasing licit trade, notably at points such as Kinsembo, Chincoxo and Landana.[4] From 1865, therefore, river and coast joined in a steady commercial progress. Small steam launches began to ply on the Congo,[5] distributing trade goods to branch factories and collecting produce, which soon came to include sesame seed, rubber and groundnut oil, for onward shipment to Europe, usually from each company's main establishment. Two more British firms appeared in the area in the mid-sixties—the Company of African Merchants with local headquarters at Cabinda,[6] and Taylor, Laughland & Co. of Glasgow.[7] Likewise indicative of a growing trade is Commander Peile's surprise when, towards the end of 1866, he visited Boma and found a thriving legitimate trade being carried on there.[8] Early the next year Commodore Hornby could speak of a 20 per cent. increase in (apparently) the coastal

[1] *FO84/1228*, Wilmot to Ad., 31 Dec. 1863, Encl. in Ad. to F.O., 29 Apr. 1864.
[2] Ibid.
[3] Richard Burton, the explorer, ascended the Congo during 1863 and his report on the state of legitimate trade runs counter to those of the various naval officers familiar with the river. He could speak of 'the rapidly growing licit trade in ground nut and palm oil' (*FO84/1221*, Burton to F.O., 30 Nov. 1863, Confidential). His observations, however, were based on a single visit, whilst the consensus of naval opinion was that legitimate trade on the river only began a rapid development in 1865–6, or 1864 at the earliest.
[4] *FO84/1183*, Edmonstone to Walker, 7 Nov. 1861, Encl. in Ad. to F.O., 6 Jan. 1862. *FO84/1228*, Wilmot to Ad., 31 Dec. 1863, Encl. in Ad. to F.O., 29 Apr. 1864. *FO84/1252*, Wilmot to Ad., 1 Dec. 1864, Encl. in Ad. to F.O. 6 Jan. 1865.
[5] *FO84/1268*, Comdr. Grubbe to Comm. Hornby, 30 June 1866, Encl. in Ad. to F.O., 28 Sept. 1866.
[6] *FO84/1267*, Comm. Wilmot to Ad., 19 Dec. 1865, Copy, Encl. in Ad. to F.O., 12 Jan. 1866.
[7] *FO84/1268*, Grubbe to Hornby, 30 June 1866, Encl. in Ad. to F.O., 28 Sept. 1866.
[8] *FO84/1281*, Hornby to Ad., 23 Dec. 1866, Encl. in Ad. to F.O., 26 Jan. 1867.

trade, whilst on the same occasion he remarked that former slave traders, African and European alike, had commonly turned to licit trade, the latter as intermediaries between African, and European trading houses. So pronounced was this new face of things, Hornby added, that a temporary shortage of trade goods had resulted, and he ventured the suggestion that in a few years the Congo was likely to rival Bonny in productiveness.[1]

For a time this happy state of affairs continued. W. H. Wylde, head of the Slave Trade department at the Foreign Office, succinctly showed why this was so in a minute of March 1869 (written as a warning against too severe a reduction of the naval squadron).

It must be borne in mind that the valuable and rapidly increasing trade on the West Coast [Evidently the Congo and adjoining coast is meant] has been brought into existence and developed entirely by the protection afforded by our Cruisers, and it is only the constant pressure, or the knowledge on the part of the Native Chiefs that a ship of war is within reach, that prevents them from engaging in petty wars among themselves, or getting into disputes with the European traders, the effects of which are to put a stop for a time to a profitable trade.[2]

But the strength of the squadron was reduced (the West African and Cape Stations were combined in 1870)[3] and piracy, it has been seen, again broke out, persisting until 1875. This wave of piracy did not cripple the trade of the river, but without the punitive action undertaken no less than six times between 1869 and 1875[4] it might well have done so. Even though this counter action was being taken, Commander Jones reported in March 1871, for example, that it was difficult for trading vessels to get up to Boma,[5] and in 1873 Vacca actually stopped the entire trade of the river for a space.[6] It

[1] *FO84/1281*, Hornby to Ad., 12 Feb. 1867, Encl. in Ad. to F.O., 9 Apr. 1867. See also *FO84/1294*, Hornby to Ad., 1 Dec. 1867, Encl. in Ad. to F.O., 9 Jan. 1868, and other naval reports of the years 1865–9.
[2] *FO84/1310*, Wylde, Minute, 25 Mar. 1869 on Ad. to F.O., 23 Mar. 1869. See also *FO84/1419*, Wylde, Minute, 4 May 1875 on Hopkins to F.O. 26 Mar. 1875.
[3] Lloyd, op. cit., 284.
[4] *FO84/1310*, Ad. to F.O., 31 Mar. 1869 and Encls. *FO84/1328*, Comm. Dowell to Ad. 30 Apr. 1870, and other Encls. in Ad. to F.O., 20 June 1870. *FO84/1329*, Dowell to Ad., 18 Nov. 1870, and other Encls. in Ad. to F.O., 21 Dec. 1870. *FO84/1345*, Ad. to F.O., 23 Mar. 1871 and Encls. *FO84/1358*, Ad. to F.O., 6 June 1872. See also pp. 16–18 above.
[5] *FO84/1345*, Ad. to F.O., 23 Mar. 1871 and Encls.
[6] *FO84/1380*, Ad. to F.O., 13 June 1873 and Encls.

was only with Hewett's large-scale expedition against pirate towns in 1875 that piracy on the river came to an end.

The piracy of the 1869–75 period appears to have had a rather different inspiration from that of the early sixties. In the earlier period Vacca, encouraged by the Portuguese slave traders, urged on his followers with the promise (which he probably believed) that if legitimate traders were driven from the river then the palmy days of 1859–62, the last big boom time of the slave trade, would return. By the early seventies, he and other pirates can hardly have believed that the slave trade would revive again. Whether this second wave of piracy had an aim beyond the mere plunder of merchant vessels is difficult to say. It is probable that, reconciled as they must now have been to the ending of the slave trade, the pirates hoped to dominate the Lower Congo and use their domination to extract high payments from ships seeking to trade, on threat of pillage and destruction. A more positive aim than this seems unlikely. They can scarcely have hoped to establish themselves as monopolistic middlemen as the men of Bonny and other city states of the Niger Delta had done, for the petty tribal organization of the Lower Congo was simply not conducive to such a development.

Undoubtedly piracy on the Congo checked the rate of development of the trade on the river, but, in the sixties and seventies as a whole, British commerce with the Congo region nevertheless increased. In 1870 the commercial prospects were sufficient for a line of British mail steamers to call at the Congo mouth;[1] by 1874 the service was a monthly one, operated alternately by the African Steam Ship Company and the British & African Steam Navigation Company.[2] By this time, too, British merchants were established not only at Banana Point, Punta da Lenha and Boma on the Congo itself, but had establishments at fourteen points between Landana and Kinsembo. In 1873 the Loanda consul, Hartley, hazarded an estimate of the value of the British trade. He put the annual value of British manufactures imported in the Congo region,

---

[1] *FO84/1809*, Paper by Mr. Phillips (a Congo trader), on the Congo question, undated, and forwarded to F.O. by Sir F. Goldsmid, 9 Feb. 1884.

[2] *A. & P.*, 1875, C1132, lxxv (Report by Consul Hopkins on the Trade, Commerce, Navigation, etc., of the Province of Angola and its dependencies for the year 1874), 236.

'together with the exports of native produce which are principally shipped to British ports' at over £500,000. 'I feel satisfied', he added, 'that the trade is steadily increasing.'[1]

With a modicum of law and order now general on coast and river alike, British merchants could turn to the further expansion of their trade. Indeed, in the quinquennium 1879–84 the total British trade increased about fourfold, and by the latter year the increase had assumed such proportions that in addition to several steamers of 800 to 1,000 tons which ran at frequent intervals, a mailboat ran fortnightly.[2] Underlying this growth in the trade was the continuing ability of African products, of which palm produce was the most important, to find a market. In other terms, the increase was a result of the natural extension of the activities of the various firms already established in the area, and of the appearance of a number of new houses. Stuart & Douglas, J. McFarlane, the Congo & Central African Co., Ltd. (whose management was soon taken over by John Holt), Messrs. Rattray, and McLesh, Wylie & Co. all appeared in the seventies or early eighties, whilst James Irvine & Co. and John Capper & Co., who had also appeared in the seventies, had first amalgamated and then gone bankrupt before the end of the decade.

The growth of the coast trade must also have owed something to the system of inter-tribal commerce which Stanley found established on the Upper Congo on his descent of the river in 1877 and which may have been in existence long before. The system had two feeders which converged on Stanley Pool. The first lay along the cataracts and first part of the upper river and consisted of a line of markets beginning near European trading houses at Boma and elsewhere on the Lower Congo, and along which, in small stages, European manufactures passed in exchange for African produce. Basically, the trade was in the hands of individual Africans, no trader or tribe being powerful enough to dominate this trade, save perhaps the Bakongo and Bazombo on the stretch above Manyanga. The other feeder began at various points between the Congo mouth and Loanda.

[1] *A. & P.*, 1875, C1132, lxxv (Report by Consul Hopkins on the Trade, Commerce, Navigation, etc., of the Districts comprised within the northern limits of Angola and Black Point, including the River Congo), 243. *FO63/1008*, Hartley to F.O., 7 Jan. 1873 and Encl.
[2] *FO84/1809*, Encl. in Manch. Ch. Comm. to F.O., 6 Mar. 1884.

Its way to Stanley Pool lay through San Salvador, the Portuguese inspired name for the capital of the old Kingdom of the Congo, and Tungwa. Trade along this route appears to have been more in the hands of strong tribal groups, including notably the Bazombo, again, in the Tungwa region and a Bateke tribe established on the route's junction with Stanley Pool. At the Pool the two feeders of the system converged and from there onwards longer stages were covered. The peoples on the banks of Stanley Pool would journey in large canoes to the Buyanzi country, a hundred miles upstream, by which point ivory predominated as the principal item for which European goods were exchanged. The Bayanzi people then carried on the trade over a 150-mile stage to the Irebu, whom Stanley described as the champion traders of the Congo. It continued thereafter on a similar pattern as far up as Upoto (Bopoto) on the crest of the inverted U-shaped bend which the Congo describes north of the Equator, and a good third of the way across the continent. This was the point which Stanley, in 1877, found to be 'the present ultimate reach of anything arriving from the west coast'.[1] (Six years later he was to find that the Arabs had advanced to within 250 miles of that place.)[2]

By a variously organized trade route, therefore, European goods landed on the coast or Lower Congo could penetrate 1,000 miles into the interior, whilst some of the produce for which European manufactures were exchanged came from no less distance. It took about five years for an imported article to reach the Upoto district,[3] but it is the existence of this pipeline, rather than the speed at which trade flowed, which is important as helping to explain the growth of British trade —and the commerce of other European nations—with the Lower Congo and adjoining coast.

The commercial stake of Britain in the Congo region was appreciably larger than a mere enumeration of the British firms trading there, and assessment of their activities, might suggest. A considerable proportion of the 1,990,000 florin (£165,833) capital of the *Afrikaansche Handelsvereeniging*, a

---

[1] H. M. Stanley, *Through the Dark Continent*, cheap ed. (London, 1890), 554, 595. H. M. Stanley, *The Congo and the Founding of its Free State* (London, 1885), II, 21. Miss R. Slade, *English-speaking Missions in the Congo Independent State* (Brussels, 1959), 40–41.
[2] Stanley, *Congo*, II, 139.   [3] Stanley, *Dark Continent*, 554.

Dutch house and the largest in the Congo region—in 1878 it employed over fifty Europeans at Banana, its African headquarters, alone—was owned by British subjects. Moreover small British-owned coasting vessels were also largely responsible for carrying on the firm's commerce along the coast and in the Lower Congo.[1] In addition, both the Dutch company and a French company operating in the area re-exported to the Congo cotton and other British manufactures originally consigned to the Continent.[2] Most of the exports of the Dutch company, at least, were British goods.[3] In 1879, for example, it shipped to the Congo region British cotton goods to the value of $690,000, guns from Britain to the value of $105,000, powder worth $30,000 and, making the rough assumption that half its exports of hardware originated in Britain, $50,000 worth of brass, rods, pots and pans—$875,000 or £175,000 sterling in total value,[4] much of it, it may be presumed, re-exported from Holland, and thus not included in estimates of the direct British trade. Indeed, by the early eighties, Britain had the largest share in Europe's trade with the Congo region, estimates varying from 'more than one-half' to three-quarters.[5]

Estimates of the value of the trade in this final period of rapid growth emanated almost exclusively from Manchester, then in the forefront of the campaign against the projected Anglo-Portuguese treaty, because commercial opinion there held that the admission of Portugal to the Congo, as proposed in the treaty, would injure British trade. Manchester estimates of its value must therefore be examined with some care since there was every temptation to infla' ; hem in the interests of the case. An estimate made in 1883 reckoned British exports to the Congo region at £540,000,[6] whilst in the following year it

[1] *FO63/1116*, Carnegie (Loanda) to F.O., 14 Sept. 1876, No. 32. *M. des A. E., C. et D., Afrique, A.I.C. 1883—Vol. 2, No. 58*, Belgian Minister at The Hague to Belgian Foreign Minister, 2 June 1883. W. Holman Bentley, *Pioneering on the Congo* (London, 1900), I, 69–73. See also *The Times*, 24 Apr. 1878, 4.
[2] *FO63/1116*, J. F. Hutton to F.O., 7 Dec. 1876.
[3] *FO84/1817*, Extract from letter, no author given, headed 'Berlin, 1 Dec. 1884', apparently given to Granville by Hutton and Helm at interview of 15 Dec. 1884 (see p. 177 below).
[4] *FO84/1810*, U.S. Senate Report No. 393, 26 Mar. 1884, 14–15, Encl. in West to F.O., 30 Mar. 1884, Africa No. 2.
[5] *FO84/1640*, Cohen (Loanda) to F.O., 6 Aug. 1883, Africa No. 21, Confidential. *FO84/1802*, Liverpool African Association to F.O., 1 Dec. 1882. H. M. Stanley, *Address to the Manchester Chamber of Commerce* (? London, 1884), 4–5. *New York Herald*, 24 June 1885, Report of interview with General H. S. Sanford.
[6] *FO84/1803*, Manch. Ch. Comm. to Granville, Memorial, 29 Jan. 1883.

was claimed that the figure 'now approaches a million sterling per annum'. On the same occasion the total volume of the trade was stated to be 'not less than £2,000,000 per annum',[1] a figure which was frequently quoted in circles which clearly drew their inspiration from Manchester. The only other source —the British & African Steam Navigation Company—which made an estimate, is subject to the same suspicion of bias but the very detail of its figures imparts a certain authenticity. In December 1883 it communicated to the Foreign Office particulars of the direct trade to and from the Congo river and six specified points on the adjoining coast carried on by the Company and its business partner, the African Steam Ship Company, and by Hatton & Cookson who had their own vessels. In the period covered—1 July 1882 to 30 June 1883—exports to the Congo totalled £256,401 and imports £202,790, an overall direct trade of £459,191.[2] This is not at first sight an impressive amount and may appear difficult to reconcile with the claim of a commerce valued at £2,000,000. But it excluded important branches of the trade. The Liverpool African Association specifically pointed out that the figures did not include the large shipments made from the Congo to the Continent on British account, probably amounting to a further £150,000.[3] They also excluded British manufactures re-exported from the Continent by the French, Dutch and probably the Belgian and Portuguese houses. When it is remembered that in 1879, £175,000 worth, or 61 per cent. of the exports shipped to the Congo region on the account of the Dutch company alone had originated in Britain, that this was before the almost fourfold increase in the trade predicated by the Manchester Chamber of Commerce,[4] that a large proportion of the manufactures sold on the Congo by Continental houses was re-exported from the Continent and was not reckoned as direct British exports, that the goods or bullion remitted to Britain as payment for these manufactures should be regarded as part of the Congo trade, then the estimate of £2,000,000 becomes

[1] *FO84/1809*, Encl. in Manch. Ch. Comm. to F.O., 6 Mar. 1884.
[2] *FO84/1808*, Statement, Encl. in B. & A.S.N. Co. to F.O., 13 Dec. 1883.
[3] *FO84/1808*, Liverpool African Assoc. to F.O., 12 Dec. 1883.
[4] See p. 29 above. The *Afrikaansche Handelsvereeniging* had gone bankrupt in 1879, but had been immediately succeeded by the *Afrikaansche Venootshcap*, without, it seems, Dutch activities in the Congo region being markedly affected.

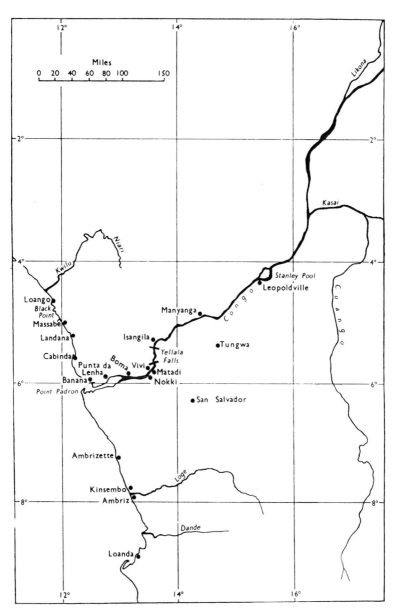

Western portion of the River Congo, and adjoining coast

more convincing. The final consideration in support of Manchester's estimate is that the British & African Steam Navigation Co.'s figures did not include the value of the cargoes carried by the British tramp steamers engaged in the Congo trade. Although the lack of precise information makes proof of the Manchester claim impossible, it appears from the evidence available to be reasonably accurate.[1] What is more, Britain's trade with the Congo region was commensurate with her trade with the Niger Delta. Unofficial estimates—the only kind available—put the value of the British trade in the *whole* of the Bights of Benin and Biafra in 1883–4 at only £3,000,000, a figure which apparently included the indirect trade.[2] The implied rough equivalence of the trade of the Niger Delta with that of the Congo region contrasts both with the view which contemporaries seem to have had of the relative value and importance of the two trades, and with what later students of British expansion have supposed. To each category of observer Britain's commerce with the Congo seems not to have been regarded as of comparable extent or importance with that with the Niger. Contemporaries were perhaps disposed to undervalue the Congo because a more obvious British paramountcy had been established in the Bight of Benin; because of Britain's leading role in the Niger quest; because the Niger, unbroken by cataracts in its lower reaches, appeared an easier route into the African interior; because earlier in the century the Niger had been an important focus of humanitarian zeal; and because a relatively powerful and influential British company—the National African Company—was established on the Niger. Later students, as well as being similarly influenced, have possibly also assumed that the region which eventually became British must always have been more important to

[1] In November 1884 the Board of Trade, on the basis of Customs returns, estimated the trade in 1883 between Liverpool and the West African coast between 5° and 8° south latitude at £408,000. It added, however, that the customs authorities were doubtful of the accuracy of these figures and that the indirect trade through Hamburg, Antwerp, and Havre was 'very large'. The Board's conclusion was that 'without agreeing with the large figures put forward by the Manchester Chamber we may admit that it is a growing and important trade'. But the disagreement with the Manchester estimate was principally over the extent of the very important indirect trade and on this point the Board of Trade spoke with no detailed knowledge. (*FO84/1814*, B.o.T. to F.O., 5 Nov. 1884, and Encls. 'G', 'H', and 'Congo Treaty'.)

[2] *FO84/1683*, Lord Aberdare to F.O., 28 Mar. 1884. *FO84/1684*, Manch. Ch. Comm. to Granville, Memorial, 4 Apr. 1884.

Britain than the one which did not fall under her control.

By the early eighties, therefore, Britain had an important commercial stake in the Congo region: but already in the late seventies the Congo had also come to have in England an appeal of a quite different nature—as an exceptionally promising field for missionary work. Two British missionary societies responded to this appeal and their response led them not to the estuary of the river and the adjoining coast but far into the interior.

Robert Arthington, a wealthy Leeds industrialist of strongly evangelical outlook, inspired the first missionary expedition on the Congo. Convinced that if Cameron, in 1874, had followed the flow of the Lualaba downstream from Nyangwe he would have conclusively proved the identity of that river with the Congo, he saw a relatively easy route for the entry of Christianity into Central Africa, and in 1877 offered to the Baptist Missionary Society £1,000 if it would begin the evangelization of the Upper Congo lands. The B.M.S. accepted Arthington's offer—and a subsequent one of £500 for a pioneering expedition—and an appeal for missionary volunteers and further funds was immediately made.[1]

The pioneering expedition was entrusted to George Grenfell and Thomas Comber of the Society's Cameroons mission. They arrived on the Congo early in 1878 but the line of advance to the upper river which they first planned—via San Salvador, capital of the now moribund Kingdom of the Congo—proved impracticable. The king himself was friendly but a series of attempts to penetrate to Stanley Pool from San Salvador was repulsed by the tribes in the intervening territory who saw in the missionary invasion a threat of European competition in the profitable ivory trade which they carried on along this very route. But whilst Comber persevered with this route, another B.M.S. expedition, consisting of Henry Crudgington and Holman Bentley, decided to try to reach Stanley Pool by by-passing the cataracts on the north bank, a route which Stanley had in part already opened up. They were immediately

---

[1] Slade, *English-speaking Missions*, 33–34. Miss R. Slade, 'L'Attitude des Missions Protestants vis-à-vis des Puissances Européenes au Congo avant 1885', *Bulletin des Séances de l'Institut Royal Colonial Belge*, XXV-1954-1, 685–6. W. H. Bentley, *Pioneering on the Congo* (London, 1900), I, 57–60. H. H. Johnston, *George Grenfell and the Congo* (London, 1908), I, 63.

successful and in July 1881 reached Stanley Pool after a journey of twenty-one days from Vivi.[1]

In the same year as Arthington had made his offer to the B.M.S., Henry and Fanny Grattan Guinness had been instrumental in founding the Livingstone Inland Mission with an aim similar to Arthington's—the evangelization of Central Africa by means of the Congo. The mission's first expedition reached Boma in 1878 and by 1879 a station had been established at Matadi, above the cataracts.[2]

By the early eighties, therefore, both missions were firmly established on the Upper Congo. Inevitably their presence there, despite their own quite apolitical intentions, constituted an extension of British influence though by no means of the same kind and extent as did the activities of the Navy and of British traders on the Lower Congo and adjoining coast. But the presence of one of the societies—the B.M.S.—was soon to become important for another reason. Anxious to create in England an opinion favourable to his efforts to develop and civilize the Congo, Leopold II of Belgium had instructed H. M. Stanley and his other agents to offer every assistance to the two British missions. The L.I.M. preferred to remain independent of outside help, but the B.M.S. was glad to benefit from much arduous and expensive pioneering work which it would otherwise have had to undertake itself. Consequently when in 1882–4 the position of Leopold's *Association Internationale du Congo* on the upper river appeared threatened by a proposal of the British Government to conclude a treaty with Portugal which would admit her to the lower river, the B.M.S. actively participated in a campaign of opposition to the proposed agreement.[3]

The missionary pioneers on the Upper Congo owed nothing to official support. Nor, in a sense, did the British merchants engaged in the trade of the lower river and adjoining coast— theirs was the capital, theirs the enterprise and theirs the risk. But without the operations of the Navy nothing more than a modest coast trade, sufficient to employ two or three small firms

[1] Slade, *Bulletin*, 686–8. Slade, *English-speaking Missions*, 35. Johnston, *Grenfell*, I, 63–68, 91–96. Bentley, op. cit., I, 68–369 *passim*.
[2] Slade, *Bulletin*, 687. Slade, *English-speaking Missions*, 34–35. Bentley, op. cit. I, 90.
[3] See pp. 121–3, 154–5 below.

only, would have been possible. From the 1840's, when it began effective operations on the Congo coast, until the mid-sixties, the primary aim of the naval squadron was to crush the slave trade. Even if the Foreign Office and Admiralty had been completely indifferent to the encouragement of legitimate trade, the very success of anti-slavery measures could only have had the effect of promoting it. Such indifference, of course, there was not. Apart from the fact of the accepted duty of the British Government to promote British trade, this was an age which believed that if licit trade could be established it would of itself play a part in ending the slave trade, and which was deeply, if somewhat uncritically convinced of the moral value of commerce. Consequently the encouragement of legitimate trade was something more than a by-product of the Navy's anti-slavery operations. Right from the early days the Navy had as a conscious aim the protection and furtherance of British trade. Captains intervened in 'palavers', and concluded treaties, containing, *inter alia*, commercial clauses, with native chiefs. Of more importance and as vital, from the commercial point of view, as the operations against the slave trade itself, were the measures which the Navy took against the piracy which followed it. Only because the Navy both 'kept the ring' and opened the way for commerce were British merchants able to build up a trade whose value and importance is often, perhaps, overlooked, and which was certainly greater than that of all other nations combined. Without the Navy Great Britain could not have established that informal political supremacy on the Lower Congo and adjoining coast which was quite sufficient both to protect her interests in that region, and to keep open the gateway of what would soon become the main route to the heart of Africa.

CHAPTER III

THE ASSERTION OF BRITISH PARAMOUNTCY ON THE LOWER CONGO AND ADJOINING COAST

(2) THE DIPLOMATIC BACKGROUND

It may appear that a sufficient explanation of the establishment of British paramountcy on the Lower Congo and coast adjoining has already been given. That position was the result of the naval and commercial activities which have already been considered in some detail. But it is no less true that diplomatic factors conditioned British activity in the area in the early part of the period, and that diplomacy underlay the British position from the mid-1840's onwards. It was only after diplomacy had done the necessary groundwork that the Navy could usefully devote attention to the area. It was diplomacy, again, which helped to safeguard Britain's commerce and her freedom of action against the slave trade in the face of possible extensions of foreign influence. Most important of all, only a consistent resistance to a Portuguese claim to the Lower Congo and adjoining coast prevented Portugal from taking actual possession of it.

Before the 1840's there was little inducement for the anti-slavery squadron to devote much attention to the Congo region. Certainly its resources were only too well occupied north of the Equator. But another part of the explanation of naval neglect of the area is that the ships of the three nations —Portugal, Brazil, and Spain—principally engaged in the slave trade of that part of the African coastline could not be touched by British cruisers. By a treaty of 1817 Portugal had agreed to certain restrictions on the slave trade then being carried on by her nationals. But these restrictions were operative only north of the Equator, and the considerable trade in Africans between Angola and Brazil was left untouched. Neither did the position improve after Brazil became independent in the early 1820's—the new nation merely agreed to continue the 1817 treaty. Nor was the position in regard to the third nation—Spain—any better, for until 1835 her nationals enjoyed the same immunity south of the Line as did those of Portugal and Brazil.

Conventional diplomatic pressure on Spain was able to secure an effective slave trade treaty in that year, but ability to take effective action against slavers wearing Portuguese or Brazilian colours was not accorded to naval captains until 1839 and 1845 respectively. After unsuccessfully trying to persuade Portugal to grant more effective powers of search, visit, and condemnation, Palmerston threw International Law overboard and secured the passage of an Act of Parliament which gave to the Royal Navy power to seize Portuguese slavers in any waters, be they loaded or merely equipped for the slave trade, and bring them before Vice-Admiralty courts as pirates. 'The ships of Portugal', he told the Commons in a typically Palmerstonian manner, 'now prowl about the ocean pandering to the crimes of other nations; and when her own ships are not sufficiently numerous for the purpose, her flag is lent as a shield to protect the misdeeds of foreign pirates.'[1] Similar powers were taken against Brazilian slavers under the terms of the so-called 'Aberdeen Act' of 1845. It was the passage of these acts, which for the first time made operations against slavers in the Congo region worth while, that led, during the forties, to the first significant activity of the naval squadron in the area.[2]

The treaties concluded with eleven native authorities in the Congo region between 1848 and 1877 have already been cited as evidence of the dual aim of British policy.[3] Their very conclusion constituted, of course, the use of diplomacy, backed in an unusually immanent sense by force, to obtain from native chiefs freedom of trade for British subjects and the right, in certain circumstances, to use force against the slave trade, but these treaties must also be seen as precautionary diplomatic measures directed against other European powers. Palmerston was the impetus behind the treaty-making policy. Acting on a proposal by Bandinel, the Superintendent of the Slave Trade department of the Foreign Office, he had instituted the policy in 1838 and reinvigorated it shortly after he returned to the

[1] Quoted in Lloyd, op. cit., 47. [2] See pp. 10–11 above.
[3] See pp. 15–16 above.

Foreign Office in July 1846. On inquiry in the Office he learned that in a four-month period of the previous year France had concluded nine treaties with native chiefs on various parts of the Western African coast.[1] None of these agreements was avowedly protectionist:[2] nevertheless, the Admiralty was informed, the French 'have during a very short and recent period obtained for themselves important commercial advantages and a friendly footing on large districts of the West Coast'.[3] Then followed the instruction that similar treaties be concluded with all those chiefs with whom the French had made treaties, and that naval officers should go on to make treaties 'for Commerce and against slave trade' with chiefs along the whole length of the African coastline, East and West. A determination to guard against the possible consequences of any extensions of the influence of other European nations is particularly demonstrated by the inclusion of the clause stipulating that British commerce and British subjects should enjoy most favoured nation treatment.[4]

This treaty-making policy did not apply only to the Congo region, as Palmerston's minute makes clear. As far as that region is concerned it was not, in fact, immediately prosecuted with any vigour. But over the next thirty years, as circumstance demanded or opportunity offered, treaties were signed with eleven native authorities in the region. These were with the Chiefs of Molembo on 31 March 1848, of Cabinda on 11 February 1853, of a portion of the Congo River on 20 June 1854, of Ambrizette on 17 September 1855, of Kinsembo on 13 July 1857, of Saint Antonio (on the banks of the Congo) on 1 June 1865, of a portion of the Congo River on 6 June 1865, of the south bank of the Congo on 27 March 1876, of the north bank on 19 April 1876, of Mellalla (on the river) on 19 March 1877, and of Luculla (also on the river) on 20 March 1877.[5]

In sum, these treaties were intended to obtain from native chiefs legal recognition of certain important privileges—principally the right to use force against those chiefs, if they

---

[1] *FO84/701*, F.O. Memo., 14 Apr. 1847. *FO84/702*, Palmerston, Minutes, 24 July 1846 and 9 Aug. 1846. Gavin, op. cit., 128, 153-4.
[2] *S.P.*, Vol. 34, 1845-6, 834 and Vol. 35, 1846-7, 678-87.
[3] *FO84/702*, F.O. to Ad., 27 Aug. 1846, Draft.
[4] *FO84/702*, Palmerston, Minute, 9 Aug. 1846. See also *FO84/702*, F.O. to Ad., 27 Aug. 1846, Draft, and Gavin, op. cit., 155-6.
[5] *A. & P.*, 1883, C3531, xlviii, 87-100.

subsequently engaged in slave trading, and freedom of trade for British subjects. But they were, no less, diplomatic moves aimed at safeguarding British commerce and freedom of action against the slave trade from the harm which those causes might suffer if the influence of other European nations was extended.

But it was by its resistance to a long series of attempts by Portugal to extend her dominion over the Lower Congo and the coastal territories lying between 5° 12′ and 8° south latitude that diplomacy contributed most to the development of British influence in the Congo region. If Portugal had been permitted thus to extend her authority, British cruisers would have been unable to hunt slavers in Portuguese waters and it seems certain that Portugal's traditionally protective colonial system would have made impossible the development of a worth while British trade. Still less, obviously, would the development of an informal British paramountcy have been possible.

Portugal's claim to this territory could scarcely have been of longer standing since it rested on the right of prior discovery. Diego Cam had reached the mouth of the Congo in 1483 during the great period of Portuguese overseas expansion, and subsequently ascended the river as far as the first cataracts. He also established relations with the King of the Congo, the paramount chief of a loose confederation of tribes. This confederation was bounded by the Atlantic Ocean, the River Congo, the Cuango River in the east (running very roughly in a north-south line from the confluence of the Kasai with the Congo and about 300 miles from the coast), and the Dande River (running inland from a point on the coast between Loanda and Ambriz) in the south. For the next century or so Portugal enjoyed a lively connexion with this kingdom. Up to 200 Portuguese may have lived in it and a quite considerable missionary effort was made, marked notably by the conversion of the Congo royal house to Christianity and the administration of a number of other baptisms, and, symbolically, by the changing of the name of Mbanza, the capital city, to San Salvador. It was made the seat of a diocese in 1596, but already Portuguese power was in marked decline. The moderately good intentions of the Portuguese crown foundered on its limited resources, severely strained in any case by the maintenance of the Portuguese trading empire in the East, and its consequent inability to carry those intentions into practice. Portuguese residents on the Congo, and the Portuguese *donatário* (lord proprietor) of the island of San Thomé in the Gulf of Guinea, increasingly regarded the Congo kingdom as a reservoir of slave labour for the plantations of that island, and against these disruptive forces, neither the will of the Portuguese monarchy, the desire of Afonso I, the most notable of the Congo kings of the sixteenth century, for the extension of Christianity and the establishment of European civilization, nor the missionary orders, could prevail. By the early seventeenth century, most of the Portuguese had left and most traces of Christian life had disappeared. The Portuguese presence was no more.[1] Nor did Portugal ever regain the influence she had enjoyed in the sixteenth century. Despite the existence of the Portuguese colony of Angola, immediately to the south, Portugal was not able to extend lasting, effective dominion over the Lower Congo and adjoining coast by pushing northwards. Cabinda, on the coast to the north of the Congo mouth was, it is true, occupied in 1783, but it fell to the French soon afterwards. What Portugal could claim was a vague suzerainty over the territories north of Angola and as far up, for most of the time, as Cabinda.[2] But certainly, in the earlier years of the nineteenth century, there was no sign of actual Portuguese jurisdiction. In broad terms the explanation of Portugal's neglect of the region is probably that her resources in men and wealth were insufficient, whilst Angola itself was content with the prosperity, albeit superficial, which the supply of slaves to Brazil brought it. Such resources as Portugal did devote to empire were, from the late seventeenth century onwards, devoted to the exploitation of the mineral and agricultural wealth of Brazil. It would seem to be no coincidence that the revival of Portuguese interest in the Congo began little more than a decade after the independence of Brazil had been recognized.

This new interest took concrete form, from the mid-nineteenth century onwards, in the repeated assertion by Portugal of a claim to Cabinda and Molembo, the coastal territory between 5° 12' and 8° south latitude. The claim rested, as

[1] James Duffy, *Portuguese Africa* (Harvard, 1959), 5–23.
[2] Duffy, op. cit., 70–71. For further information on the early history of the Congo see especially J. Cuvelier and L. Jadin, *L'Ancien Congo d'après les Archives Romaines* (Brussels 1954), and J. Cuvelier, *L'Ancien Royaume de Congo* (Bruges, 1946).

Portugal on various occasions attested, on the threefold basis of prior discovery, possession, at least of an intermittent kind, and recognition, implied or expressed.[1] The existence of this claim was first taken note of, and its validity almost recognized by the British Government in a clause of the Treaty of Friendship and Alliance signed by Great Britain and Portugal in 1810. It ran: 'It is, however, to be distinctly understood that the stipulations of the present Article are not to be considered as invalidating or otherwise affecting the rights of the Crown of Portugal to the territories of Cabinda and Molembo.'[2] The existence of the claim was further acknowledged in Castlereagh's treaty with Portugal for the restriction of the Portuguese slave trade, concluded in 1815, though this treaty's nullification of the 1810 treaty consequently withdrew the virtual recognition accorded in that agreement.[3] In a supplementary convention of 1817 the claim was specifically defined by latitude.[4] Nine years later, in the Portuguese constitutional charter of 1826, Cabinda and Molembo were specifically enumerated, without British protest, as dominions of the Crown of Portugal. Now Canning, the British Foreign Secretary at that time, certainly endorsed the grant of this charter and Great Britain gave the appearance of having fathered it. But the ambiguous circumstances of Britain's paternity and her qualified recognition of the offspring as her own refute the view that she must be held responsible for its every characteristic.[5] Nevertheless the British failure to protest at this assertion by Portugal of the validity of her claim was one more step towards tacit acceptance of it, and no less so because as Morier later commented, 'at that time nobody thought anything about the question'.[6]

The failure of the Foreign Office to make a protest had no immediate consequences. It was twelve years at the earliest

[1] See *inter alia*, *FO63/1112*, d'Athoguia to Ward, 3 Oct. 1855, Encl. in Ward to F.O., 8 Oct. 1855, S/T No. 18, and *FO63/1116*, Memo., n.d., Encl. in Corvo to de Saldanha, 4 Dec. 1875, communicated to F.O. in translation, by Senor Quiliman, 24 Jan. 1876.
[2] *A. & P.*, 1883, C3531, xlviii, 1. *FO63/1116*, Hertslet, Memo., 23 Mar. 1876, 2–3.
[3] *A. & P.*, 1883, C3531, xlviii, 1–2.
[4] *FO63/1116*, Memo., 23 Mar. 1876, 5. *A. & P.*, 1883, C3531, xlviii, 3.
[5] For this episode see *Cambridge History of Foreign Policy* (Cambridge, 1923), II, 78–83.
[6] *FO84/1801*, Morier, Memorandum on the Claims of Portugal, 26 June 1880.

before Portugal sought to make good her claim. This was during the negotiations of 1838–9 for an Anglo-Portuguese slave trade treaty. After the negotiations had foundered, Palmerston, at least, expressed the opinion that the real reason why the Portuguese Government had been so anxious to include in the treaty a British guarantee of Portugal's African colonies was 'an intention to entrap the British Government into an acknowledgement of the Rights of the Portuguese Crown to Parts of the African Coast which do not in fact belong to Portugal'.[1]

Lord Aberdeen, on the other hand, who had returned to the Foreign Office in September 1841, took a further step towards the admission of the validity of the Portuguese claim four years later. Portugal had protested that a recent Anglo-French slave trade agreement was in danger of infringing Portuguese rights in West Central Africa since, *inter alia*, it could be held to permit French and British naval captains to conclude and enforce anti-slavery treaties with native chiefs in Portuguese territory, or in territory over which Portugal maintained her rights.[2] In reply, Aberdeen assured Baron Moncorvo, the Portuguese minister in London, that 'undoubtedly neither of the Articles in question apply to those parts of the Coast which are under the dominion of the Portuguese Crown, or over which the Rights of Portugal have been acknowledged.'[3] To speak thus was to accord to Portugal at the very least a privileged position on the disputed coast.

The complacent attitude of the Foreign Office under Aberdeen was, however, reversed when Palmerston again became Foreign Secretary in July 1846. In that year the Loanda Commissioners reported the condemnation by a Portuguese court at Loanda of a Brazilian slave vessel seized off the coast between 5° 12' and 8° south latitude by a Portuguese corvette. Now the court's claim to competence in the matter rested on the assertion that it was off the coast of *Portuguese African territory* that the seizure had been effected.[4]

[1] *FO84/303*, Palmerston, Minute, 7 Nov. 1839, on Adm. Elliott to Ad., 20 Aug. 1839, Copy, Encl. in Ad. to F.O., 2 Nov. 1839.
[2] *FO63/1112*, Moncorvo to F.O., 28 July 1845, Translation.
[3] *FO63/1112*, F.O. to Moncorvo, 20 Sept. 1845, Draft.
[4] *FO84/826*, Loanda Commissioners to F.O., 25 Mar. 1846, No. 18. *FO84/659*, Consul Brand to Comm. Jones, 28 July 1846, Copy, Encl. in Ad. to F.O., 6 July 1846.

Palmerston at once saw the issue involved. He instructed Lord Howard de Walden, the British minister at Lisbon, to approve Portuguese zeal but at the same time to give a warning. Reference to the Anglo-Portuguese Convention of 1817, he said, showed that the British Government did not recognize the validity of the Portuguese rights from 5° 12′ down to 8° south latitude. In consequence,

> Her Majesty's Government are not wholly without apprehension that, if allowed to pass without notice, this sentence of the Portuguese court at Loanda, which involves a claim of exclusive Territorial Possession, might prejudice the right, which it is important, in the interests of Commerce, for Her Majesty's Government to maintain, to unrestricted intercourse with that part of the West Coast of Africa which lies between the 5th degree 12 minutes of South Latitude, and the 8th degree of South Latitude.[1]

Portugal appears not to have replied to Palmerston's statement of the British position—but only, no doubt, because a *coup d'état* took place, to be followed by civil war, within days of Palmerston's instructions being dispatched to Howard de Walden.[2]

Three years later, in 1849, on hearing that Ambriz was notorious as a centre of the slave trade, Palmerston considered recognizing Portuguese dominion there 'if the Portuguese Government would in good faith put down and prevent revival of the Slave Trade in the African Dominions of the Portuguese Crown'. He added the interesting rider: 'It might not be equally expedient to acknowledge Portuguese jurisdiction and dominion further North because by doing so we might shut ourselves out of the Congo.'[3] The Board of Trade was asked the value of the British trade at Ambriz, it being pointed out that the possible inconvenience to that trade must be weighed against the assistance to anti-slavery operations which the recognition of Portuguese authority at Ambriz might be expected to give.[4] The Board of Trade replied that Ambriz was an important, if not the most important commercial port on that portion of the coast and that Portuguese occupation

---

[1] *FO63/1112*, F.O. to Howard de Walden, 26 Sept. 1846, S/T No. 44, Draft.
[2] H. V. Livermore, *A History of Portugal* (Cambridge, 1947), 429.
[3] *FO84/764*, Brand to F.O., 19 Apr. 1849, S/T No. 1 and Palmerston Minute thereon, 25 July 1849. Palmerston, Minute, 31 July 1849.
[4] *FO84/787*, F.O. to B.o.T., 4 Aug. 1849, Draft.

would be a great impediment to trade.¹ Hearing this, Palmerston ruled that the question be left as it stood for the time being.²

In both 1850 and 1851 Portugal put out feelers designed to secure British acquiescence in the occupation of Ambriz but both moves came to nothing.³ On the second occasion, Palmerston, in approving the reply given by Pakenham, now the British minister at Lisbon, that he could hold out no hope that his Government would view the proposal favourably, made it clear that he had abandoned the notion of doing a deal with Portugal with which he had flirted two years previously. Rather, he went on to say that the anti-slavery cause, no less than British trade, was better served in districts unoccupied by Portugal and still in the hands of native chiefs.⁴ Hearing shortly afterwards that Portugal might proceed to occupy Ambriz, Palmerston instructed Pakenham to be watchful to prevent this in the interests of commerce and anti-slavery work alike.⁵

In 1853 the question of jurisdiction over the whole of the disputed coast was again raised when Count Lavradio, Portuguese minister in London, protested against the attempt of Captain Wilmot, R.N. to make slave trade treaties with certain Cabinda chiefs, on the ground that they were under Portugal's jurisdiction.⁶ Lord Clarendon, who had succeeded Palmerston as Foreign Secretary, persevered in refusing to acknowledge the Portuguese claim, adding a counter to that part of the Portuguese claim which cited the right of prior discovery.

It is manifest and notorious that the African Tribes inhabiting the line of coast claimed by Portugal ... are in reality independent, and that the rights which Portugal acquired by priority of discovery at the close of

¹ *FO84/787*, B.o.T. to F.O., 13 Aug. 1849 and Encl. 2, Foster & Smith to B.o.T., 9 Aug. 1849.
² *FO84/764*, Palmerston, Minute, 23 Aug. 1849.
³ *FO84/799*, Seymour to F.O., 8 Nov. 1850, S/T No. 3 and Encl., Tojal to Seymour, 6 Nov. 1850. *FO63/1112*, Pakenham to F.O., 28 Sept. 1851, S/T No. 9, Confidential.
⁴ *FO63/1112*, Palmerston, Minute, 7 Oct. 1851. *FO84/840*, F.O. to Pakenham, 17 Oct. 1851, S/T No. 50, Draft.
⁵ *FO63/1112*, Pakenham to F.O., 18 Oct. 1851, S/T No. 15, Confidential, and Encls. Palmerston, Minute, 25 Oct. 1851. *FO84/840*, F.O. to Pakenham, 7 Nov. 1851, S/T No. 54, Draft.
⁶ *FO63/1112*, Lavradio to F.O., 17 Sept. 1853 and Encls.

the fifteenth century have been long since suffered to lapse, in consequence of the Portuguese Government having neglected to occupy the countries so discovered.[1]

Frustrated in her attempts to occupy the disputed coast, or a portion of it, by agreement, Portugal resolved to occupy Ambriz and confront Britain with a *fait accompli*. In April 1855 the Foreign Office had wind of this through the Admiralty, and Pakenham was instructed to express to the Portuguese Government the hope that the Governor-General of Angola would immediately be ordered not to persist in the project.[2] When it became apparent that Portugal was persevering in her intention, the British representative at Lisbon was on three further occasions in August and September instructed to renew his protests.[3] On 8 September, Ward, acting for Pakenham, informed Viscount d'Athoguia, the Portuguese Foreign Minister, that his Government would never assent to the occupation of Ambriz,[4] and on the 19th, when news had been received that the occupation had actually taken place, Pakenham demanded the immediate withdrawal of the Portuguese force.[5]

Portugal paid no heed to this demand but in November, Lavradio, in London, privately proposed a compromise settlement. Great Britain was to recognize Portugal's immediate right to Ambriz and her future right to occupy the coast up to 5° 12'. As a *quid pro quo* Portugal would promise at once to abolish slavery at Ambriz, and on other parts of the coast when she occupied them. No duties would be levied at Ambriz for one year after the signature of the treaty embodying the compromise, and thereafter duties would only be levied as agreed in the treaty; these duties would also be levied on other parts of the coast when occupied.[6]

Clarendon was prepared to negotiate over Ambriz, his attitude being that 'the Portuguese . . . I think have right on their side and we are playing a dog in the manger game with

---

[1] *FO63/1112*, F.O. to Lavradio, 26 Nov. 1853, Draft.
[2] *FO63/1112*, F.O. to Pakenham, 6 Apr. 1855, S/T No. 11, Draft.
[3] *FO63/1112*, F.O. to Ward, 17 Aug. 1855, S/T No. 7; F.O. to Pakenham, 29 Aug. 1855, S/T No. 18; and 8 Sept. 1855, S/T No. 19, Drafts.
[4] *FO63/1112*, Ward to d'Athoguia, 8 Sept. 1855, Copy, Encl. in Ward to F.O., 8 Sept. 1855, S/T No. 14.
[5] *FO63/1112*, Pakenham to d'Athoguia, 19 Sept. 1855, Copy, Encl. in Pakenham to F.O., 28 Sept. 1855, S/T No. 18.
[6] *FO63/1112*, Lavradio to Clarendon, 9 Nov. 1855, Private. Draft Convention, n.d.

THE DIPLOMATIC BACKGROUND

them'.[1] Discussions continued for five months, the British position being that the Portuguese occupation of Ambriz would be recognized, but only if certain guarantees for British trade were given and if Portugal gave an assurance that she would not extend her boundaries northward of Ambriz. This last demand was unacceptable to Lavradio on the understandable ground that it involved the renunciation of his country's historic rights.[2]

With these negotiations still in train in London, the Portuguese Government took action in the *Cortes* which implicitly asserted the sovereignty of Portugal not only over Ambriz but, once again, over the whole disputed coast. A law was introduced abolishing slavery in Ambriz and throughout the disputed territory—a somewhat transparent stratagem, it would seem, for securing British acquiescence. When the Foreign Office was informed of this action,[3] Clarendon was away and Palmerston was supervising its work. He immediately ruled that the Portuguese claim to the disputed territory was ill-founded and that Portugal should be warned that further encroachments upon it would be resisted by armed force.[4] Backed by a favourable opinion from the Law Officers[5] this was done. On instructions from London,[6] Howard, the British Minister at Lisbon, sent a strong warning to d'Athoguia.

> The Earl of Clarendon . . . instructs me to say that without prejudging the question now under discussion between the British and Portuguese Governments as to Ambriz, and without implying any acquiescence in the occupation of that district by the Portuguese authorities, Her Majesty's Government deem it right to warn the Government of His Most Faithful Majesty that any attempt of the Portuguese authorities in Africa to extend that occupation will be opposed by Her Majesty's Naval Forces.[7]

At the end of July Howard was instructed to underline this warning.[8] In the following month Clarendon decided that

[1] *FO63/1112*, Clarendon, Minute, 9 Nov. 1855.
[2] *FO63/1112*, Wodehouse, Minute, 18 Nov. 1855. *FO63/1113*, Lavradio to Clarendon, 9 Feb. 1856, Private, and Encl. and Clarendon, Minute thereon, 10 Feb. 1856. F.O. to Lavradio, 23 Feb. 1856, Counter Proposal and Memo., Drafts. Lavradio to F.O., 29 Feb. 1856.
[3] *FO63/1113*, Howard to F.O., 18 Apr. 1856, S/T No. 27 and Encl.
[4] *FO63/1113*, Palmerston, Minute, 30 Apr. 1856.
[5] *FO63/1113*, Queen's Advocate to F.O., 19 May 1856.
[6] *FO63/1113*, F.O. to Howard, 26 May 1856, S/T No. 36, Draft.
[7] *FO63/1113*, Howard to F.O., 3 June 1856, S/T No. 43 and Encl., Howard to d'Athoguia, 2 June 1856.
[8] *FO63/1113*, F.O. to Howard, 26 July 1856, S/T No. 49, Draft.

there was little chance of reaching agreement with Portugal over Ambriz, that the Portuguese occupation of that place should be tacitly accepted, and that otherwise matters had best be left in their present state. 'The best way of securing this,' he wrote to Howard, 'will probably be a conviction on the part of the Portuguese Government that any attempt at territorial expansion will be resisted by force.'[1]

There, apart from an attempt by Lavradio to re-open discussions in London, which Clarendon courteously rebuffed,[2] the matter rested. The outcome of these events of 1856 was to make the British attitude to the Portuguese territorial claim in west Central Africa starkly clear. The Portuguese occupation of Ambriz was tacitly accepted but it was affirmed, in stronger terms than before, that future expansion to the north would not be tolerated by Britain. This policy, essentially Palmerston's, was a logical development of the stand he had made in 1846 when the Portuguese case was in danger of being conceded. The grounds of his attitude are not far to seek. Of all British ministers of the mid-nineteenth century Palmerston had the clearest conception of Britain's role in tropical Africa. The crushing of the Atlantic slave trade and the extension of British commerce—these were his complementary aims. As far as west Central Africa was concerned, this meant resistance to any extension of Portuguese jurisdiction—or, for that matter, of any other exclusive sovereignty. Until 1839, when Palmerston had taken the law into his own hands, Portugal's record as a slave trading nation was, perhaps, the least enviable of any European state, whilst she believed in a virtually exclusive system of colonial commerce. Also informing his attitude was an insular, arrogant, Victorian conviction of British superiority and Portuguese inferiority. 'The plain truth is', he once told Russell, 'that the Portuguese are of all European nations the lowest in the moral scale.'[3] Palmerston was not unmindful of the ancient tradition of Anglo-Portuguese friendship. But in his estimation Portugal was very definitely a client state which should be made to pay a higher price for

[1] *FO63/1113*, F.O. to Howard, 15 Aug. 1856, S/T No. 55, Confidential, Draft.
[2] *FO63/1113*, Lavradio to F.O., 11 Oct. 1856 and Translation. *FO63/1113*, Clarendon, Memo., 22 Oct. 1856. F.O. to Lavradio, 25 Nov. 1856, Draft.
[3] Palmerston to Russell, 5 Oct. 1864, quoted in H. C. F. Bell, *Lord Palmerston* (London, 1936, 2 vols.), II, 411.

THE DIPLOMATIC BACKGROUND

Britain's friendship than Britain paid for hers. Since 1826, Britain had ranged herself behind the cause of constitutional government in Portugal, but this would not be allowed to stand in the way of a firm policy when that was called for. As he said at the time of the passage of the 1839 Act against the Portuguese slave trade,

he could assure the hon. Baronet (Peel) that no predilection of his in favour of the system of government now fortunately established in that country, or any degree in which he might have identified himself with the support of that system . . . would he allow to interfere by mitigating, in the slightest degree, the indignation which he felt on this subject.[1]

For twenty years no serious attempt was made to alter Palmerston's policy towards the Portuguese Congo claim, and during that time it undoubtedly secured Britain's commercial and humanitarian interests. The chance of a settlement had been lost but it is difficult to believe either that Portugal could reasonably have given up her claim to the disputed territory or that Great Britain could have accepted at that time a change inimical both to her trade and to the success of the operations of her cruisers, and which would have lost to the first commercial nation the control of the mouth of the Congo.

At the time when the occupation of Ambriz was still only threatened, the Liverpool merchants engaged in its trade expressed alarm to the Foreign Office.[2] When the occupation had taken place they protested.[3] Neither action availed them anything, but a year later they again expressed their concern to the Foreign Office. Despite the fact that the occupation was now a *fait accompli*, the Liverpool African Association urged in August 1856 that a request of the kings and chiefs of Ambriz for a treaty with Britain should be met,[4] whilst in October and November alarm was voiced at the establishment of a Customs House at Ambriz and the promulgation of a scale of duties unfavourable to British commerce.[5] In a further letter of December the Liverpool Association also turned its attention

---
[1] Quoted in Bell, op. cit., I, 234.
[2] *FO84/977*, T. B. Horsfall, M.P., to F.O., 17 Aug. 1855 and Encl., Hatton & Cookson to F.O., 17 Aug. 1855. Tobin & Son to F.O., 17 Aug. 1855.
[3] *FO84/977*, Liverpool African Association to F.O., 23 Oct. 1855.
[4] *FO63/1113*, T. B. Horsfall (on behalf of Liv. Afr. Assoc.), to F.O., 6 Aug., 1856 and Encl.
[5] *FO63/1113*, T. B. Horsfall (on behalf of Liv. Afr. Assoc.), to F.O., 18 Oct., and Encl., and 10 Nov. 1856.

to the countering of future Portuguese expansion. If such expansion was permitted, the transfer of the British factories northwards to Kinsembo, an action which the merchants must already have been considering, would be futile. The Liverpool Association therefore advocated treaty-making with native chiefs along the coast to the northward, a course which would ensure the free operation of British commerce, whose humanitarian consequences they had, in their previous letter, not omitted to contrast with the harmful effect on anti-slavery work of Portuguese occupation. The Association also sought reassurance that Portugal would not be allowed to extend her frontier beyond the River Loge since it was imperative to protect the growing trade at Ambrizette and on the Congo.[1] Fears that Portugal would extend her authority northward of Ambriz were again expressed in February of the following year.[2]

On resistance to future Portuguese expansion the Foreign Office was reassuring. Formally, it displayed official caution, saying it could offer no guarantee beyond the instructions given to naval officers in accordance with the warning given to Portugal in June 1856. But the accompanying statement of the British Government's view of the case was, in its very forthrightness, encouraging.

> Her Majesty's Government object to . . . the extension of the Portuguese restrictive system of commerce to parts of the Sea Coast of Africa which have hitherto been free from it, and open more advantageously to British commerce; and we object, secondly, to the Extension of Portuguese rule to Parts of the Coast which have hitherto been free from it, because where Portuguese rule does not extend we can, by Treaties with native chiefs and by the action of our Cruisers more effectually prevent Slave Trade than we are able to do at places where Portuguese rule exists.[3]

The response to the Liverpool African Association's last representation was also encouraging. Howard was instructed to inform the Portuguese Foreign Minister that Her Majesty's Government hoped that 'no cause for discussion between the two Governments would arise over this matter'.[4] The instructions

---

[1] *FO63/1113*, Liv. Afr. Assoc. to F.O., 10 Nov. and 2 Dec. 1856.
[2] *FO63/1114*, Liv. Afr. Assoc. to F.O., 18 Feb. 1857.
[3] *FO63/1113*, F.O. to T. B. Horsfall (Liv. Afr. Assoc.), 6 Dec. 1856, Draft.
[4] *FO63/1114*, F.O. to Howard, 23 Feb. 1857, S/T No. 10, Draft.

to naval officers were treated as seriously as it was intended they should be. In 1857 Commander Hickley intervened to prevent the Portuguese authorities interfering with the construction of a new factory at Kinsembo, north of Ambriz, by Hatton & Cookson's agent. In the same year this officer also obliged a Portuguese military detachment to quit Punta da Lenha, on the Congo, where it had established itself.[1]

However effective it was for the moment, the policy confirmed in the 1856 instructions to naval captains had the limitation that it rested on coercion and that its legality was disputable. Moreover it made no positive provision for securing the freedom of the Congo. These limitations, together with a sense of the traditional Anglo-Portuguese alliance and that it might be made good use of, would seem to explain the periodic flirtation of the Foreign Office with the notion of a settlement with Portugal. The next such occasion was in April 1858 in response to a proposal of Viscount de Bandeira, the Portuguese Foreign Minister, that Britain should admit Portugal to the Congo and adjoining coastline in order, so he alleged, to prevent a French and (threatened) American export of slaves from the river in the guise of free labourers.[2]

Commenting on the proposal, Wylde adumbrated, though tentatively, the policy advocated by Morier two decades later for the protection of British interests in the region. Despite the fact that, in the meantime, the project for introducing African 'free labourers' into the American Southern States, at least, had been dropped, the proposal had certain attractions.

> In some respects, it would be advantageous if Portugal were permitted to take possession of the Territory in dispute. The slave trade would then doubtless be put a stop to in the Congo River from whence the greater part of the cargoes shipped from the South Coast are now obtained and the French Emigration scheme would also be prevented from being carried out in Portuguese Territory, and above all the other European Powers would thereby be prevented from taking possession of an important line of Coast including the embouchure of a River (the Congo) which cannot fail before many years have elapsed to become one of the great highways and channels of Trade into the Interior of

[1] *FO63/1114*, Gabriel to F.O., 9 July 1857, No. 43 and Encl. F.O. 'Memo on Portuguese Encroachments on the West Coast of Africa', 11 Sept. 1857. *Ad.1/5684*, Hickley to Adm. Grey, 10 July 1857, Copy, Encl. in Hickley to Ad., 10 July 1857.
[2] *FO63/1114*, Howard to Malmesbury, 7 Apr. 1858, Private and Encl., de Bandeira to Howard, 1 Apr. 1858, Private and Confidential, Copy.

Africa. The Trade on the African Coast has within the last few years become a very valuable one and in the Congo River a very great increase has lately taken place in licit trade. . . .

It would be more to our advantage that that part of the African Coast should be in the hands of a country like Portugal than in the possession of France or any other Power that might be disposed to make use of it for the purpose of fostering a system of African Emigration.

But at this point Wylde contradicted a part of what he had said earlier and weakened the force of his memorandum by expressing doubt of Portugal's ability to crush the slave trade and to protect lawful commerce. In conclusion he made the interesting point that Portuguese occupation 'would also be very unpopular amongst the British merchants trading with Africa for it would destroy the Monopoly which is now practically enjoyed by a few large Firms which have the trade almost entirely in their own hands'.[1]

Despite Wylde's indecision, Lord Malmesbury, who had succeeded Clarendon at the Foreign Office, considered that a settlement might be negotiated. After approaching France, 'a convention might be signed between the three Powers recognizing Portugal's jurisdiction but securing equal rights of trade for the three powers'. But the approach to France did not take place for Fitzgerald, the Parliamentary Under-Secretary, persuaded Malmesbury against it though there is no evidence on what grounds.[2] Nevertheless, the proposal for a settlement still had its advocates. Within a year the C.-in-C. of the Cape of Good Hope Station urged that the Portuguese claim should be admitted provided that guarantees for freedom of commerce were obtained, and Wylde endorsed the proposal.[3] But the conservative view prevailed, and, indeed, found utterance at this very time in a negative response to a Portuguese attempt to obtain British recognition of her Congo claim in compensation for the support which Britain had failed to give her in the *Charles et Georges* affair.[4] (France had made a prestige issue of the seizure by the Portuguese of the *Charles et Georges* which was

[1] *FO63/1114*, Wylde, Memo., 29 Apr. 1858, on Howard to Malmesbury, Private, 7 Apr. 1858. 'Large' is an exaggeration.
[2] *FO63/1114*, Malmesbury, Minute, 1 May 1858, and pencilled note appended to it.
[3] *FO84/1070*, Adm. Grey to Ad., 12 Nov. 1858, Encl. in Ad. to F.O., 30 Dec. 1858, and Wylde, Minute thereon, n.d. *FO84/1097*, Comm. Wise to Adm. Grey, 20 Jan. 1859, Copy, Encl. in Ad. to F.O., 11 Mar. 1859.
[4] *FO84/1082*, F.O. Memo. on slave trade, 23 June 1859.

engaged in a veiled form of the slave trade, and largely because British support was not forthcoming, had forced a diplomatic humiliation on Portugal.) As on this occasion, so in 1860, 1862 and 1867, when Portugal, in one form or another, again raised the question of her claim, the British attitude was unyielding.[1] On this last occasion Wylde, whose opinion as the head of the Slave Trade Department carried particular weight, made it clear that he had abandoned his readiness for a settlement, and, rather, developed the second thoughts which he had had in April 1858. The latest attempt of Portugal to assert her sovereignty, he wrote, should not be allowed to pass unnoticed. What was more—and here he testified to a consideration which, with the passing of the slave trade, the general progress of exploration, and the growth of legitimate trade on the Congo, was now of greater consequence—if the Lower Congo and adjoining coast

were to fall into the hands of the Portuguese it is needless to say the trade would be trammelled to such an extent that there would be little chance of the River becoming as it someday surely will, one of the main channels of Trade into the interior of Africa.[2]

So matters stood until 1876: but that year heralded the end of an era in the Congo region for in February Lord Derby set in train the process of reconsideration of Great Britain's Congo policy which, with many setbacks, and forced on by the pressure of events, was to lead to the negotiation of a treaty with Portugal. Once more Portugal had protested against British naval activity in waters which she claimed as her own —in this case Commodore Hewett's large-scale expedition against piracy in the Lower Congo—and utilized this opportunity to request the reopening of negotiations on the Portuguese territorial claim. Added to the request was a clear intimation that even if the negotiations were unsuccessful, they would be followed by the affirmation 'by means of actual possession of the validity of . . . [Portugal's] reserved rights'.[3] Derby's

[1] *FO63/1114*, Lavradio to F.O., 29 June and 9 July 1860 and Translations. F.O. to Lavradio, 28 July and 13 Oct. 1860, Drafts. R. W. Bixler, 'Anglo-Portuguese Rivalry for Delagoa Bay', *Journal of Modern History*, vi, 1934, 434–5. *FO63/1115*, Lavradio to F.O., 20 Aug. 1867, Encls. and Translations. F.O. to Harriss, 21 Aug. 1867, S/T No. 2, Draft.
[2] *FO63/1115*, Wylde, Minute, 10 Aug. 1867.
[3] *FO63/1116*, Corvo to de Saldanha, 4 Dec. 1875, communicated to F.O., 24 Jan. 1876.

immediate reply was mere repetition—the 1856 instructions remained in force: but at the same time he deferred a final reply until he had acquainted himself with the history of the question,[1] and it is clear from a departmental minute of this period[2] and from his subsequent actions, that he was, in fact, resolved to reconsider British policy towards the Portuguese claim.

Derby's motive in reopening the question is not completely clear. He certainly appears to have felt moved to act fairly by Portugal who, after all, was Britain's traditional ally. The high-handed course advocated by T. V. Lister, then an Assistant Under-Secretary, had been rejected. 'Whatever our right may be', Lister had written, 'I am sure that all Portuguese encroachments in Africa should be resisted. It is far better to have to deal with the worst savages than with the best intentioned Portuguese.' Derby's rejection of this course was based on the simple, aristocratic ground that 'You can't keep a man out of his estate because you do not think him likely to be a good landlord.'[3] At the same time there was a particular reason why Derby may have reasoned that the old Palmerstonian policy, effective though it had been, was not likely to prove adequate for much longer. The reason lay in Commander V. L. Cameron's recently completed journey across Africa. During the course of it he had signed numerous treaties with native chiefs and on the strength of these had actually declared a British protectorate over the Congo basin by a proclamation of 28 December 1874. Cameron had duly submitted the treaties and the proclamation to the Foreign Office for its approval[4] and the matter was almost certainly under the Office's consideration at the end of January 1876, the time when the latest Portuguese representation was under discussion. The official decision not to recognize Cameron's protectorate was not taken until the end of February when the Colonial Office had advised in that sense:[5] but the whole tradition of British policy in the matter of extensions of sovereignty suggests that in such a case the Foreign Office must have been in favour of rejection all along. At the same time it had long

[1] *FO63/1116*, F.O. to de Saldanha, 8 Feb. 1876, Draft.
[2] *FO63/1116*, Derby, Minute, 30 Jan. 1876.
[3] *FO63/1116*, Lister, 29 Jan. 1876 and Derby, 30 Jan. 1876, Minutes.
[4] *FO84/1459*, F.O. to C.O., 8 Feb. 1876, Draft.
[5] *FO84/1459*, C.O. to F.O., Feb. 1876, n.d.

been accepted that the Congo would one day be a commercial artery of great importance—an importance, the realization of which by the European powers, Cameron's discoveries could only accelerate. Therefore it is not far-fetched to suppose that at the end of January Derby, although, or rather, because he was against acceptance of Cameron's protectorate would be very ready to consider the admission to a vital portion of that part of Africa of a power friendly to Great Britain and in a measure subordinate to her.

The immediate fruit of Derby's promise was, in the Foreign Office itself, a long memorandum by Sir Edward Hertslet, the Librarian, detailing the history of the question and cautiously advocating a settlement[1] and, outside the Office, an instruction to Morier, who became Minister at Lisbon in the same year, to investigate and report on the whole matter.[2]

Diplomacy, backed, of course, by the might of Great Britain, had for thirty years played an important part in keeping the Congo region open to British commerce and Free Trade. In addition, while the slave trade lasted, diplomacy had secured for the naval squadron considerable freedom of action against the trade in that region. During the next half-dozen years the pace of events in the whole of west Central Africa quickened. Trade on the Lower Congo and adjoining coast steadily grew; atrocities—perpetrated by Europeans—took place, disorder increased; Stanley completed Cameron's work by actually following the course of the Congo from its source in the heart of the continent to the coast, and publicized its immense potentialities; Leopold II of Belgium formed the *Comité d'Etudes du Haut Congo* to pave the way for the development of the Upper Congo lands; Lieutenant Savorgnan de Brazza brought under French jurisdiction territory on the Upper Congo. Such a situation Britain's traditional policy was not able to meet and the Foreign Office eventually realized this. Necessity now demanded what previously only equity had tentatively suggested. Portugal was to be admitted to the Lower Congo—as the watchdog of Free Trade.

As the Foreign Office responded to the changed conditions

[1] *FO63/1116*, Hertslet, Memo., 23 Mar. 1876.
[2] *FO63/1117*, Draft, n.d., Morier to Braamcamp, Encl. in Morier to F.O., 12 Mar. 1880, No. 13, Confidential. *FO84/1801*, Morier, Memo., 17 Aug. 1877.

so also, but even more slowly, did the British merchants. But their response was different and involved them in opposition to the Government's new Congo policy. This opposition was utilized, energized and directed by the British supporters of Leopold II of Belgium and his Congo project who had their own good reasons for opposing the admission of Portugal to the Lower Congo. The outcome was a head-on collision over the negotiations for a treaty with Portugal.

CHAPTER IV

THE BEGINNINGS OF BRITISH COLLABORATION WITH LEOPOLD OF THE BELGIANS

SOVEREIGN of a small European State which scarcely provided him with sufficient outlets for his energy and enthusiasm, Leopold II of Belgium had for some time before 1876 interested himself in various overseas projects. The year 1855, in which, as Duke of Brabant, he first visited Africa, marks the beginning of his interest in schemes of overseas expansion. In the next decade he not only made a close study of colonial affairs, but, in the years 1861-5, considered no less than five overseas projects, including a Belgian company or society for the exploration of the Far East, and plans for the purchase of Sarawak and of an Argentine province. The latter, at least, had he acquired it, would have been made over to Belgium. Shortly after he ascended the throne, however, Leopold became convinced of the national lukewarmness to the idea of colonies and by December 1866 was thinking in different terms—of an international company, but with its headquarters in Brussels, which would gradually become for China what the East India Company had become for India. But nothing came of this scheme nor of attempts to acquire concessions in Mozambique and the Philippines. By 1875 his hopes had, if only in disappointment become centred on Africa. He first considered the possibilities of the unstable and near-bankrupt Transvaal, but his main attention soon became fixed on the convocation of an International Geographical Conference to consider the opening up of Central Africa.[1]

The precise intention that lay behind the calling of the Brussels Geographical Conference of 1876 is not entirely clear. Leopold may already have had in view the creation of

[1] This summary of Leopold's thinking on overseas projects before 1876 is based on A. Roeykens, *Léopold II et l'Afrique, 1855-1880* (Brussels, 1958), 13-39, 55-56, though it does not always share his conclusions. This book is itself a summary of a number of previous works of Father Roeykens, the most important of which are *Les Débuts de l'œuvre Africaine de Léopold II, 1876-1879* (Brussels, 1955), and *Léopold II et la Conférence Géographique de Bruxelles, 1876* (Brussels, 1956).

an independent state of which he was to become King and which would be linked to Belgium in the person of the common sovereign (he may, indeed, have cherished such a design since the mid-sixties), and conceived of the Conference as the initial step in the fulfilment of this plan. He may, on the other hand, at this time, have had in mind only broad and tentative steps for the future. Whichever was the case, the concern of this chapter is, rather, with the proposal for a conference as it was presented to a group of Englishmen and as it appeared to them.

Leopold appears to have prepared the ground by a private visit to London in May–June 1876 during which he met Cameron, the Baroness Burdett-Coutts—whose wide-ranging philanthropy embraced alike amenities for the poor of East London and a water supply for the humbler inhabitants of Jerusalem—and Sir Henry Rawlinson, a member of the Council of the Royal Geographical Society.[1] In the following weeks general preparations for the Conference proceeded apace and on 3 August Leopold wrote to his second cousin, the Prince of Wales, asking his advice on the manner of the British representation. The Prince of Wales' response, after taking the advice of Sir Bartle Frere, a former Indian administrator of note who had also a lively interest in and experience of African questions, was to propose that three explorers—Sir Samuel Baker, Colonel J. A. Grant and Cameron—and a few persons 'with handles to their names' should be invited to represent Great Britain at the Conference.[2] This suggestion was accepted and the outcome was that the British delegation to the Conference consisted of Grant and Cameron (Baker was unable to be present) and eight others, mostly Council members of the R.G.S.—Sir Rutherford Alcock (President of the Society), Admiral Sir Leopold Heath, Sir T. Fowell Buxton, Sir John Kennaway, Sir Harry Verney, Mr. William Mackinnon, Frere and Rawlinson.[3]

What did the British representatives conceive to be the purpose of the Conference? Their notions must largely have been formed by a confidential note sent them—as to the other

[1] Roeykens, Débuts, 122–8.
[2] Sir Sidney Lee, King Edward VII, a biography (London, 1925–7), I, 629.
[3] R. S. Thomson, La Fondation de l'Etat Indépendant du Congo (Brussels, 1933), 42.

members—as a statement of the Conference's inspiration and purpose. It presented Leopold's initiative as a response to a general feeling, and his project in terms of a civilizing crusade. The Conference would be asked how best to implement certain broad principles of action. These comprised the establishment of two main bases, one at the Congo mouth and the other on the Zanzibar coast, a proposal which immediately made clear the geographical scope of the operations in contemplation; the progressive opening up of routes into the interior along which would be founded '*des stations hospitalières, scientifiques et pacificatrices*'; and the creation of an international organization to superintend and publicize the work and attract the support of philanthropy.

'I insist', wrote the King in conclusion '... on the completely charitable, completely scientific and philanthropic nature of the aim to be achieved. It is not a question of a business proposition, it is matter of a completely spontaneous collaboration between all those who wish to engage in introducing civilisation to Africa.'[1]

In the innaugural address to the Conference itself, which met on 12 September 1876, Leopold somewhat elaborated the ideas sketched out in his confidential note, and took care to retain the original emphasis on the civilizing and humanitarian ends to be served.[2] To the somewhat heady atmosphere generated by royal charm and benevolent intention the British representatives appear to have wholeheartedly responded. Alcock endorsed the proposal for a chain of stations, urging that it should start from Bagamoyo, on the coast opposite Zanzibar island, and that it include a large establishment at Ujiji, on Lake Tanganyika, in the very centre of the Continent. At this place, Alcock added the interesting suggestion, Leopold could establish a consulate. If, he concluded, appeal were made to the public, these vast and fertile regions could be civilized by the introduction of commerce and the suppression of the Arab slave trade. Central Africa would then be completely opened up.[3]

When the Conference divided into two groups to consider in more detail the establishment of stations and lines of

[1] Roeykens, *Conférence Géographique*, 28–29.
[2] Roeykens, *Conférence Géographique*, 197–9.
[3] *M. des A.E.*, Report of Proceedings of 1876 Geographical Conference, 10.

communication, the group which included the British representatives made the more ambitious proposals. It urged

the establishment of a continual line of communication between the eastern and western coasts of the continent south of the Equator, with subsidiary lines through the Lake regions which would connect the trunk road with the Nile basin and the lower course of the Congo to the north, and with the Zambezi country to the south, and would debouch at convenient points on the sea-coast.

The east-west line, the report continued, in the general vein of Alcock's earlier remarks, should run from Zanzibar to Loanda and, if it was possible to establish permanent stations, they should in the first instance be at Ujiji, and Nyangwe on the Upper Congo. Steamers should be placed on the Upper Congo and on Lakes Victoria and Tanganyika to assist in the opening up of a trade route between the Zambesi and the Nile.[1]

The British attitude at the Conference was, then, wholeheartedly to support the proposal for the opening up of Central Africa by international action working through national committees. (It was actually a British delegate, Frere, who responded to Leopold's clear wish and proposed that he be president of the body set up by the conference—the *Association Internationale Africaine*.) There is scant evidence for seeing in Alcock's suggestion that Leopold establish a (Belgian) consul at Ujiji either a move to probe the secret intentions of the King or an attempt to use Belgium to reserve Central Africa for Great Britain. Nor is there more justification for seeing in the importance attached by the British representatives to the coastal bases—which, it was argued, would have to be placed under the protection of a European power—the hope of placing the whole venture under British tutelage.[2] Each suggestion is an exercise in over-subtlety and, even were it true, would only have the significance of the proposal of a private individual—the Foreign Office had to be *told* what the Conference was all about by the British delegates on their return.[3]

The enthusiasm of the British representatives for international action did not diminish on their return to England. Formation

[1] *M. des A.E.*, Proceedings of Geographical Conference, 19–21.
[2] Roeykens, *Léopold et l'Afrique*, 112. Roeykens, *Conférence Géographique*, 228–33, 239–41.
[3] *FO84/1463*, Tenterden, Memo., 5 Dec. 1876. Quoted in Roeykens, *Léopold et l'Afrique*, 344–5.

of the British national committee had been entrusted to the R.G.S., and at meetings of the Society in November Alcock and Frere spoke enthusiastically of the whole project.[1] But the British Committee never materialized. The Council of the R.G.S. decided in the New Year that 'looking... at the subject from a practical point of view, African exploration will be more effectually prosecuted by England . . . through national enterprise than by international association.'[2]

Why the change?

It is possible that doubts first entered the minds of Alcock and his associates early in December. On the fifth of that month Alcock had an interview with Lord Tenterden, the Permanent Under-Secretary at the Foreign Office, at which the President of the R.G.S. outlined the functions of the proposed British national committee. (Its first task was to be the construction of a road from opposite Zanzibar to Lake Tanganyika and thence to Lake Nyasa.) Tenterden immediately drew attention to what he clearly considered to be the inadequate provision which was contemplated for the protection of the Committee's operations. He pressed Alcock on this point and the latter could only make the feeble rejoinder that it was hoped no protection would be required.[3] Here, possibly, was a first realization of an important limitation of internationally inspired action. Derby himself, in a completely noncommital statement to a deputation comprising Alcock, Frere and Rawlinson, six days later, did nothing more to upset faith[4] but in the middle of the month the circulation of a memorandum drawn up by Sir Henry Thring, the Home Office Counsel and an eminent authority on International Law, raised more serious objections. Thring's opinion had been sought on the particular point of whether the Prince of Wales should accept the presidency of the British national committee. But the grounds on which Thring based his submission against acceptance necessarily drew attention to the hazards of a general British participation in the work of the International Association. Thring based his opinion on three considerations

---

[1] *Royal Geographical Society Proceedings, 1876–7*, 16–20, 60. Roeykens, *Léopold et l'Afrique*, 342, 343–4.
[2] *R.G.S. Proceedings, 1876–7*, 391–2, 475.
[3] *FO84/1463*, Tenterden, Memo., 7 Dec. 1876.
[4] *FO84/1463*, Derby, Memo., 11 Dec. 1876.

—the suppression of the slave trade, an avowed object of the Association, was properly a matter for individual governments; the establishment of stations would both involve interference in local disputes and was likely to lead to the establishment of territorial jurisdiction; and it was conceivable that funds subscribed to the central organization by the British committee might be used for purposes inimical to British interests.[1]

Thring's memorandum certainly convinced one of the British representatives at the Brussels Conference that though a committee of some sort should still be formed in England, it should have no integral connexion with the International Association, and it is not unlikely that others reached the same conclusion. Buxton made his opinion clear in a note to Mackinnon of 16 December written in reference to Thring's memorandum.

> It was alarming to find [what] tremendous duties we, according to his view, had taken upon our shoulders—War, conquest, trade and Government—We shall look to you Scotchmen to pull us through. It is clear however that H.R.H. cannot join any committee that is not purely consultative and recording. *It will be a very good thing if those limits are fully laid down and recognised.*[2] (My italics.)

Three weeks later Mackinnon, for his part, still envisaged the creation of a British committee. The terms in which he writes suggest, on balance, that he had not accepted Buxton's restricted view and that he still assumed the creation of a British committee on the lines originally laid down, but the evidence is by no means conclusive.

> 'There is some legal difficulty', he wrote to his friend Kirk, the consul at Zanzibar, 'about the Prince of Wales becoming president of the British Section of the International Society formed at Brussels and in the meantime the formation of a committee in London is delayed.'[3]

Evidence of the reaction of the other British representatives at the Brussels Conference to the Thring memorandum is lacking: but it is not unlikely that some, at least, would have reacted as Buxton had. Religion was a factor in determining

[1] *M.P.*, Thring, Confidential Memo. on International African Association, 13 Dec. 1876, Encl., in Buxton to Mackinnon, 16 Dec. 1876.
[2] *M.P.*, Buxton to Mackinnon, 16 Dec. 1876.
[3] *M.P.*, Mackinnon to Kirk, 9 Jan. 1877, Copy.

the rejection of international action, and on one view was reckoned as decisive as far as Scottish opinion was concerned. As it was put seven years later,

When they [the Glasgow Committee] came to examine the constitution of the International Association, they found that the Roman Catholic Powers would have a majority of votes, Belgium and other small powers having so many, and that the subscribers would be raising money for them to pay away. The Committee was accordingly dissolved.[1]

Of most debatable importance as a factor leading to rejection was a letter from the Sultan of Zanzibar to Lord Derby promising his support in the exploitation and development of his dominions. The proposal resulted from Kirk's initiative. In the Sultan's own words:

I have seen from the newspapers and it has been explained to me by my friend Dr. Kirk, Agent of the Government, what passed at a conference held by invitation of the King of the Belgians for the object of opening up the interior of Africa and I have also been told what took place at a meeting held in Scotland at which were present some of those gentlemen who take an interest in developing the lands of the Interior of Africa. . . .

I should wish these my friends to know by Your Lordship that it is my desire to help them all that I can and to render every assistance to them throughout my dominions.[2]

Father A. Roeykens contends that the receipt of this letter —a copy was sent to Frere on 12 January and to Alcock at about the same time[3]—was the decisive influence in leading the R.G.S. not to form a national committee because, he argues, the Sultan's letter was an invitation to England to extend *her* influence and *her* commerce in East Africa.[4] Within a week of Alcock and Frere being told of the Sultan's offer, a subcommittee of the R.G.S. had been convened and had resolved to recommend that the R.G.S. should co-operate in the attainment of the aims declared by the Brussels Conference, yes, but through the creation of an 'African Exploration Fund' —in other words by direct and independent action.[5] Moreover

---
[1] *FO84/1811*, J. C. Stevenson to Lord Edmond Fitzmaurice, 15 May 1884.
[2] *FO84/1454*, Sultan to F.O., 13 Dec. 1876, Encl. in Kirk to F.O., 13 Dec. 1876. See also this covering dispatch.
[3] Roeykens, *Léopold II et l'Afrique*, 364–5, 367.
[4] Ibid., 367–8.
[5] Alcock to Greindl, 19 Jan. 1877 and 22 Jan. 1877, quoted in Roeykens, *Débuts*, 213–15.

the receipt of the Sultan's proposal was immediately followed by Mackinnon and a group of British associates setting on foot a project for the economic development of East Africa.

The conclusion suggested by this juxtaposition of events may be the correct one. But against this, it is quite clear that as far as Mackinnon himself was concerned, he was, as will be seen in more detail, seriously considering an East African scheme of his own, which had first been conceived twelve months previously anyway, *before* he heard of the Sultan's approach and *before* the R.G.S. decided on abstention.[1] Neither need Mackinnon and the R.G.S. have necessarily regarded it as essential *not* to form a national committee as a condition of respectively promoting or leaving scope for a purely British enterprise. After all, why need the programme agreed at Brussels—the construction under international auspices of transcontinental lines of communication and stations—have been regarded as incompatible with an unofficial national enterprise whose aim, the economic development of East Africa, was not included in the Brussels programme?

What is clear is that after the British delegates to the Conference left Brussels, the limitations and disadvantages of international action were brought home in a number of ways. The relative importance of each consideration and of the Sultan's offer is a matter of conjecture.

The changed attitude of the R.G.S. did not mean that thenceforth British support for Leopold's work would be completely denied. In the early eighties such influential bodies as the Manchester Chamber of Commerce, followed by many other Chambers, the Anti-Slavery Society and the Baptist Missionary Society came to range themselves behind it, whilst a number of influential politicians—Jacob Bright, W. E. Forster and others—also championed his work. But there were three—an Englishman and two Scotsmen—whose support was of a different character, for it was distinguished by a measure of intimacy with Leopold and his Brussels coadjutors and was inspired by more positive hopes of the outcome of the king's African work. The three do not include those Englishmen who took service under him, of whom H. M. Stanley was much the

---

[1] *M.P.*, Mackinnon to Kirk, 9 Jan. 1877, Copy. H. Waller to Mackinnon, 12 Jan. 1877. See also pp. 70–71 below.

most important, though, as will be seen, by 1885 and 1886, when Stanley had returned from his great work for Leopold on the Congo, he can no longer be considered as a mere agent.

Of the three, John Kirk, later Sir John Kirk, is perhaps the least expected. In the consular service at Zanzibar since 1866 and consul since 1873, he had established a position of unique influence at the court of the Sultan of Zanzibar. But he did not allow his official duties to monopolize a deep interest in the opening up of Africa which dated from his membership of Livingstone's Zambesi expedition. What seems to have drawn him to Leopold was a deep sense that the Upper Congo offered unrivalled access to the heart of Africa and that Leopold, who from 1878, and especially 1880, onwards, was striving to open up this route, was in a position to confirm its promise. 'The country is the richest in Africa and the river the only waterway of any consequence.'[1] 'I have myself perfect faith in the eventual success of the Congo navigation scheme and the profits to come from it. . . .'[2] These are the sort of terms in which he expressed his conviction.[3] Also significant is the expression, in 1882, of the hope that 'the Congo scheme could be diverted into English hands'.[4] In the seventies and up till 1883 the only help that Kirk could give Leopold was assistance to the various expeditions which the *A.I.A.* sent to the Lake Tanganyika region via the East Coast. But in 1883 he was able to give more valuable help when, since he chanced to be on leave in England, he played a very active part in opposing the Anglo-Portuguese treaty negotiations.

James F. Hutton of Manchester had a longer and closer association with Leopold. He began his commercial career as the Manchester superintendent of the family firm of W. B. Hutton & Sons, West African merchants, of London, in 1848. But within a few years he had wound up this firm, recommencing business in Manchester in the early 1850's as James F. Hutton & Co. and in partnership with a brother. The business of the firm was the supplying of European and native West African merchants with goods for the African market, and was

---
[1] *M.P.*, Kirk to Mackinnon, 7 June 1886.
[2] *M.P.*, Kirk to Mackinnon, 10 Dec. 1879.
[3] See also *M.P.*, Kirk to Mackinnon, 22 July 1882, 25 Nov. 1884 and 31 Aug. 1885.
[4] *M.P.*, Kirk to Mackinnnon, 30 Sept. 1882.

sufficiently prosperous to carry J. F. Hutton to a position of some eminence in his adopted city. He became Belgian consul in Manchester, and in 1877 a director of its Chamber of Commerce. He was later to become its president (1884–5), the first M.P. for North Manchester, one of the founders of the Manchester Geographical Society, a director of the Royal Niger Company and a founder of the British East Africa Company. In his house at Victoria Park he was host to a number of African explorers,[1] whilst his interest in Africa, if centred on its economic prospects, extended also to the support of missionary work. His first notable assistance to Leopold was a subscription of £800 to the *Comité d'Etudes du Haut Congo*,[2] a body inspired by Leopold in the autumn of 1878 to finance a second expedition by Stanley to investigate the potentialities of the Congo in more detail. The *Comité*'s ultimate intentions were ambitious. If Stanley's findings were favourable, the subscribers to the *Comité* were to be again called together with a view to the formation of two companies, one for the construction of a link between the Lower and Upper Congo, and the other to establish navigation and develop commerce on the upper reaches of the river.[3] Meanwhile, probably with the construction of a railway to join the upper and lower river in mind, should Stanley report favourably, Hutton was asked to invite a few Englishmen of note to join the *Comité*. Certainly those whom he approached were a group centring on the Duke of Sutherland and Stafford House, names much associated with the financing of railway construction at this time. Two members of the group, General Kemball and Mr. Donald Currie, had an interview with Leopold, but the approach came to nothing. The group feared that difficulties with Portugal would result from the intention apparently professed by the *Comité* to restrict trade on the Lower Congo to one firm—the Dutch company—an intention which is something of an augury when the subsequent development of the Congo Free State is recalled. The Foreign Office, in a semi-official way, confirmed this fear: Her Majesty's

---

[1] Information on the Hutton family and its commercial activities has been obtained from J. A. and P. C. Hutton, *Hutton Families* (1939, published privately), a copy of which the late J. Arthur Hutton kindly gave to the present writer.

[2] *M.P.*, Strauch to Mackinnon, 25 Apr. 1879. *FO84/1556*, Memorandum of Association, 25 Nov. 1878, Encl. 2 in Reay to Currie, 4 Apr. 1879, Private.

[3] Thomson. op. cit., 66–67.

Government would not recognize such a monopoly. Participation was therefore refused.[1]

The four years after 1882 were the period of Hutton's most active support for Leopold's work. The third of Leopold's British collaborators—William Mackinnon, later Sir William Mackinnon—on the other hand, was consistently active from 1878 to 1886, and later. Although he may not have displayed the fierce energy which Hutton from time to time put forth, his collaboration, because of his national as opposed to Hutton's provincial eminence, was probably of greater importance to Leopold. Moreover Mackinnon's interest in Leopold's schemes is significant because Mackinnon was one of the foremost figures in that small group of Englishmen who played a decisive part in Britain's African expansion.

William Mackinnon was a self-made man. Born in Campbeltown, Lanarkshire, in 1823, of poor parents, he received some sort of education and was then put to train for the grocery trade. Quite soon, however, he moved to Glasgow where he was first employed in a silk warehouse, and then in the office of a merchant engaged in the Eastern trade. A decisive step was taken in 1847 when he went to India and joined an old schoolfellow, Robert Mackenzie, probably at the latter's suggestion. Mackenzie was then engaged in the coasting trade of the Bay of Bengal, apparently in a quite humble way. Mackinnon became his partner and the immediate fruit of the partnership was the foundation of the trading company later to be known as Mackinnon & Mackenzie and which became a considerable business. It would appear that Mackenzie thenceforth devoted himself principally to the affairs of this company whilst Mackinnon channelled his energies into shipping. In 1854 Mackinnon bought a steam vessel and formed the Calcutta & Burma Steam Navigation Co. Eight years later the name was changed to the British India Steam Navigation Co. The company grew rapidly.

Following a common Victorian mould, Mackinnon combined a deep piety with his considerable business abilities. Up

[1] *FO84/1556*, Kemball to Tenterden, 1 Apr. 1879, and Encl.(?), Minute, 1 Apr. 1879, Copy. Wylde, Memo., 1 Apr. 1879. Reay to Currie, 4 Apr. 1879 and Encl. 1, Private Memo. 4 Apr. 1879; Encl. 2, Memorandum of Association, 25 Nov. 1878; and Encl. 3, Translation thereof, Strictly Private and Confidential, with which is included Strauch to Hutton, 30 Jan. 1879, and Extract of minutes of Executive Committee of *Comité d'Etudes*, 29 Jan. 1879, both in translation. Currie to Reay, 4 Apr. 1879, Copy. *M.P.*, Strauch to Mackinnon, 25 Apr. 1879.

to the closing years of his life he was a firm member of the Free Church of Scotland, but certain disagreements with the leaders of that church led to his giving active assistance to secessionist congregations in the Highlands.[1] Harry Johnston, the explorer and builder of empire, and then a very positive agnostic, paints a gloomy picture of the influence of secessionist religion on the Mackinnon household, as he interpreted it on a week-end visit in 1883.[2] But the evidence of Mackinnon's life as a whole quite contradicts Johnston's suggestion that his religion had a narrowing effect upon him. Personally unextravagant, he was the most generous of men. His correspondence is full of requests for help and assistance from all sorts of people, and to most response was made. In his friendships he was likewise generous. When Jules Devaux, Leopold II's *chef du cabinet*, lay ill, Mackinnon sent him wines and delicacies to speed his recovery, whilst he gave financial assistance to General H. S. Sanford, U.S. Minister in Brussels, with whom he was associated both over African projects and in the Florida Land & Colonisation Company, and later, to Sanford's widow. Another direction which his generosity took may seem more questionable. In the early 1880's he helped a Foreign Office official to repay the debts he owed to various money-lenders. But there is no evidence of an improper understanding. Certainly the official kept Mackinnon informed of the progress of the Anglo-Portuguese treaty negotiations, but the information Mackinnon thus received was of the semi-confidential order only, and conferred upon him no vital advantage. The benefits gained by his connexion with the official were not such as Mackinnon could not have obtained by the means normally open to a man of his standing. The whole episode is best seen as a commentary on the *mores* of the time, which in this respect were probably less rigid than is commonly supposed.

More of Mackinnon's character is displayed in his correspondence with a number of the men of African importance— Kirk, Rev. Horace Waller, H. M. Stanley, Sanford, Devaux, General Strauch (Secretary-General of the *A.I.A.* and President of the *Comité d'Etudes du Haut Congo*), M. Lambert (Leopold II's banker) and others. In his relationships with them he

[1] *D.N.B.*, Supplement, Vol. III, 127–8. Sheriff J. Macmaster Campbell, *Sir William Mackinnon, Bart.*, (reprinted from *Campbeltown Courier*, n.d.). I am indebted to Sir William Currie for this source of biographical information.
[2] H. H. Johnston, *The Story of My Life* (London, 1923), 146–8.

appears to have maintained a kind of Olympian charity which stood above their passions and the attacks which some of them sometimes made on each other. But clearly Mackinnon did not amass a fortune of half a million merely by the exercise of benevolence. Johnston's description of his appearance and bearing attests the more assertive side of his character. He depicts Mackinnon as 'a leetle, dapper, upright man, with an acquiline nose, side whiskers, a pouting mouth, and a strutting manner of walking and holding himself'.[1] There, it would seem, lay his more thrustful side. Vigorous and positive as he must in his prime have been, there were in the last decade of Mackinnon's life—he died in 1893—signs of a certain indecisiveness of character, tokens of more than the mellowing of time. Salisbury, in 1890, clearly thought that Mackinnon had lost his grip on East African affairs,[2] and Kirk could write privately to Lugard in 1892 that 'Sir William is one of the most impractical men I have ever had to do with and with all his success in India he is ignorant of Africa'.[3] The explanation is probably indifferent health and overwork, and, as Kirk said, an unfamiliarity with African affairs.[4]

Mackinnon's interest in tropical Africa appears to have stemmed from Christianity, commerce and, perhaps, simple curiosity. As a devout Christian he felt the need of missionary operations and demonstrated a readiness to give them more than usual support by, for example, subscribing £500 to the Livingstonia mission in the seven-year period 1874–80,[5] and by founding, with his fellow-directors of the Imperial British East African Co., an Industrial Mission, the East African Scottish Mission, in 1891.[6] As a man whose religion

---

[1] Johnston, *Life*, 147.
[2] Lady Gwendolen Cecil, *Life of Robert Marquis of Salisbury*, Vol. IV (London, 1931), 280 1.
[3] *Kirk Papers*, Kirk to Lugard, 20 Jan. 1892, Copy. See also *Kirk Papers*, Kitchener to Kirk, 12 July 1890, 'I hope you will now take up the East African Co. strongly and get rid of Mackinnon. Otherwise I greatly fear that our future work in Africa will become the laughing stock of Europe', quoted in R. Coupland, *The Exploitation of East Africa, 1856–1890* (London, 1939), 469, f.n.
[4] The principal source for the assessment of Mackinnon's character is the *Mackinnon Papers*.
[5] *FO84/1657*, Report of the Glasgow Auxiliary Committee of the Livingstonia Mission, Encl. in Dr. J. Smith to F.O., 10 Feb. 1883.
[6] Information kindly supplied to the writer by the Rev. John W. Arthur. The directors transferred the mission to the Church of Scotland in 1898 with an endowment of £38,000.

reinforced his essential humanity he wanted to strike at the slave trade. As a shipowner and man of business he wished to share in and profit from the work of African development. His membership of the Royal Geographical Society from 1862, and of its council after 1877, suggests that he was also interested in the extension of geographical knowledge. In Mackinnon's view these aims could best be served—and without discord—by engaging actively in the economic development of what was still the Dark Continent.

When Mackinnon began to collaborate with Leopold in 1876, he had already begun to interest himself in African affairs and was contemplating a wider extension of that interest. He had first been led to Africa by a commercial opportunity for the British India Company on the East Coast, the taking of which at the same time served the humanitarian cause. This was in 1872 when, persuaded that an extension of legitimate commerce, rather than a further reinforcement of the anti-slavery squadron, would be both a more effective and a more economical means of slave trade prevention, the Imperial Government had accepted the British India Company's tender for a subsidized monthly mail service between Aden and Durban via Zanzibar.[1] Probably because the mail service drew his attention to East Africa, Mackinnon began, early in 1876, with a group of friends, of whom the Rev. Horace Waller (a noted Africanist who had been associated with Livingstone and had worked in the Universities' Mission to Central Africa) was one, and the Baroness Burdett-Coutts possibly another, to consider an expedition on the East African mainland to open up commerce and to put down the slave trade.[2] Kirk was told of the scheme[3] but before the matter could go further the Brussels Conference supervened. As will be remembered, however, there was nothing exclusive and no intention to acquire large blocks of territory in the early plans of the *A.I.A.* as they were represented to the members of the Brussels Geographical Conference. Acceptance of the offer of facilities —implicitly to a British consortium—made in the Sultan of Zanzibar's proposal of December 1876, a proposal inspired by Kirk and perhaps more remotely by Mackinnon himself,

[1] Coupland, op. cit., 85.   [2] *M.P.*, H. Waller to Mackinnon, 12 Jan. 1877.
[3] *M.P.*, Mackinnon to Kirk, 9 Jan. 1877, Copy.

would not therefore involve action consciously inimical to Leopold. To respond would be to take a particularly favourable opportunity for the realization of a project which had not been called into question by the Brussels Conference and which Mackinnon is on record as hoping to push forward before he heard of the Sultan's approach.[1] A final spur to action was the availability of 'Chinese' Gordon on whose services as leader of the enterprise great store was put.[2] For these reasons, therefore, Mackinnon revived his East African project in the second half of January 1877. (There appears to have been a possibility that Mackinnon would in some way associate his scheme with Leopold's plans, but Gordon's opposition, probably on account of the consequential divided control, scotched this—if, indeed, it was ever seriously considered.)[3]

Mackinnon's project was for the formation of a company which would obtain from the Sultan concessions for the leasing of the whole of his commercial and administrative rights on the mainland. The powers the company sought were so wide as to place it in the position of a colonial government—indeed Waller used the analogy of the East India Company. The company would be empowered to make and administer laws, to raise an armed force, to make treaties with native chiefs, to dispose of unoccupied land and to levy and collect taxes. It would have exclusive mining and forestry rights and would lease the customs at the coast ports, whilst its sphere of operations would extend up to Lake Victoria. The Sultan would enjoy in return a yearly rental and a percentage of the profits.[4]

The concession negotiations failed on account, as Miss M. de Kiewiet has shown, of Lord Salisbury's secret opposition (made known to the Sultan privately and apparently dictated by an unreadiness to accept what would inevitably be a British commitment in East Africa).[5] But Mackinnon did not yet give up hope. At the turn of 1876–7, at the time of what he then

[1] Ibid. See also pp. 63–64 above.
[2] Ibid., *M.P.*, H. Waller to Mackinnon, 12 Jan. 1877.
[3] 'I am sure it is utterly useless to try and make him (Gordon) work in with the King of the Belgians' scheme, so in all your cogitations put that notion altogether out of the question.' (*M.P.*, H. Waller to Mackinnon, 12 Jan. 1877).
[4] *M.P.*, H. Waller to Mackinnon, 12 Jan. 1877. Gray, Dawes & Co. to G. Waller, 8 Mar. 1877, Copy. *FO84/1485*, Encl. in Kirk to F.O., 10 Apr. 1877. Miss M. J. de Kiewiet, *History of the Imperial British East Africa Company, 1876–1895* (Univ. of London, Ph.D. thesis, 1955), 24. Coupland, op. cit., 306–8.
[5] De Kiewiet, op. cit., 23–45.

regarded as a delay in the formation of the British national committee of the *A.I.A.*, and impatient at it, Mackinnon had joined with Buxton and a few of their friends to make an independent beginning on the construction of a road from Dar es Salaam to Lake Nyasa.[1] The British national committee and the concession scheme alike failed, but Mackinnon and Buxton still had their road. On Mackinnon's initiative it was decided to try to make it the basis of a more modest concession scheme. From the beginning it had been hoped that the Sultan might be induced to grant certain land concessions along the line of road, together with the lease of a port and a farm of its customs.[2] In March 1879, therefore, Mackinnon asked Sultan Barghash for the lease or purchase of 'the houses and land of Dar es Salaam . . . including all harbour rights . . . (and) . . . the lease of the customs and taxes', together with the lease of strips of land along the course of the road. Added to the request was a plea for mineral rights in the land to be made over to the concessionaires, and for the grant of authority to regulate native affairs.[3] The concession was on a smaller scale than the previous one but was something more than an amateurish road-building venture. A company was to be formed[4] and, with the privileges it was to possess, the undertaking could have developed into something quite big. Vice-Consul Holmwood, at least, thought the project of sufficient importance to urge Mackinnon to make a personal visit to the Sultan in order to secure it.[5]

But again Mackinnon met failure. Kirk considered that Stanley, who was then in Zanzibar, was putting the Sultan against England,[6] whilst Holmwood, also, tentatively cited this as a cause of failure and went on to name additional causes, of which the hostile influence of the French and American consuls was the most important.[7] Most of all, perhaps, the Sultan could scarcely have forgotten the view Salisbury had been at pains to express in the previous year. The upshot was a letter to Mackinnon early in May 1879 in

---

[1] *M.P.*, Mackinnon to Kirk, 9 Jan. 1877, Copy.   [2] Ibid.
[3] *PRO 30/29/367*, Mackinnon to Sultan, 7 Mar. 1879, Copy.
[4] *M.P.*, Mackinnon to Lambert, Copy, 22 Mar. 1879,
[5] *M.P.*, Holmwood to Mackinnon, 3 May and 1 June 1879.
[6] *M.P.*, Kirk to Dawes, 28 Apr. 1879, Copy. Kirk to G. Waller, 1 May 1879.
[7] *M.P.*, Holmwood to Mackinnon, 3 May 1879.

which the Sultan promised him every assistance in road-making efforts, an assistance he would lend to others engaged in similar projects, but regretted he could not cede Dar es Salaam since this would make it impossible to resist demands by others for ports. Moreover it would attract trade away from Bagamoyo with consequent loss of customs revenue.[1]

Even before this second rebuff Mackinnon was growing despondent at the lack of success of his African ventures. In June 1879, before news of the failure to obtain the second concession had been received in London, Gerald Waller, brother of Horace and a personal assistant to Mackinnon, wrote him a letter which testifies to this despondency. He expressed the hope that news of the safe arrival at Dar es Salaam of 'the Royal Belgian Elephant Expedition' (a scheme for the use of elephants as a means of transport, with which Mackinnon had had much to do) and Kirk's promise to devote more time to the task of securing the concession from the Sultan 'may . . . keep your interest in Tropical Africa alive'. More encouraging times, he added, were at hand.[2] Again, at about this time it was decided to call a halt to work on the road when the Kingani river (short of Lake Nyasa) was reached.[3] By the end of the year Mackinnon had had enough. Gerald Waller wrote to Mackinnon in January 1880 that Holmwood had informed him that 'you "have quite given up African schemes which is a pity" '.[4]

Mackinnon's disillusionment, apparent in mid-1879 and reaching a climax in the second half of the year, would appear to have had an important effect on his African thinking—and on his relations with Leopold. Disappointed at the failure of his own African schemes, Mackinnon still cherished a desire to develop the commerce of tropical Africa and, quite simply, to do something useful there. Nor were the possibilities exhausted. In particular there was the rather different mode of procedure offered by Leopold, with whom his relations had continued to be of the most cordial.

Up till 1880, at least, Leopold himself wanted an East African concession, but not as an end in itself. Ever since 1877

[1] M.P., Sultan to Mackinnon, 3 May 1879.
[2] M.P., G. Waller to Mackinnon, 10 June 1879.
[3] Ibid., 12 June 1879.   [4] Ibid., 12 Jan. 1880.

when Stanley's epic descent of the Congo had confirmed that it offered the best way into Central Africa, Leopold's thinking had centred increasingly on that river, and by the summer of 1880 his intention, as far as East Africa was concerned, was to acquire a concession but merely as the base for a line of communication with the Upper Congo. Strauch expressed quite clearly what the *A.I.A.* had in mind in a letter to Mackinnon in October 1879. 'The African Association proposes, as you in any case know, to establish in Africa a chain of stations. . . . This chain will begin from the east coast and end on the Upper Congo.'[1]

In Leopold's plans lay a vision to appeal to Mackinnon. Opportunity was offered to penetrate to the heart of Central Africa and to strike at the Arab slave trade in the vital catchment area, and at the same time to share in opening up for commerce an area possessing considerable possibilities of development. Collaboration with Leopold would also, Mackinnon may possibly have reasoned, forestall French and German ambitions.[2] Compared with this an East African concession could only offer more limited prospects—and in any case had twice been found impossible to obtain. Hence during the second half of 1879 Mackinnon appears to have come to regard the *A.I.A.* and the *Comité d'Etudes du Haut Congo* as the best instruments for the penetration of Central Africa, at least in the immediate future. From this time onwards Mackinnon gave increasing assistance to Leopold.

Mackinnon had already given active co-operation. Early in 1879 he had been to considerable trouble in the matter of the Belgian elephant expedition. This was an interesting attempt to find one answer to the transport problem by importing Indian elephants, which were thought to be immune to the infection carried by the tsetse fly, both as beasts of burden, and, if the experiment was successful, to train African elephants in the habits of industry. Mackinnon went to great pains to obtain the elephants in India and to recruit attendants and an Englishman, Carter, to superintend the venture, and made himself responsible for the arrangement of the shipment of the

---

[1] *M.P.*, Strauch to Mackinnon, 16 Oct. 1879.
[2] *Strauch MSS., No. 8*, Leopold to Strauch, (?)17 Aug. 1879, but certainly between 16 Aug. and 14 Oct. 1879.

animals.[1] (There was no harbour on the East African coast at which the elephants could conveniently be landed and the difficulties of getting the beasts ashore may readily be imagined. After the vessel in which they had been shipped had been run into shallow water, the elephants were lowered over the side in slings in the expectation that they would then make their own way ashore. On the contrary, the elephants sought to clamber back on board and, when an attempt was made to tow them ashore by the ship's boats, the beasts began to tow the boats out to sea. Eventually it was not by the wit of man but by the sagacity of the elephants that a safe landing was made, the animals eventually deciding that there was no choice but to strike out for the shore, which they successfully reached.) The experiment, however, was a failure. Two of the elephants died, Carter was murdered and a similar fate overtook a second Englishman also recruited by Mackinnon for the expedition.[2]

Whilst he was busy with the elephant expedition, Mackinnon had given additional proof of his readiness to co-operate with the *A.I.A.* In March 1879 he had agreed to reserve for the Belgian national committee of the Association a certain number of shares in the company he intended to form should the negotiations for the Dar es Salaam concession be successful. He had also agreed with Lambert that the Belgian committee should appoint one director and that a certain number of shares would be offered to M. Rabaud, a Marseilles merchant and Zanzibar consul at that port—a curious stipulation until it is realized that Rabaud was a personal friend of Leopold, a fact presumably known to Mackinnon, but even then not fully explained. In the third place, Mackinnon had promised:

'Should the Sultan grant the concessions asked, I shall with great pleasure, subject to his concurrence, reserve a part of the land near the harbour of Dar Es Salam for the Belgian Committee and I shall also reserve for them the necessary lands [for] four or five stations at intervals along the line of road towards the Lake Nyasa to facilitate the establishment by them of four or five stations according to the programme of the International Committee for African Exploration.' 'And

[1] *M.P.*, Strauch to Mackinnon, 15 Apr. 1879. Mackinnon to Strauch, 24 Apr. 1879, Copy.
[2] Coupland, op. cit., 263. *M.P.*, Strauch to Mackinnon, 4 Oct. and 5 Nov. 1879.

in general', added Mackinnon, 'I shall gladly do everything in my power to promote and facilitate the objects of the Belgian Committee International and Special' ['national' is clearly meant].[1]

The way was prepared, therefore, for Mackinnon to give Leopold his undivided support on the East Coast. Opportunity came in the autumn of 1879 when Leopold initiated a second attempt to gain a foothold in East Africa as the necessary base for the creation of a line of communication with the Upper Congo.[2] In August he had broached to Strauch the possibility of 'Chinese' Gordon entering the service of the *A.I.A.* in order, principally, to establish the necessary chain of stations.[3] The outcome was that, after preliminary approaches earlier in October, Strauch, on the 16th, specifically requested Mackinnon to sound out Gordon and ask him if he would be prepared to take service under Leopold for this purpose.[4] To tempt Gordon the more, to persuade him that here was an excellent opportunity for him to continue his personal crusade against the slave trade, Strauch, on Leopold's instructions, asked Mackinnon a few days later to make it clear to Gordon that the opening of a chain of stations was only a first step. More

---

[1] *M.P.*, Mackinnon to Lambert, 22 Mar. 1879, Copy. In view of the readiness of Mackinnon to assist the *A.I.A.*, the attitude of that body to him in the spring of 1879 was, on one hypothesis, unscrupulous. Kirk and Holmwood both thought that plotting by Stanley (now, of course, in Leopold's employ) in Zanzibar, whither he had departed from Brussels on 10 Feb. 1879, was one reason for the Sultan's refusal of Mackinnon's (second) request for a concession. This may have been the case. Stanley had called at Zanzibar *en route* for the Congo partly, so his biographer says, 'to obtain concessions from the Sultan for a free port, and for trading rights for the *Association Internationale Africaine*'. It is possible that, in the interests of his own negotiations, and either on instructions from Brussels or independently, he sought to put the Sultan against a scheme which could be regarded as a rival. Alternatively, his own negotiations having failed, it is conceivable that in pique, and perhaps believing that Kirk, whom he strongly disliked, had had something to do with that failure, he did his best to put the Sultan against the scheme Kirk was advocating. This theory must presuppose that the *A.I.A.* sought to participate in Mackinnon's scheme only as an alternative to gaining its own concession, and that it either failed, or was unable quickly enough to tell Stanley not to oppose that scheme, or that Stanley acted from personal dislike of Kirk. It is relevant to note that Stanley and Mackinnon had not yet established that intimacy which was to characterize their relationship from about 1884 onwards.

Alternative explanations are either that Kirk allowed his antipathy towards Stanley to affect his diagnosis of the situation, or that he was misinformed.

M.P., Holmwood to Mackinnon, 3 May and 1 June 1879. Kirk to Dawes, 28 Apr. 1879. Kirk to G. Waller, 1 May, 1879. F. Hird, *H. M. Stanley, The Authorised Life* (London, 1935), 176.

[2] *Strauch MSS.*, *No. 9*, Leopold to Strauch, 17 Aug. 1879.

[3] Ibid.

[4] *M.P.*, Strauch to Mackinnon, 3, 6 and 16 Oct. 1879.

exploration, the further opening up of communications, agricultural development on a large scale—all efficacious against the slave trade—would follow.¹

Mackinnon made clear to the king his readiness to approach Gordon and to commend Leopold's invitation to him,² though he also put to Strauch certain 'suggestions in regard to Colonel Gordon'.³ Of the nature of these suggestions there is no available record. Mackinnon probably wanted Gordon's work to be based on a concession to be obtained by Leopold from the Sultan of Zanzibar.⁴ Nor are the implications of Mackinnons' attitude on this point, and on the larger point of his readiness to encourage Gordon to enter Leopold's service entirely clear. What is clear is that Mackinnon, disillusioned at the failure of his own East African projects,⁵ was now not only prepared to allow the *A.I.A.* to take the lead in East Africa but was also ready to give vital assistance by helping to recruit for Leopold the man who had been his own chosen agent for the abortive 1877 concession—and whom he would not have been ready to yield up had he himself had any immediate intention of reviving any considerable East African scheme.

Towards the end of February Mackinnon relayed to Gordon an invitation to visit Brussels and discuss the whole question with Leopold.⁶ Meanwhile Gordon himself had conceived the alternative idea of entering the Sultan's service and striking an effective blow at the slave trade by extending the Sultan's effective authority inland⁷—the Sultan was, in fact, ready, on conditions, to employ an Englishman for such a purpose.⁸

¹ *M.P.*, Strauch to Mackinnon, 20 Oct. 1879.
² Mackinnon explicitly states his willingness that Gordon should take service under Leopold in the draft of a letter to Strauch, dated 2 Feb. 1880. But the implication of that same letter is that Mackinnon's general agreement had been made known earlier, whilst the likely implication of a note from Leopold to Strauch of 27 Nov. 1879 is that Mackinnon's general agreement had been made known before that date (*M.P.*, Mackinnon to Strauch, 2 Feb. 1880, Draft). *Strauch MSS.*, Leopold to Strauch, 27 Nov. 1879 (the year is missing in the document but its contents make it clear that it belongs to 1879).
³ *M.P.*, Mackinnon to Strauch, Draft, 2 Feb. 1880.
⁴ *M.P.*, H. Waller to Mackinnon, 2 Mar. 1880. *Waller Papers, II*, Gordon to H. Waller, 8 Feb. 1880. Gordon to H. Waller, 4 Mar. 1880.
⁵ See p. 73 above.
⁶ *M.P.*, Strauch to Mackinnon, 24 Feb. 1880.
⁷ *M.P.*, H. Waller to Mackinnon, 2 Mar. 1880. *Waller Papers, II*, Gordon to H. Waller, 6 Apr. 1880. P. Ceulemans, 'Les tentatives de Léopold II pour engager le Colonel Charles Gordon au service de l'Association Internationale Africaine (1880)', *Zaire*, XII–3–1958, 260.
⁸ *Zaire*, XII–3–1958, 260, 271–2.

With his mind still open, Gordon accepted Leopold's invitation and had a number of conversations with him early in March. But an episode already significant for its revelation of Mackinnon's readiness to allow the *A.I.A.* to take the lead in East Africa, failed to acquire the additional significance of gaining another Englishman of Stanley's calibre for Leopold's service, for the discussions between Leopold and Gordon soon reached deadlock. Gordon believed that the *A.I.A.*'s lack of international status—of a flag—must necessarily involve the obtaining of a concession from the Sultan and the use of his flag. Leopold, on the other hand, refused to consider this since all Gordon's efforts would then merely serve to extend the Sultan's territory and would leave the *A.I.A.* as far removed as ever from establishing itself in a manner which would constitute a claim to international recognition. Nor did Gordon suppose —and he was to be proved right—that the British Government would permit, as Leopold believed Britain and the other European powers would permit, the establishment by the *A.I.A.* of a port between the northern limits of the Sultan's territory and the border claimed by Egypt, if such intervening territory were found to exist. From Gordon's point of view, finally, the fact of having visited Brussels and receiving the king's confidence effectually prevented him from subsequently seeking service under the Sultan, for to do so would involve him in blocking Leopold's ambitions.[1] The sole fruit of the discussions—save that an introduction had been performed that was to lead to Gordon agreeing two and a half years later to enter Leopold's service—was that Gordon apparently gave Leopold six months in which to gain a *pied-à-terre* on the coast, though he can have had little hope of anything coming of this.[2] Leopold did in fact make a last attempt to acquire a concession on the East African coast in June, probably in order to gain the port on which Gordon had insisted. Mackinnon's advice was sought and the suggestion made that Mackinnon might be interested in a joint operation, in which case the king

---

[1] *Waller Papers II*, Gordon to H. Waller, 3, 4, 12, 20, 30 Mar., 4 and 6 Apr. 1880. *FO84/1585*, Minutes by Anderson, n.d., Lister, n.d., Pauncefote, 13 May 1880 and Granville, 24 May 1880 on Gordon to Tenterden, 7 May 1880 and Encl., Gordon to Tenterden, 10 Mar. 1880, quoted in *Zaire*, XII–3–1958, 266–9.

[2] *Waller Papers, II*, Gordon to H. Waller, 8 Sept. 1880. For the whole episode see also P. Ceulemans' above-mentioned article, *Zaire*, XII–3–1958, 251–4.

would be delighted.[1] But nothing came of this suggestion nor the project in general.

Mackinnon continued to co-operate with Leopold on the East Coast, notably by giving assistance to the various expeditions which the Belgian Committee sent into the interior via Zanzibar right up to 1885. But in this period the direction of Mackinnon's energies reflected Leopold's increasing concentration on the Congo as the really promising way into Central Africa. Active co-operation on the Congo had begun in November 1878 when Mackinnon had subscribed to the original capital of the *Comité d'Etudes du Haut Congo*. The *Comité*'s ultimate intentions were ambitious. If Stanley's findings were favourable, it will be recalled, the subscribers to the *Comité* were to be again called together with a view to forming two companies, one for the construction of a link between the Lower and Upper Congo and the other to establish navigation and develop commerce on the upper reaches of the river.[2]

Mackinnon's share in the original capital of £30,269 was between £800 and £1,000.[3] Apart from Hutton he was the only British contributor. Like Hutton's, Mackinnon's immediate financial stake in the Congo was therefore small, and even this came to an end in 1879 when all non-Belgian subscriptions were returned. But because of the conditions under which the subscriptions were returned, Mackinnon, with Hutton, came to have an important, albeit veiled stake in the Congo.

Leopold's reason for wishing to return all foreign subscriptions was to make possible untrammelled personal control. After a preliminary sounding in June[4] he went cleverly to work. The subscribers were called together in November 1879 and told, comparatively soon after they had made their original contributions, that a further sum was required, since three-quarters of the initial capital had been spent. Taking advantage of a probable reluctance to subscribe again so soon, Leopold then offered to provide the new capital himself on the sole

---

[1] *M.P.*, Strauch to Mackinnon, 5 June 1880. See also Coupland, op. cit., 346-8.
[2] Thomson, op. cit., 66-67.
[3] *M.P.*, Mackinnon to Lambert, 22 Mar. 1879, Copy. Strauch to Mackinnon, 26 Mar. and 25 Apr. 1879.
[4] *M.P.*, Sanford to Mackinnon, 7 June 1879, Confidential.

condition that the *Comité* as originally constituted be dissolved. He offered the subscribers further inducements to accept dissolution. The new capital which he, Leopold, would provide would be used, *inter alia*, for the establishment of three new stations, and a portion of their profits (Leopold envisaged commercial operations for the reconstituted *Comité*) would be divided amongst those subscribers who accepted Leopold's proposal. This distribution of profits would continue until the original sums invested by the subscribers, increased at 5 per cent. per annum, had been redeemed. In addition, when conditions permitted, the subscribers would be handed bonds for the amount of their instalments bearing interest at 5 per cent. per annum, to be derived from the further profits of the stations. Of greater importance was the last part of Leopold's offer.

From this time hence he assures a right of preference to the original subscribers who accept his proposals, for every commercial, industrial or financial operation issued by the stations or by himself in connection with the Congo, in all public adjudications or subscriptions. That right will be exercised in proportion to the funds paid up by every original subscriber.[1]

Mackinnon and Hutton accepted Leopold's proposals.[2] The promise of interest payments and capital redemption can scarcely have weighed greatly with them—Mackinnon was a wealthy man and Hutton very well off—but Leopold's final inducement offered them entry on the ground floor of what they believed to be an immense potential market. It is even probable, suggests one authority, that Mackinnon and Hutton, together with Stanley, were promised the concession for the construction of a railway.[3] Paradoxically, therefore, the withdrawal of the British subscribers from the *Comité*, because one of the conditions of their withdrawal made their expectations more precise, increased rather than diminished their stake in the Congo.

The readiness of Mackinnon and Hutton to assist Leopold is even more understandable in the light of this arrangement. In a letter to Strauch in the autumn of 1881 Mackinnon attests

---

[1] *M.P.*, Report of General Meeting of *Comité d'Etudes du Haut Congo*, 17 Nov. 1879. Thomson, op. cit., 74–75.
[2] Thomson, op. cit., 75.
[3] R. J. Cornet, *La Bataille du Rail* (Brussels, 1947), 53.

his continuing interest in Leopold's work and his willingness to further it. In this same letter he says that he is arranging the charter of a ship to convey Zanzibaris round Africa for work on the Congo and makes a conditional offer to pay up to £1,000 of the cost. He is also, he continues, trying to recruit some Scotsmen for service on the Congo.[1] It was, in fact, in the recruitment of agents and labour for Leopold that Mackinnon was most active in this period. From Strauch's letters to him in 1881 and 1882 it is apparent that he endeavoured to secure for the *Comité* the services of Englishmen and time-served Indian soldiers, as well as Indian and Chinese coolies and West Africans as porters. He also seems to have assisted in the arrangements for the purchase in England of a steamer for the *Comité*.[2] Stanley, in his preface to *The Congo and the Founding of its Free State*, the narrative of his work between 1879 and 1884, singles out only three people for especial thanks; one of them is Mackinnon.

'The British reader', he says, 'must be persuaded by the Author to believe that the expedition has been largely indebted to the munificence of William Mackinnon Esq. . . . from whom at various times we obtained substantial help, and invariably the most generous sympathy with the kindliest advice.'[3]

In July 1882, on Leopold's behalf, Mackinnon again approached Gordon, seeking to persuade him, this time, to take charge of the pioneering work of the *Association Internationale du Congo* (this title was substituted for *Comité d'Etudes du Haut Congo* during 1882), and supported his approach with a long and rosy account of Congo developments and prospects.[4] By the end of the year Gordon had agreed to enter Leopold's service at any time the king might require him. The call came in October 1883 in a telegram from Mackinnon, when Gordon was asked to go out as Stanley's successor,[5] but before Gordon could leave for the Congo he was required to take charge of the Sudan expedition which was to lead to his death. Mackinnon

[1] *M.P.*, Mackinnon to Strauch, n.d. but probably Autumn 1882, Draft.
[2] *M.P.*, Strauch to Mackinnon, 10 Nov. 1881, 7 Dec. 1882, and 1881–2 *passim*.
[3] H. M. Stanley, *The Congo and the Founding of its Free State* (London, 1885), I, xiii.
[4] *Gordon MSS.*, Mackinnon to Gordon, 22 July 1882. (Kindly communicated by Dr. J. R. Gray.)
[5] *M.P.*, Devaux to Mackinnon, 2 Nov. 1883. H. W. Gordon, *Events in the Life of Charles George Gordon* (London, 1886), 238–40, 286–7.

gave further help in the engagement of high-level administrators for Leopold's service. When Strauch visited London in June 1883, Mackinnon assisted him by giving introductions to General Sir Arnold Kemball, Lieutenant General Sir Lewis Pelly, Sir Frederick Goldsmid, and others from amongst whom Leopold hoped to engage an administrator.[1]

Of immense importance to Leopold's Congo venture was the work of the Englishman whom he had engaged as his principal agent—Stanley.[2] The Welsh orphan, who fled to America and after meeting both kindness and hazard became a journalist, had sprung to fame as the man who found Livingstone. The character he discerned in Livingstone profoundly influenced him—though he retained something of the harshness and the haunting inferiority complex for both of which his miserable childhood was probably responsible. When in August 1877 he reached Boma after a 999 day crossing of Africa, he had also proved Cameron's strong presumption of the importance of the Congo as the route into the interior of Central Africa. Stanley's first move was to urge Englishmen to avail themselves of this rich opportunity for commerce and active humanitarianism.

'I had hoped', he wrote in his journal, 'to have inspired Englishmen with something of my own belief in the future of the Congo. I delivered addresses, after-dinner speeches, and in private have spoken earnestly to try and rouse them to adopt early means to secure the Congo basin for England.'[3]

Only when unsuccessful did Stanley accept service under Leopold but even then he continued to hope that Britain would share largely in the economic development of the Congo region.[4]

Stanley was in overall charge of the work on the Congo from early in 1879 until mid-1884. He was responsible for the construction of a road linking the lower to the upper river, for

---

[1] *Strauch MSS., No. 194*, Strauch to Leopold, 17 June 1883.
[2] Stanley believed himself at this time to be an American citizen by virtue of his army oath (he had fought in the Civil War). In fact, up till 1885 he was a British citizen. In any case the distinction is unimportant for he was a constant supporter of British interests on the Congo. For the character and career of Stanley see Lady Dorothy Stanley (Ed.), *The Autobiography of Sir Henry Morton Stanley* (London, 1909) and F. Hird, *H. M. Stanley, the Authorised Life* (London, 1935).
[3] Stanley's Journal, quoted, n.d., in Hird, op. cit., 171.
[4] For an interpretation of Stanley's hopes of the Congo, see pp. 202–5 below.

Hauling canoes round the Inkisi Falls on the Congo during Stanley's trans-African journey, 1874-7
(From a sketch by Stanley, reproduced by kind permission of the *Illustrated London News.*)

penetrating to Stanley Falls in prefabricated boats, for the conclusion of the most important of the treaties with native chiefs and for the establishment and maintenance of the key stations. The title of the book in which he describes his work, *The Congo and the Founding of its Free State*, is in every way justified. To him Leopold owed everything.

In September 1883 General Goldsmid went out to assist Stanley and in May 1884 another Englishman, Colonel Sir Francis de Winton, took over from Stanley who by that time needed leave in Europe. Both did a valuable work of consolidation.

In the early stages of Leopold's Congo venture the work of Stanley, his agent, was more important than that of Mackinnon and the other British sympathizers. Their activity is significant more as an indication of their own hopes of the Congo than as a practical contribution, though that was not negligible. But at the end of 1882 the decision of the Imperial Government to negotiate a Congo treaty with Portugal appeared to Leopold and his British sympathizers to threaten the whole future of the work of the *A.I.C.* by giving up to Portugal the control of the Congo mouth. In this situation Leopold needed all the help in resisting the treaty which his British supporters could give him. They for their part were fully prepared to give it, for on the *Association Internationale du Congo* depended their hopes of an immense new field for British commercial enterprise.

CHAPTER V

THE EVOLUTION OF BRITAIN'S NEW CONGO POLICY

WHEN Morier took up his appointment in Lisbon he found that Portugal's claim to the Congo was the question of the hour. Nevertheless for over a year he kept his own counsel in the matter, only breaking silence when certain atrocities perpetrated by Europeans (torture, and execution by drowning of thirty-two Africans for alleged incendiarism) drew attention to the fragile basis of law and order on the river.[1] The report which he then made was succinct and cogent. The Portuguese claim, stated Morier, was stronger than the Foreign Office had hitherto assumed, and Britain had no tenable basis for resisting it. Even if she had, more harm than good would probably result from the continued absence of a responsible European jurisdiction on the Congo. Yet more compelling, circumstances were combining to make the maintenance of the existing order not only inadvisable but impossible. Recourse to arms, or to arbitration, since Britain had no claim of her own, Morier dismissed: a settlement should be reached by negotiation.

In this settlement, continued Morier, three major points should be kept in mind—the extreme importance of the Congo 'as the great arterial communication from the west with the centre of Africa', the impossibility of allowing the present anarchy to continue, and the undesirability of the river 'getting into other hands than ours'.

'Our proper policy', he advised, 'would be to acknowledge the Portuguese claims, and to make them in return cede the portion of the territory claimed from the mouth of the Congo to 5° 12', a short strip of territory, but which would give us the right bank of the Congo and the full command of its mouth.

'We could in the same treaty', Morier added, 'make the Portuguese engage to regulate the whole of their traffic and commerce along the coast by the rules we laid down for our portion of the coast. It seems to me that with the docility the Portuguese have always shown to our handling [sic] such a plan would give us the virtual control for all

[1] *FO 84/1538*, Morier to Salisbury, 26 Sept. 1879, Private.

purposes of commerce and Slave Trade of the west coast.' Morier concluded: 'Of course, if this idea was entertained, we should have to manœuvre so that the proposal should come from Portugal and not be made by us. I think that if, as is likely, Corvo returns to power next year I could manage this.'[1]

The Foreign Office took no action on Morier's memorandum and Morier himself did not immediately press for any. This unusual silence—Morier was never one to conceal his opinions —was dictated, just as his silence in the first year of his appointment had been, by the strategy of a wider plan which he had conceived since his arrival at Lisbon.[2] The conception of this plan testified to the breadth of Morier's vision, whilst the persistence with which he pressed it bore witness to the independence of mind which a diplomat of his aristocratic background could afford to have. It provided for joint Anglo-Portuguese action against the remnants of the external slave trade of Portuguese Africa and against the internal slave trade and, beyond this, for the fiscal liberalization of the Portuguese empire, for Anglo-Portuguese co-operation in its economic development, and for the assertion of the right of free access to those interior parts of Africa served by the two great rivers, the Zambesi and the Congo, the mouths of which Portugal either possessed or might be permitted to occupy.[3] Britain would benefit considerably from the wider extension of Free Trade and the growth of commerce, but the benefit to Portugal would be at least as great, whilst the advantages to other nations would be only less. Morier's rejection of the theoretical alternative of trying to purchase key points in the Portuguese colonial empire both amplifies his motives and constitutes a classic exposition of informal imperialism. It is the burden of a confidential despatch to Derby of May 1877 which began by retailing information of an Italian attempt to buy a portion of Mozambique (for a penal settlement), by reporting rumours that Germany was also in the market, and by asserting Morier's belief that Portugal would reject, or would already have rejected any approaches by Germany just as she had spurned those of Italy. Morier continued:

[1] *FO63/1117*, Morier, Memorandum, 17 Aug. 1877.
[2] *FO84/1538*, Morier to Salisbury, 26 Sept. 1879, Private.
[3] Ibid. *FO63/1131*, Draft of Congo Treaty, Encl. in Morier to F.O., 20 Apr. 1881, No. 101. A. J. Hanna, *The Beginnings of Nyasaland and North-Eastern Rhodesia, 1859–1895* (Oxford, 1956), 110–17.

Now although, when the immense extent of territory owned by Portugal in Africa, and the impossibility, with her limited resources, of availing herself of that territory, are considered, such a policy as that described [i.e. of refusal to sell] seems to border on infatuation, it yet appears to me to be a matter of serious consideration whether it is in our interests, even with the result of acquiring such valuable properties as Goa and Lourenço Marques, that this policy should be changed, and the spirit of commerce dethrone the spirit of history and tradition in Portugal.

One thing appears to me certain, viz. that were the spell once broken by the sale of even of one square kilometre of territory, the process of turning these vast and useless possessions into ready money would not stop there, but in all probability [would] degenerate into an auction at which vast portions of the sea-board of Africa would be sold to the highest bidder.

Now it may fairly be asked whether we should not find the neighbourhood of the powerful and ambitious states who would be the most likely to bid the highest for such prizes, less to our convenience than the sluggish do-nothingness of Portugal. As matters stand, there are four great landlords in Africa: ourselves, Portugal, Egypt and Zanzibar. Egypt and Zanzibar do pretty well what we tell them to do. Portugal, if we know how to set about it, with a little humouring (and it is no difficult task to humour fancies whose abiding home is mostly in the sixteenth century) can, I am convinced, be equally coaxed into the way she should go. If once she has been induced to do away with all commercial and administrative restrictions, and she is now fairly engaged along this course, an immense coastal territory will be open to the capital and enterprise of mankind, from which we shall be the first to derive the benefit, with the agreeable reflection that the increase of wealth and comparative power which must result to the owners of the property thus utilised, will accrue to a country whose European interests compel her to look to us as her only certain and reliable ally.

In a word, with the right of territorial ownership as at present distributed in Africa, it appears to me that we have it in our power to exercise a paramount influence over that continent. I do not feel sure that this would continue to be the case if young and ambitious states with decided notions of their own, like Germany and Italy, shared between them the conquests of Vasco da Gama.[1]

The first stage in the fulfilment of Morier's plan was to assist and encourage the Portuguese Government, and Senor Corvo, the Foreign Minister and Minister of Marine and the Colonies, in particular, in their project for the reduction of the Mozambique tariff, including a reduction in the transit duties payable on goods destined for the interior. By the spring of 1877 this

[1] *FO63/1062*, Morier to Derby, 15 May 1877, No. 31, Most Confidential, quoted in A. J. Hanna, *History of Nyasaland and North-Eastern Rhodesia, 1875–1895* (Univ. of London, Ph.D. thesis, 1948), 436–8.

had been achieved, due, in no small part, to Corvo and Morier and the friendship, based partly on a similar view of colonial development, which had grown up between them.[1] This, however, was achievement only in the limited sense that it removed an obstacle. Morier's next step was more positive. It was made possible by an instruction he received, shortly after his arrival in Lisbon, to negotiate with Portugal on an Anglo-Portuguese Indian dispute. The negotiations had been envisaged before Morier's appointment to Lisbon and, from the British point of view, had initially been intended simply to deal with a fiscal question. A privilege originally enjoyed by the director of the Portuguese factory at Surat, in the Portuguese settlement of Damao, had led to a serious abuse whereby certain goods, notably wines and spirits, were re-exported into adjacent British India at a lower rate of duty than was payable on the commodities if imported direct, and on such a scale as to involve a loss to the British Indian revenue reckoned at £150,000 a year. Arbitrary suspension of the privilege by the Indian Government followed, but the British authorities later showed a readiness to negotiate. The opening of negotiations was delayed, however, with the result that it was Morier who was entrusted with the task of bringing about a settlement of this dispute shortly after his arrival in Lisbon.[2]

If, in a narrow sense, Morier acted on instructions, he brought to the negotiations his own vision and gave to them his own particular impress. Notably, he did not limit himself to the removal of a fiscal grievance, but rather took up a suggestion which had originated with Lord Lytton, his predecessor at Lisbon—and which was the more likely to be received with favour by the Government of India in that Lytton had since become Viceroy—that Portuguese acquiescence and goodwill should be secured by providing in the treaty for Anglo-Portuguese co-operation in the construction of a railway linking Marmagao, the port of the Portuguese colony of Goa, with the British Indian railway system at New Hubli. This was an object much desired by the Portuguese and one which strongly appealed to Morier. Goa was the natural port for a very large

[1] Hanna, *History*, 53–55, 61–63. Hanna, *Beginnings*, 110–14.
[2] Miss I. Bains, *British Policy in relation to Portuguese Claims in West Africa, 1876–1884* (Univ. of London, M.A. thesis, 1940), 37–44, 58.

hinterland. The construction of a railway link would both enhance the prosperity of that (British Indian) hinterland and enable Goa to fulfil its natural *raison d'être* and secure its prosperity as a colony. In these terms he wrote to Corvo who, indeed, needed no persuasion.

Negotiations, though protracted, were eventually successful, not least because of Morier's exertions, and a 'Treaty of Commerce and Extradition between Great Britain and Portugal, with reference to their Indian Possessions' was signed on 26 December 1878. It provided for the establishment of a customs union between the Indian possessions of Britain and Portugal, for an annual compensation payment to the Portuguese Government, and laid down terms on which Britain and Portugal could co-operate in the construction of a railway. Ratification proved a difficulty owing, in Morier's view, to the anti-British influence of Count Casal Ribeiro, and the treaty was, in Morier's opinion, only eventually ratified because he obtained permission to use 'strong language . . . as coming directly from Her Majesty's Government' and because he was able to bring pressure to bear from another quarter. He represented that the Stafford House group, which he had successfully interested in the Goa railway project, would dissolve the committee it had set up to pursue the matter if the treaty was not ratified within a reasonable time. Ratified it was in August 1879.[1]

Whilst the Goa negotiations were still in progress, Morier was given a further opportunity to implement his plans for colonial co-operation between Britain and Portugal. This opportunity was furnished by a Colonial Office initiative of August 1878 which, in its turn, had been prompted by the annexation of the Transvaal in the previous year. This move necessarily directed attention to the Portuguese port of Lourenço Marques in Delagoa Bay and the Transvaal's natural outlet

---

[1] *FO63/1091*, Morier to F.O., 7 June 1879, No. 23 Commercial, Confidential. *S.P.*, 1877-8, LXIX, 19-63. Bains, op. cit., 42-43, 77-85. See also p. 66 above. The reasons advanced in this chapter for the difficulties which Morier's policies encountered in Lisbon are those adduced by Morier himself. Looked at from a Portuguese point of view it is reasonable to envisage other reasons. For instance he may not always have successfully concealed his patronizing attitude to Portugal and the Portuguese, and it may have been believed that his various schemes were exclusively for England's benefit, and thus prejudicial to Portugal.

to the sea. It followed, therefore, that Britain's government of that province would be strengthened by an agreement with Portugal providing for the construction of a railway link between Lourenço Marques and the Transvaal, and for the regulation of the import of arms (necessary for the prevention of native risings, for which task, since the Transvaal's annexation, Britain now had an increased responsibility). At the same time, before the railway could have the prospect of significant traffic and thus become an economic possibility and a means of opening up the Transvaal, an agreement on tariffs would have to be negotiated with Portugal. These, then, were the reasons for the Colonial Office initiative. It resulted in an instruction to Morier to sound the Portuguese Government as to their willingness to conclude an agreement on these points.[1] Here was Morier's opportunity. With the purely South African objects of the project he seems to have been in full agreement[2] but, as might be supposed, he also saw in this instruction an opportunity to put forward a wider scheme for a settlement with Portugal in south-east Africa. By January 1879 he was ready to submit a draft treaty to the Foreign Office, a treaty whose terms, *mutatis mutandis*, evince marked similarities to the Goa treaty. The Portuguese, he said, greatly desired a Lourenço Marques–Transvaal railway. If Great Britain were to offer 'the powerful bribe of immediate action' and a liberal attitude to the financing of the project, he believed that Portugal could be brought to agree to the other terms he proposed. The most important of these were the grant to Britain of the free use of the harbour at Delagoa Bay for commercial and military purposes, the introduction of a common tariff there, the enunciation of the general principle of the freedom of the great waterways linking the interior to the coast (the principal reference here is to the Zambesi—it has been seen that Morier had already obtained a reduction in transit dues payable on goods destined for the interior. He had also exerted himself in opposing a Portuguese monopoly of the trade and navigation of that river, even when a British subject had been like to obtain it),[3] and provision for common action against the

[1] Hanna, *History*, 106.
[2] J. Martineau, *Life of Sir Bartle Frere* (London, 1895), II, 371–2.
[3] Hanna, *History*, 65–68. Hanna, *Beginnings*, 115.

internal and external slave trade of Mozambique. Morier eventually got his treaty signed—but only after surmounting more opposition from his own Colonial and Foreign Offices than he received from Corvo, only after he had made a special journey to London in the spring of 1879 to press his case, and only on condition that ratification be, by agreement, postponed until Britain's relations with the Transvaal and with the Zulu empire of Cetewayo became more stable. When Morier returned towards the end of May he was only just in time. The Fontes–Corvo ministry was on the point of resigning and virtually the last official action of Corvo was to sign the treaty. But it had still to be ratified, and Morier immediately took steps to obtain in Lisbon a disposition favourable to Portuguese ratification, contravening, on this point, at least the spirit of his instructions. However, since the new ministry was, in his view, governed by anglophobe influences, all he could immediately do was to urge the King of Portugal to use all his influence on the ministry, and to point out that he, Morier, had persuaded the Duke of Sutherland, of that same Stafford House group which Morier had interested in the Goa railway, to assist in the formation of a company to build the Lourenço Marques–Transvaal railway, but that the duke would not wait indefinitely for ratification.[1] This, of course, was a tactic similar to the one Morier had used to obtain Portuguese ratification of the Goa treaty. Notwithstanding, a Press campaign against ratification was soon launched, whilst in any case the chances of ratification were not improved by the fact of the treaty's signature—and its terms had aroused a good deal of opposition—being the last act of a dying ministry. Indeed, over the following months it became quite clear that ratification would be obtained only with considerable difficulty.

Whilst Morier was in London trying to obtain approval of the Lourenço Marques treaty he had been asked for his opinion on what should be the British response to the recent conclusion by the Portuguese of treaties with certain native chiefs in the disputed Congo territory. He used this opportunity to urge that 'a radical solution' should be taken in hand on the basis

[1] Hanna, *History*, 102–14. Hanna, *Beginnings*. 115–20. See also Bains, op. cit., 88–90.

of his 1877 memorandum, and that the successful conclusion of the Goa and Lourenço Marques treaties would be the propitious moment for the negotiation of a Congo settlement.[1]

This new representation evoked Wylde's qualified approval. The situation which Great Britain's traditional policy had been designed to meet had now entirely changed. Not only was the slave trade a thing of the past but also, during the last two years, Morier had contrived to persuade the Portuguese to substitute a liberal colonial fiscal system for the previous almost prohibitive code. In sum

If we could be certain that the liberal policy recently inaugurated would be permanent, the grounds on which we have hitherto objected to the extension of Portuguese sovereignty on the West African Coast would no longer hold good, and should it be considered advisable to come to an understanding with the Portuguese on the subject of their territorial claims on that coast, there would be no insuperable objection to our doing so—always provided that the free navigation of the Congo be preserved for all nations.[2]

There the matter for the moment rested but early in the following month news came from the Loanda consul of friction over Portuguese claims at Ambrizette. This drew from Salisbury the comment that 'the whole case will have to be renewed when the Portuguese King (?) crisis is over'.[3]

The ground was thus well prepared when in September 1879 Morier began seriously to press for what he had from the first regarded as the last stage in the transformation of the Anglo-Portuguese colonial relationship—the settlement of the Congo question. In a private letter of 26 September, in which he informed Salisbury of the nature of his overall plan for a colonial settlement with Portugal, and the measure of success which he had so far achieved, he also made clear the reason why he had not previously pressed for a Congo settlement.

It is just because it is [a question] of . . . [a] burning and momentous kind that I have kept it at arms length waiting for the moment when it

[1] *FO84/1801*, Morier, Memo., 3 May 1879 (Confidential Print 3915). *FO84/1538*, Morier to Salisbury, 26 Sept. 1879, Private.
[2] *FO84/1801*, Wylde, Minute, 9 May 1879, on Memo. by Morier of 3 May 1879 on Congo question.
[3] *FO63/1087*, Hunt to F.O., 10 Apr. 1879, No. 17, and Minute thereon by Salisbury, 8 June 1879. This Portuguese crisis appears to have been connected with the coming to power of Braamcamp's (*Progressista*) ministry.

could be conveniently dealt with once for all. I found it ready to burst upon me when I first came out here but I induced Corvo, as a matter of policy, to keep it absolutely dormant until all the other questions had been first settled and Portugal had earned by the manner in which she settled them the right to claim that this, the one to her most vital, should be taken in hand.

My whole work accordingly for the last three years has been systematically carried out upon a prearranged plan leading up to this last treaty and having succeeded with every portion of my plan up to this point I think I may fairly claim to be listened to in regard to the 'crowning of the edifice'.

He then summarized his work so far and the large measure of success which had attended it, and went on:

All this I got by engaging that when all these results were apparent I would use my best endeavours to obtain a satisfactory settlement of the Congo question. . . . I never pledged H.M. Govt. or exaggerated my personal influence in the matter but I pointed out the almost irresistible force with which Portugal would be able to plead her cause if she could produce a long chain of accomplished facts in support of her pleadings before she entered into Court.

But there was now an imperative reason why the Congo question should be taken in hand. Casal Ribeiro, the dominant influence behind the Braamcamp ministry, had, Morier believed, a grudge against him and was in any case against closer treaty relations with Britain. Consequently Ribeiro was utilizing the fact that the all important last agreement in Morier's package deal had not been concluded, and that Portugal had apparently made all the concessions, to embarrass not only Morier but also the pro-British Corvo. The Braamcamp ministry could not last more than six months, but in order to spike Ribeiro's guns during that time and to assist in the ministry's replacement 'by a colourless ministry whom I shall have in hand and with whom Corvo could work not as Minister but as negotiator for my last treaty', he needed permission to state

as from myself and not as speaking on behalf of H.M. Govt. that with a friendly ministry, and one desirous of international co-operation with us, I have every reason to believe that H.M. Govt. would not refuse to take a settlement of the Congo question into consideration.

He would thus have in his hand, Morier concluded with feeling, 'a strong weapon of offence and defence and with these tribes of Bashan surrounding me on every side I am much in need of both'.[1]

Salisbury's reply, presumably private, to Morier's request is not on record. Events, however, took a surprising turn. Quite unknown to Morier the Braamcamp ministry intimated to Salisbury that it would itself shortly 'submit a proposal' to the Foreign Office on the Congo question. To d'Antas, the Portuguese minister in London and bearer of the intimation, Salisbury replied that he would be very glad to discuss the matter.[2] Because the Lourenço Marques treaty was still unratified, Morier's response when Salisbury told him of what had happened, was to telegraph urging that the Portuguese be told that any formal discussion of their Congo claim must wait upon Portuguese ratification of that treaty.[3] Salisbury now immediately agreed to this, authorizing Morier to make that condition clear to the Portuguese Government.[4] In the months which followed, the question of the Congo negotiations became somewhat confused owing largely to Salisbury's failure to give precise instructions—doubtless because he was unable properly to attend to the matter. So tangled, indeed, did it become that by May 1880 Tenterden was obliged to minute: 'This affair is evidently in a dreadful mess.'[5] Confusion began early in December. When Morier reported to the Foreign Office that Braamcamp had pressed upon him that the Congo negotiations be begun as a means of getting Portuguese ratification of the Lourenço Marques treaty, and that he had replied that he would maintain his original insistence on prior ratification unless his government instructed him otherwise, Salisbury merely minuted that Morier's language be approved.[6] Three

---

[1] *FO84/1538*, Morier to Salisbury, 26 Sept. 1879, Private. See also the advice Morier gave to Corvo in 1877: 'Do not now moot the question [of the Congo] ... show that you are in earnest in changing your colonial system root and branch. Then let us take in hand all the other questions which require settlement in the Colonies. You will thus have a ground of vantage for urging your Congo claims which you have not now' (quoted in *FO63/1117*, Morier, Memo., June 1880). See also Bains, op. cit., 59–98 *passim*.

[2] *FO63/1117*, F.O. to Morier, 31 Oct. 1879, S/T No. 66, Draft. *FO84/1801*, Salisbury, Memorandum, 24 Oct. 1879.

[3] *FO84/1801*, Morier to F.O., 14 Nov. 1879, Telegram.

[4] *FO84/1801*, F.O. to Morier, 15 Nov. 1879, Telegram, Copy.

[5] *FO84/1801*, Tenterden, Memo., 24 May 1880. But he went on to clarify it in a memo. 'Lourenço Marques and Congo Negotiations', 3 June 1880 (*FO63/1101*).

[6] *FO63/1117*, Morier to F.O., 19 Nov. 1879, S/T No. 76, and Salisbury, Minute thereon, 10 Dec. 1879.

weeks later Morier reported a fresh approach by Braamcamp—*ad misericordiam* as Morier put it—and forwarded a note from the Portuguese Foreign Minister containing a plea for prior British *admission* of Portugal's Congo claim. To this representation Morier had replied that it was for Lord Salisbury 'to decide when the matter should be taken in hand', and—a curious addition—that he himself had not at the moment the data available on which to base an opinion.[1] In reply Salisbury merely said: 'I approve your remarks generally.'[2] The question therefore remained in the air.

In January, on Pauncefote's prompting (Julian Pauncefote was at this time the Legal Assistant Under-Secretary at the Foreign Office, but owing to Tenterden's poor health was also much involved in the general work of the Office), Morier was asked to state the bases on which he would wish to treat in any discussion of Portugal's Congo claim,[3] but to this request he for some reason did not reply. Two months elapsed before Morier made any further move. By that time he had abandoned any thought he may possibly have entertained of yielding to the Braamcamp ministry's entreaties, and had rather, it seems, come to feel that the virulence of the ministerial press was such that he needed clear evidence of the ministry's intention to pursue a policy of inter-colonial co-operation with Britain before he would proffer any co-operation at all. As he put it, in a typically Morier metaphor, in a note intended for Braamcamp:

As between the ministers themselves and the ministerial press, 'I am placed in the difficulty of having to decide for myself who is the true oracle. The voice is the voice of Esau, the hands are the hands of Jacob. Am I dealing with Jacob or with Esau, with the rough voice or the smooth hand?'[4]

Morier therefore sought permission to put the Portuguese ministry to the test, and at the same time to try to bring on an important step in his overall plan. He requested Foreign Office approval of a draft note he wished to send to Braamcamp in

[1] *FO63/1117*, Morier to F.O., 6 Dec. 1879, S/T No. 80 and Encl., Braamcamp to Morier, 28 Nov. 1879, Confidential, Translation.
[2] *FO63/1117*, F.O. to Morier, 24 Dec. 1879, S/T No. 80, Draft.
[3] *FO84/1801*, Pauncefote, 8 Jan. 1880 and Salisbury, 12 Jan. 1880, Minutes. *FO63/1117*, F.O. to Morier, 17 Jan. 1880, No. 6, Draft.
[4] *FO63/1117*, Draft Note, Morier to Braamcamp, n.d., Encl. in Morier to F.O. 12 Mar. 1880, No. 13, Confidential.

which he stated that if the Lourenço Marques treaty was ratified by the *Cortes* he would inform his government that in his opinion the moment had arrived to open discussions on the Congo question.[1] When Morier's request reached the Foreign Office, Salisbury was on holiday at Biarritz.[2] The Office's reply was consequently delayed and before it was received Morier sent the note in on his own responsibility.[3] But within a fortnight Salisbury forbade any immediate action over the Congo. He does not appear to have been opposed to it in principle but was, rather, reluctantly obliged to prohibit the opening of negotiations because of Conservative defeat at the polls and the impropriety of committing his successor, in whose hands, he told Morier, the decision must lie. Salisbury nevertheless expressed the hope—pious in the circumstances, as was proved early in June by rejection in the *Cortes*—that it would still be possible for ratifications of the Lourenço Marques treaty to be exchanged.[4]

To the new Liberal administration Morier now addressed himself. After paving the way with a number of private letters to Lord Granville, the new Foreign Secretary (the letter of 13 June ran to forty-four pages!), and with a further memorandum on the Congo question at the end of June, Morier had an interview with Granville early in August 1880 and obtained from him the assurance that he and Lord Kimberley, the Colonial Secretary, were agreeable to the opening of negotiations on the Congo as soon as the Lourenço Marques treaty had been ratified by Portugal. Morier could, meanwhile, urge as his personal view of the form a Congo settlement should take the basis he had originally propounded in 1877, but he was not to commit Her Majesty's Government.[5]

But this was not the end of Morier's difficulties; not only

[1] *FO63/1117*, Morier to F.O., 12 Mar. 1880, No. 13, Confidential, and Encl., Draft Note, Morier to Braamcamp, n.d. See also *FO84/1801*, Morier to F.O., 20 Mar. 1880, Telegram.
[2] *FO63/1101*, Tenterden, Memo. on 'Lourenço Marques Treaty and Congo Negotiations', 3 June 1880.
[3] *FO63/1101*, Morier to F.O., 26 Mar. 1880, No. 20 and Encl., Morier to Braamcamp, 26 Mar. 1880, Copy.
[4] *FO63/1100*, Eliot, Minute, 21 Apr. 1880 on C.O. to F.O., 20 Apr. 1880. *FO84/1801*, Salisbury, Minute, 3 Apr. 1880. F.O. to Morier, 6 Apr. 1880, Telegram, Copy, and F.O. to Morier, 21 Apr. 1880.
[5] *PRO30/29/183*, Morier to Granville, Private Letters, May–Aug. 1880 *passim*. *FO84/1801*, Morier, Memorandum on the claims of Portugal, 26 June 1880, Draft. Morier to Granville, 7 Aug. 1880, Private.

were negotiations re-opened on certain points, but there was a continuing and vigorous Portuguese opposition to ratification. In June 1880 he had written of what was to him the 'bad faith and misdirected cunning of the Portuguese Government' and did not alter his view in the following months.[1] It was during this period that he wrote in frustration to his friend, Sir Charles Dilke, Under-Secretary at the Foreign Office in the new ministry, 'Goa, Lourenço Marques, Congo—these are the waters by which I have had to hang up my harp and weep'.[2] (The explanation of the Goa reference is that Morier was at this time aiding negotiations between the Stafford House group and the Portuguese Government for the construction of the Goa railway as envisaged in the treaty of 1878–1879.) Prevarication —as Morier saw it—continued until March 1881 when, at last, the Lourenço Marques ratification passed through the House of Deputies.[3] To strengthen his hand in the final stage —passage through the Upper House—Morier asked on 18 March for a public declaration in Parliament that the British Government would agree to the opening of the Congo negotiations immediately after ratification.[4] A fortnight later he modified his request, asking permission to begin negotiations on the Congo in order to obtain Portuguese ratification of the Lourenço Marques treaty, the course of action which Braamcamp had vainly urged in the autumn of 1879, though Morier made clear that the ratification of a Congo treaty would still be dependent on ratification of the Lourenço Marques agreement.[5] A draft Congo treaty followed the request some three weeks later.

Basic to the draft was recognition by Great Britain of Portuguese sovereignty over the coast between 18° south latitude, the southern boundary of Angola, and the mouth of the Congo. In addition Great Britain would engage to use her good offices to obtain a similar recognition from other powers (Article I). In return Portugal would concede that the commercial relations of the two Powers on the section of the coast not already

---

[1] *PRO30/29/183*, Morier to Granville, 13 June 1880, Private. Bains, op. cit., 94–95.
[2] *Dilke MSS., 43887, Folio 239*, Morier to Dilke, n.d. (1880), Private.
[3] Bains, op. cit., 95.
[4] *FO63/1130*, Morier to F.O., 18 Mar. 1881, Telegram.
[5] *FO63/1131*, Morier to F.O., 3 Apr. 1881, No. 82, Most Confidential.

occupied by Portugal should be determined by a separate convention (Article II) and that a joint commission should be set up to consider the rights of the native tribes and established interests of the European inhabitants of that same section of coast (Article III). A joint commission would also be set up to manage slave trade affairs for a period of twelve years along the whole coast from the Congo mouth to 18° south and on the River Congo itself (Article IV). Here would seem to lie the reason for Morier's definition of the coast to be recognized as Portuguese extending down to 18° south. Portuguese sovereignty could hardly be disputed: but only if the whole coast was made the subject of a treaty could Britain have grounds for intervention in slave trade matters along the 700-mile coastline of Angola. A veiled form of the slave trade still persisted—the *'engagé'* trade between Angola and the islands of San Thomé and Principé. Portugal would be required to make two further concessions. Although the treaty accorded her sovereignty over the right bank of the Congo and up to 5° 12′ south latitude, Portugal would, for the duration of the treaty, exercise this sovereignty jointly with those powers whose subjects had commercial or other establishments there (Article V). She would also agree to a joint Anglo-Portuguese control of the navigation and policing of the Congo itself (Article VI). The treaty would run for twelve years, and would be renewable for further periods of twelve years, whilst ratifications would be exchanged on the same day as those of the Lourenço Marques treaty (Article VII).[1]

Even as a draft treaty this was a slapdash affair. It can hardly have been intended, for instance, that Portugal's very right to the portion of the coast hitherto unoccupied by her should depend, after twelve years, on renewal of the treaty. And yet, if her right did not so depend, what was the object of providing for renewal of an agreement by which Portugal would agree to the perpetuation of limitations upon her authority? But

[1] *FO63/1131*, Morier to F.O., 20 Apr. 1881, No. 101, and Encl., Draft Congo Treaty. See also *Dilke MSS., 43888*, Folios *143–4 and 237–8*, Morier to Dilke, 19 Apr. 1881, Private, and Encl., Draft Congo Treaty, and ibid., Folios *157–8*, Morier to Dilke, 24 Apr. 1881, Private. There are certain minor differences, but not contradictions, between the official and the private drafts, and the above summary combines both versions. In his official draft, Morier confused the northern and the southern limits of the Portuguese Congo claim. He spoke of latitude 8° 15′ as its northern limit. It was, of course, 5° 12′ south latitude.

however poor his drafting, Morier's purpose is clear. He was putting forward a settlement which was to be the consummation of his plan for the reform and opening up of the Portuguese colonial empire and which would at the same time give to Portugal the form, and much of the substance, of her long coveted desire. From the British point of view the most immediate benefit would lie in the maintenance of Britain's commercial and humanitarian interests in a region which might soon attract the attention of powers more considerable and less tractable than Portugal—and quite without the burden and dangers of annexation.

But Morier's plea to be allowed to open negotiations was rejected.

'I have to inform you', wrote Granville, 'that Lord Kimberley has expressed the conviction that looking to the proceedings of the Portuguese Government with respect to the Lourenço Marques treaty, and the hostile feeling which apparently prevails in Portugal on the subject of negotiations with this country, it would not be desirable to take any steps at the present time in regard to the Congo question.'[1]

The rejection appears to have been based on a feeling that, in Pauncefote's words, 'considering the way we have been treated by Portugal we are hardly called upon to give them a sop in the shape of the Congo Treaty'.[2] In the following weeks the disturbed South African situation stemming from the British defeat at Majuba in February led the Liberal government to agree to a Portuguese request to shelve the ratification of the Lourenço Marques treaty[3]—though the Portuguese Government was prepared, as payment of a debt of honour, to allow it to take its chance in the House of Peers, if Granville so insisted[4] —just at the time when Morier had become certain that ratification in the Upper House could be obtained without even the promise to open Congo negotiations.[5]

There was some justification for Granville's withholding of the backing that Morier needed in the crucial final stage of

[1] *FO63/1104*, F.O. to Morier, 30 Apr. 1881, No. 52, Draft.
[2] *FO63/1131*, Pauncefote, Minute, n.d., on Morier to F.O., 3 Apr. 1881, No. 82, Most Confidential. C.O. to F.O., 23 Apr. 1881, Confidential. Granville, Endorsement of Pauncefote Minute, n.d., on Morier to F.O., 27 Apr. 1881, Telegram.
[3] *FO63/1132*, F.O. to Morier, 18 May 1881, No. 57, Draft.
[4] *FO63/1131*, Morier to F.O., 27 Apr. 1881, Telegram.
[5] *FO63/1132*, Morier to F.O., 5 and 10 May 1881, Telegrams, and 7 May 1881, Telegram Recorder, No. 116a, Confidential.

his 'grand design'. Nevertheless an opportunity for a most advantageous reform of the Anglo-Portuguese colonial relationship, made possible because Morier saw it whole instead of consisting of distinct questions, had been largely lost by the British Government. The indifferent support which Morier's proposal commanded is not difficult to explain.

There was in the Foreign Office a *vis inertiae*, not incompatible with overwork on the part of the Secretary of State and senior officials, which prevented attention being given to any but pressing problems, and a distrust of ambitious new departures in policy. In addition there was the antipathy which Morier aroused amongst the permanent officials. Morier's understanding of African problems was more acute than that of any of them (Anderson was not in a position of authority at this time), but the vigour and enthusiasm with which he pressed his schemes was somewhat intemperate and merely aroused antagonism in the Foreign Office, where he was clearly regarded as an *enfant terrible*. Morier nevertheless came close to success over the final phase of his grand design. Salisbury, with his magisterial independence of mind, had seen the desirability of reaching agreement with Portugal but had had to suspend action on the fall of the Beaconsfield Government. He stood a chance, also, of gaining for his plan the sponsorship of Granville and Dilke, with whom he was apparently on terms of personal friendship. But both appear to have remained unconvinced by Morier's arguments and Dilke, at least, grew weary of the numerous and lengthy letters which descended on him from Lisbon. Certainly he observed on one occasion, 'I have twice urged him not to write me these private letters, and to put the whole thing into dispatches.'[1]

Morier himself was bitterly disappointed at failure when success was within his grasp, and the Foreign Office's *nolle prosequi* no doubt underlined the opinion of its officials which he had expressed privately to Dilke earlier in the year. There was, he said, an 'utter absence of co-operation' between the Foreign Office and its servants abroad, and continued, 'You who are still a human being and able to see things from the general home point of view, will be over-weighted by two such

[1] *Dilke MSS., 43888*, Dilke, Memo., 4 May 1881; *43887–43891*, Morier to Dilke, 1880–2 *passim*. PRO 30/29/183, Morier to Granville, 1880–1 *passim*.

bureaucrats as ―――― and ――――.'[1] He told Granville, in the peroration of a dispatch which was scorching, no less, that

> This want of confidence in the judgment of a public servant in regard to matters which it is his special business to be acquainted with, is discouraging to a man who strives earnestly to promote the interests of his country.
> I do not believe that in my case it has been deserved.[2]

On his transfer to Madrid, two months later, he wrote of his conviction that he was leaving Lisbon—

> in the eyes of the Portuguese public and of the *diplomatic gallery* as one whose policy ... has been successfully resisted by public opinion and by the machinations of both the political parties, and therefore *pro tanto* as a man who has failed and whose failure is acknowledged by his Government.[3]

If Morier could treat his chiefs thus, one can see the force of Granville's remark made in 1884 when the question of Lord Dufferin's successor as ambassador at Constantinople was being discussed. 'The Turk', he observed, 'has behaved so badly that it would pay him out to send him Morier.'[4]

* * *

But within eighteen months of Granville's negative reply to Morier the Foreign Office was impelled, by the manifestation of just such a threat to the Congo basin as Morier had envisaged and sought to guard against, to take essentially similar action to that which Morier had unavailingly proposed. This threat was from France. The Foreign Office had first had wind of French designs when in June 1881 the Baptist Missionary Society reported that the French explorer, Lieutenant de Brazza, had taken possession of the northern shore of Stanley Pool. Lister had commented, 'This is serious if true', but no action had been taken other than to ask Lord Lyons at Paris for information.[5] Nine months later more definite news reached the Foreign Office from the same source when the B.M.S. forwarded a

---

[1] S. Gwynn and G. M. Tuckwell, *The Life of the Rt. Hon. Sir Charles Dilke, M.P.* (London 1917), I, 417.
[2] *FO63/1132*, Morier to F.O., 21 May 1881, No. 129.
[3] *PRO30/29/183*, Morier to Granville, 29 July 1881, Private and Confidential.
[4] Quoted in Lord E. Fitzmaurice, *The Life of Lord Granville* (London, 1905), II, 364.
[5] *FO84/1801*, B.M.S. to F.O., 25 June 1881, and Lister, Minute thereon, n.d. F.O. to Lyons, 2 July 1881, S/T No. 23, Draft.

copy of a treaty which de Brazza had concluded with Makoko, a chief holding authority on the right bank of Stanley Pool.[1] Anglo-French rivalry, fed on the British side by fear of the wider extension of a protectionist fiscal system, had long been a key feature of the politics of western Africa. French intentions on the Upper Congo, therefore, demanded urgent inquiry and on 10 April Lord Lyons was instructed to find out if the French Government regarded the Makoko treaty as genuine. Despite promptings from London in June and August,[2] the Paris Embassy was unable to give any information until October when it reported on the 6th, that the French Government had been urged in the Press to ratify, and, on the 25th, the French Government's belated reply to its official inquiries—that it was examining the clauses of the treaty. Not until 22 November could Lyons report that the Chamber actually had ratified it,[3] but the possibility, interpreted as probability, was sufficient for the Foreign Office and it had decided, sometime before 9 November, to do a deal with Portugal.[4] Lister elaborated on the reasons for this decision in a dispatch to the Colonial Office. The first part was a justification of a *volte face* of policy. As the (export) slave trade had now ceased, Portugal having indeed in recent years actively assisted in its extirpation, the British objection to the Portuguese claim to sovereignty over the Lower Congo and adjoining coast was no longer sufficiently strong to justify the risk of complication with the Portuguese Government which might arise by maintaining it. In his concluding section Lister gave the vital reason for the change in policy—the establishment of France on the Congo threatened to be detrimental to British commerce.[5] The French threat, immediately at least, being on the Upper Congo, it may appear at first sight that the decision to negotiate a treaty concerning the Lower Congo was only indirect counter action. But, as a recent study of Anglo-French relations in West Africa in this

[1] *FO84/1802*, B.M.S. to F.O., 23 Mar. 1882, and Encl., De Brazza Treaty, Copy.
[2] *FO84/1802*, F.O. to Lyons, 10 Apr. 1882, S/T No. 23; 20 June 1882, S/T No. 40; 23 Aug. 1882, S/T No. 63, Drafts.
[3] *FO84/1802*, Lyons to F.O., 25 Oct. 1882, S/T No. 69; 22 Nov. 1882, S/T No. 83. Plunkett (Paris) to F.O., 6 Oct. 1882, S/T No. 62. See also Lyons to F.O., 16 Nov. 1882, S/T No. 78; 19 Nov. 1882, S/T No. 81.
[4] *FO84/1802*, Lister, Memo., 9 Nov. 1882.
[5] *FO84/1802*, F.O. to C.O., 25 Nov. 1882. See also *FO84/1803*, Anderson, Memo. 19 Feb. 1883.

period has been at pains to point out, British policy had for some time been dominated by a concern to maintain possession of, or paramountcy over the coast and, more especially, control of the mouths of rivers. As a development of this policy it was also held desirable that England should exercise paramountcy over a solid belt of coastal territory so that France—until 1884 no other power had any importance in this context—could not infiltrate behind portions of the coast dominated by England. Hence the abortive proposal put up in 1875 for an agreement with France whereby, in return, notably, for the cession of the Gambia, France would forgo all present and future claims to any part of the West African coast between the River Pongas and the River Gaboon. It is significant that in 1883, that is when the Anglo-Portuguese negotiations were under way, the Foreign Office revived this project and sought to extend this belt southwards so as to include the French colony of Gaboon. The Gambia, the almost traditional bargaining counter, was, in effect, to be exchanged for it.[1] Thus, since the territory which Britain was prepared to recognize as Portuguese extended northwards to the frontier of Gaboon, the 'coastal' policy would perfectly have achieved its object. Although by 1883 Anglo-French relations were much too acrimonious for negotiations to be successful, this episode suggests that the decision to do a deal with Portugal was a more considered and promising policy than might at first sight appear, whilst to place the decision in the general context of a 'coastal' policy is, at the very least, to make it more comprehensible.

That the new British resolve to admit Portugal's Congo claim was, in an immediate sense, a *volte face* there can be no doubt. But there was also a real sense in which the new policy was not a change of front but rather a reversion to a traditional harmony, albeit of the type which prevails between patron and client. Since the Marriage Treaty of 1661, England and Portugal had been in alliance. In the early 1880's the existence of this bond was not in doubt, though the extent of Britain's consequential responsibilities was not clear. Certainly, in the whole period since the late 1830's, disputes and bickering— over Portuguese colonial tariffs, over Delagoa Bay, over fiscal

[1] Joan P. Schwitzer, *The British Attitude to French Colonization, 1875–1887* (Univ. of London, Ph.D. thesis, 1954), 219–35, 315–18, 353–60.

privileges in Goa, over slave trade matters as well as over the Congo itself—had overlain this harmony. Nevertheless its underlying existence is a necessary part of the explanation of why the British Government decided to admit Portugal's claim to the Congo and to appoint Portugal the watchdog of Free Trade.

The new British policy was also traditional in a yet different sense for it was but a variant of that policy of 'Informal Empire' which, since the mid-eighteenth century, had secured Britain's commercial interests in so many parts of the globe with a bare minimum of territorial acquisition. By establishing herself on a rich trade route, as at Singapore; by intervention in the affairs of areas such as South America and the obtaining of favourable commercial treaties; by the use of consular authority backed up by naval power, as at Zanzibar and in the Bight of Benin; in each of these ways Britain's fundamental commercial interest, the maintenance of Free Trade, had been secured—and with the minimum of expense.[1] To place Portugal astride the Congo mouth on specific conditions was essentially the use of the same technique.

It is probable that it was partly because of the very familiarity of this technique that the issue never became a contentious one in the Cabinet. Moreover the Congo and West Central Africa were not yet widely recognized as an important British commercial interest (which they were); consequently little heart-searching on policy to be pursued towards the region took place. Above all, of course, the policy cost nothing. It was thus acceptable to those members of the Gladstone ministry who wished to persist in its original intention of 'reverting to the tradition of non-intervention and minimum responsibility abroad'.[2]

Adoption of the new policy was further facilitated by Portugal seeking yet again, and apparently independently, British acceptance of her Congo claim. The Foreign Office heard of the likelihood of a Portuguese approach in a dispatch

[1] See Vincent T. Harlow, *The Founding of the Second British Empire, 1763–1793*, Vol. I (London, 1952), and John Gallagher and Ronald Robinson, 'The Imperialism of Free Trade', *The Economic History Review*, 2nd series, Vol. VI, No. 1, 1953, 1–15.

[2] *C.H.B.E.*, Vol. III (Cambridge, 1959), 128. For the consideration of Imperial issues in British politics see R. E. Robinson, 'Imperial Problems in British Politics, 1880–1895', *C.H.B.E.*, III, 127–80.

of 19 October from Baring at Lisbon.[1] The formal approach followed in a dispatch from M. Serpa, the Portuguese Foreign Minister, to d'Antas, and communicated to the Office on 22 November.[2] The Foreign Office naturally agreed to open negotiations, and in its reply went on to state the conditions which should form the basis of the treaty—which was also to be a settlement of certain East Central African issues, the Lourenço Marques treaty having never been ratified—namely, British recognition of Portuguese sovereignty over the coast between 5° 12′ and 8° south latitude; the navigation of the Congo and Zambesi to be free and not subject to any monopolies or exclusive concessions; a liberal tariff with a low maximum rate of duties in all Portugal's African possessions and a guarantee of most favoured nation treatment for Great Britain; due consideration for all rights enjoyed by British subjects by virtue of treaties with native chiefs; British subjects to be on the same footing as Portuguese as regards land ownership, missionary operations and taxation; the suppression of the slave trade and slavery; and, as a postscript, the transfer to Great Britain of the Portuguese fort at Whydah in Dahomey, which was wanted as a counter to French influence in that region. Appended to the treaty should be a declaration in which Portugal would disavow any claim to the southern African coastline below 18° south latitude on the west coast and 26° 30′ south latitude on the east, and would accept that her sovereignty on the African continent would nowhere extend further inland than points actually occupied.[3]

It is quite obvious that the arrangement which the Foreign Office now sought to make with Portugal owed much to Morier.[4] Unsympathetic though Granville and the Foreign Office had been to Morier's design in the previous year, they could scarcely fail to have his Congo plan at the back of their minds. Moreover, it fitted into the favoured concept of a 'coastal' policy. Hence when French treaty making on the banks of Stanley Pool compelled action of some sort, Morier's plan was taken from the shelf, dusted, and, with modifications,

---

[1] *FO84/1802*, Baring to F.O., 19 Oct. 1882, S/T No. 15.
[2] *FO84/1802*, Serpa to d'Antas, 8 Nov. 1882, Encl. in d'Antas to F.O., 22 Nov. 1882.
[3] *FO84/1802*, F.O. to d'Antas, 15 Dec. 1882.
[4] See Fitzmaurice, op. cit., II, 343.

adopted as the new Congo policy of Her Majesty's Government. This recognition of the merits of Morier's proposal was, however, 'posthumous'—and in two senses. In mid-1881 he had been moved from Lisbon to Madrid, and was shortly to be transferred to St. Petersburg. Consequently he played no part at all in the negotiations with Portugal. Recognition of the merit of Morier's proposal was 'posthumous' in the second sense that it came, as it was to prove, too late. Between 1879 and mid-1882 a Congo treaty might not only have been negotiated with Portugal but also accepted by the Powers. In 1882–4 it was quite another matter.

The Foreign Office did not seriously consider any alternative means of preserving the freedom of the Congo. There were in fact two. Great Britain might occupy the Congo mouth herself or she might recognize the sovereignty of the *A.I.C.* over the considerable sections of the river and its banks which she could claim to control. The first possibility was never seriously discussed. No British Government of this period, and in particular no Liberal government, could regard the acquisition of tropical territory as anything but a last resort to be adopted only when nothing else could preserve a vital interest. Moreover Granville, according to his biographer and sometime Parliamentary Under-Secretary, at least, foresaw that international rivalry in the Niger Delta and on the Lower Niger itself was likely soon to reach a climax and that Cabinet acceptance of the necessity of new territorial responsibilities in that region should not be prejudiced by claims to land in what was regarded as a less important sphere of interest.[1] Even Morier's mild suggestion, contained in his draft treaty, that Great Britain, amongst other powers, should share in the jurisdiction of the right bank of the Congo was never entertained.

Recognition of the International Association as the guarantor of the freedom of trade on the Congo was not perhaps a serious possibility at the time when negotiations with Portugal began. But right from their commencement the steady extension of the Association's influence on the Congo made such a course a possible alternative policy. Indeed in February 1883 Kirk pointed out to the Foreign Office the effectiveness of the International Association's stations along the rapids and up to

[1] Fitzmaurice, op. cit., II, 344. See pp. 33–34 above.

Stanley Pool as a counter to France.[1] On the face of it, support of a body active in the very region of the French threat would seem a distinctly promising policy.

But until the time of the Berlin West Africa Conference the Foreign Office never seriously considered such a course because of the undefined status of the International Association and a pessimistic view of its chances of stability and continuing independence. Until March 1884 at least, in which month the Foreign Office heard through Harry Johnston of the exclusive treaties being concluded by the Association's agents,[2] Leopold of the Belgians' venture appears to have been regarded as a piece of praiseworthy if somewhat impracticable philanthropy. But to the Foreign Office, accustomed to deal with sovereign states, the International Association, however laudable in a moral sense, was politically and diplomatically neither fish, flesh, nor red herring. It could not be a party to a diplomatic agreement for it had no existence in International Law, and since it relied on private generosity alone, its ability to maintain its independence of France and Portugal, or of any other power, could not be relied upon.[3] As a possible check to French protectionism on the Upper Congo, therefore, it did not enter the lists.[4]

Having embarked on the new policy and stated its terms the Foreign Office set itself to bargaining. The first stage of the negotiations lasted from December 1882 to April 1883. In this period agreement was virtually reached on a draft treaty comprising six fairly brief and general articles, but against a background of mounting opposition in England. This, combined with the greater perspicacity of the first head of the Africa Department of the Foreign Office, resulted in the Foreign Office sharply raising its terms and the next ten months—the

---

[1] See pp. 127–8 below.   [2] See p. 157 below.
[3] For F.O. views of the *A.I.C.* see *FO84/1803*, Lister, 28 Feb., Anderson, 1 Mar., Minutes on Leopold to Queen, 22 Feb. 1883. *FO84/1804*, Lister, Minute, 22 Mar. 1883, on Mackinnon to F.O., 19 Mar. 1883. Fitzmaurice op. cit., II, 356.
[4] In *The Partition of Africa* (London, 1895), 2nd ed., 145, J. S. Keltie makes the statement 'on very high authority' that Granville 'was under the impression that the King of the Belgians, after organizing an administration on the Congo, intended to make over all his claims to England'. Even if this is so there is no evidence in the *Granville Papers* or Foreign Office files that his actions towards Leopold and the International Association ever went beyond the dictates of aristocratic politeness and consideration for the sovereign of an allied state. Fitzmaurice's firsthand evidence (Fitzmaurice, op. cit., II, 356), that by mid-1884, at least, Granville 'was sceptical how long the King would desire to maintain the character of "the great philanthropic enterprise" ' hardly substantiates Keltie's claim.

second phase—were occupied in reaching agreement on the new basis, Portugal making most of the concessions. The treaty was signed in February 1884 and in a final phase of four months the Foreign Office unavailingly tried to get it accepted both by British and foreign opinion as a necessary preliminary to the exchange of ratifications.

The Portuguese reply to Granville's December dispatch was to forward a draft treaty founded on the basis set out in that dispatch but objecting to certain conditions. By the terms of Article I Great Britain would fully recognize Portuguese sovereignty over the coast lying between 5° 12′ and 8° south latitude whilst in Article II Portugal met the first British demand, agreeing that 'the navigation of the Congo and Zambesi and their affluents shall be free and not subject to any monopoly or exclusive concession'. Article III went part way to meeting British fiscal requirements.

The subjects of each of the high contracting parties shall in the African colonies of the other enjoy the privileges of the most favoured nation in all matters relating to navigation and commerce and to customs dues.

But Portugal was unwilling to accept a liberal tariff for all her African colonies or to agree to the indefinite duration of such fiscal concessions as she did make.

'The dues of the Portuguese customs tariffs in the African colonies', the Article ran, '[are] not to exceed during the period of ten years the dues actually in force, and those of the tariffs for the districts on or about the mouth of the Congo, when they are occupied, [are] not to exceed the maximum of 10 per cent. *ad valorem*.'

The safeguards demanded by Granville for British subjects residing in the territory to be acquired by Portugal were, in Article IV, accepted save in one particular. On the real or alleged ground of possible difficulties with the Vatican, Portugal wished 'religious worship' to be substituted for 'missionary operations'. The article ran:

The subjects of Her Britannic Majesty shall be placed on an equal footing with the subjects of His Most Faithful Majesty in the Portuguese colonies in Africa, as regards the purchase or leasing of land, religious worship and the assessment of taxes, due consideration to be shown by the Portuguese authorities for the privileges hitherto enjoyed by British subjects in virtue of any agreements made with the native chiefs in the Congo districts.

As regards the slave trade, Portugal (in Article V) responded to British insistence on its suppression by promising that 'the Portuguese legislation for the complete extinction of the slave trade shall be at once and effectively applied to the districts of the Congo referred to in Article I of this Convention'. She suggested furthermore that 'the high contracting parties bind themselves to use all possible means for the purpose of finally extinguishing the slave trade on the eastern and western coasts of Africa'.

In his accompanying dispatch Serpa objected to the fixing of definite limits to the inland frontiers of Portugal's African colonies both on account of the practical difficulties and because she would thereby be debarred from taking advantage of possible future opportunities for the extension of her dominions, and expressed the hope that the cession of the fort at Whydah would not be insisted upon. Serpa agreed, however, to the demand that Portugal should abjure any claims to territory on the southern African coastline.[1]

Granville's reply of 23 January gave promise of a rapid settlement. The British Government, he wrote to d'Antas, saw no objection to the terms of Articles I, II, and IV, and agreed that no declaration fixing the limits of her African colonies would be required of Portugal. But there were two objections. The first was to Article II, intelligence having recently been received of a significant increase in the Mozambique tariff of 1877 (the tariff in the construction of which Morier had had a part). If, however, Lisbon repudiated the revised tariff,

> Her Majesty's Government would be prepared to accept an Article, in place of the present Article II, which would provide that the tariff to be put in force in the districts in question [i.e. in the territory to be acquired by Portugal] should be similar to that settled for the Mozambique in 1877 and that none of the tariffs in the Portuguese possessions in Africa should be liable to be raised so long as the Convention, now under consideration, is in force.

The second objection was made in consequence of the past 'disinclination of the Portuguese Government to allow Her Majesty's cruisers to operate against slave traders within the

---

[1] *FO 84/1803* d'Antas to F.O., 10 Jan. 1883, *Eclaircissements*, and Encls., Serpa to d'Antas, 26 Dec. 1882 and Draft Treaty, Translations.

territorial waters of Portugal', and urged that Article V should be replaced by a modification of two articles of the abortive Lourenço Marques treaty, articles which provided for the conditional operation in Portuguese waters of British warships engaged in slave trade prevention. A third point made by Granville was scarcely an objection but the placing on record of the assumption that the local coasting trade—apparently in the Congo region only—would be open to the craft of all nations.[1]

On receiving Granville's dispatch of 23 January Serpa immediately sought to obtain agreement on outstanding points. On 29 January d'Antas addressed a note to Granville stating that Portugal agreed to the application to the Congo of the Mozambique tariff (as slightly increased in 1880 but stripped of its recent modifications) but only for ten years, and still refusing to agree to more than the maintenance of existing tariffs in the other Portuguese African colonies for the same period. Over the coasting trade Portugal prevaricated, merely promising that the freedom of this trade would be provided for by a new law. Nor did Portugal meet British wishes over the Lourenço Marques articles, either in d'Antas' January note or in a second note of 20 February.[2]

When reviewing the course of negotiations five months later Serpa claimed that immediately after Granville's dispatch of 23 January 'there were only two points to settle, and both of them of an easy settlement'. By 1 February, he continued, as a result of the concessions he had instructed d'Antas to make, 'the negotiations seemed to be in the way of coming to a speedy conclusion'.[3] In making this claim Serpa unduly minimized the differences still outstanding but this general contention was valid. Negotiation on outstanding differences might still have occupied some time but in mid-February Great Britain and Portugal were close to agreement. In the event there was no agreement on the basis of the simple draft treaty of the winter of 1882–3, and no rapid conclusion of the negotiations. The responsibility for this was Britain's for she stiffened her attitude

[1] *FO84/1803*, F.O. to d'Antas, 23 Jan. 1883. The two slave trade articles of the Lourenço Marques Treaty are printed in *FO84/1802*.
[2] *FO84/1803*, d'Antas to F.O., 29 Jan. 1883. Revised Article V, left by d'Antas at F.O., 20 Feb. 1883, and Minute by Lister thereon.
[3] *FO84/1806*, Serpa to d'Antas, 26 June 1883, forwarded to F.O., 7 July 1883 with translation.

and introduced into the negotiations a new and much more searching draft demanding many more concessions of Portugal.

The stiffening of attitude began in mid-February with H. Percy Anderson's assumption of the headship of the Africa Department of the Foreign Office, successor to the old Slave Trade Department which appears to have become moribund after Wylde's retirement in March 1880. One of Anderson's first tasks was thoroughly to study the whole question of the Anglo-Portuguese negotiations. The result of his appraisal was the conviction that Portugal was not prepared to make adequate concessions—indeed, that such had not been demanded of her—and that it was essential to press for better terms.

'The Portuguese Government', he wrote on 19 February, 'are by no means disposed at present to give us effective guarantees. They make difficulties about the vital point of the coasting trade, about definition of limits of jurisdiction, about a Slave Trade article: and they shuffle about missionaries. The only point partly conceded, the adoption of the Mozambique tariff of 1877, they wish to limit to ten years. Practically, if we were to give way to them now, they would purchase our recognition by a liberal tariff for ten years—at the end of that time when they had made their occupation good, we should be at their mercy.'

Anderson went on to comment article by article on the existing draft, specifying the amendments he thought necessary.[1]

Anderson's paper was, in fact, an implicit criticism of the previous conduct of negotiations, for as regards limits of jurisdiction and the rights of missionaries the Portuguese position had already been accepted. (It is clear that in the period before Anderson came to a position of authority, with Wylde in retirement, the conduct of negotiations suffered from the lack of anyone in the Foreign Office with a detailed knowledge of Africa and of Portugal in Africa, and with time to devote adequate attention to the matter.) Granville was nevertheless impressed, and a day or two later Anderson obtained his assent to a proposal to draft the reply which was due to d'Antas in the spirit of the views he had expressed.[2] Since his draft was not appreciably amended the dispatch which finally went off to d'Antas on 15 March was essentially Anderson's. He made Britain's position quite clear. Beginning with a general review

[1] *FO84/1803*, Anderson, Paper, 19 Feb. 1883, and notes on 'Project of Treaty respecting Congo'.
[2] *FO84/1803*, Granville, Feb. 1883, n.d., Minute.

of the inception and course of the negotiations, he went on to indicate that in the matter of the joint campaign against the slave trade Britain would not insist on the Lourenço Marques articles but only on some more effective arrangement for joint action than Portugal had yet conceded. Turning to the Congo, he prepared the way for a statement of the British requirements by a forthright declaration of the assumptions on which it was based.

When it is understood that what is proposed is not the recognition of the validity of an old claim but an admission of sovereignty over a territory, over which, in the opinion of Her Majesty's Government, Portugal has not had any right, it will be seen that the position of Her Majesty's Government from their own point of view, is not that of asking concessions as a favour but attaching them as a condition.

In view of this and of the fact that commercial and missionary operations were already being carried on by British subjects and the subjects of other European states,

it would be impossible ... to agree to the imposition of burdens which do not now exist.... No obscurity therefore must exist on the following points. There should be no differential dues, no transit dues: the freedom of Trade and Navigation of the River Congo should be absolute, involving exemption from all river dues or tolls: equality should be secured to missionaries of all creeds.

Anderson concluded his revision—it was no less—by reverting to insistence on a geographical definition of the inland frontier —though this would in no way preclude a future extension of sovereignty—and on the necessity of durable arrangements for commercial freedom, and by offering to forward a draft treaty incorporating the points he had made, should Portugal wish it.[1]

Anderson's paper and the dispatch which followed it demonstrate clearly the stiffening which Anderson put into the British attitude. He was responsible not only for a reversion to the original British position on boundaries but for a more stringent definition of freedom of navigation on the Congo and an unequivocal assertion of the necessity of freedom of trade, and for an insistence that there be no transit dues on the Congo, that the provision for commercial freedom, particularly on the Congo, be durable, and on perfect equality between missionaries of different denominations.

[1] *FO84/1804*, F.O. to d'Antas, 15 Mar. 1883.

Despite this stiffening in the British attitude, Serpa, in a dispatch communicated to the Foreign Office on 29 March, agreed in principle to the greater part of the British demands, objecting only to the immediate determination of the inland frontier on the Congo, and to the indefinite duration of the agreed tariffs (no specific counter proposal was made) and added that it only remained for Granville to draw up the articles which should be substituted for Articles III and V of the original Portuguese draft.[1] But the revised draft treaty adumbrated in March was never forwarded in the form then conceived, for in April another factor, the full flowering in England of a strong commercial and humanitarian opposition to the treaty, made the decision inspired by Anderson to obtain better conditions from Portugal no longer a step that was merely desirable but an imperative necessity. Indeed, the opposition was strong enough to bring about, between April and June, a stiffening of the British terms more considerable than had been proposed by Anderson, and to ensure in the following months that the Foreign Office would maintain its insistence on a quite exceptionally liberal treaty.

[1] *FO84/1804*, Serpa to d'Antas, 24 Mar. 1883, forwarded to F.O. 29 Mar. 1883. See also *FO84/1806*, Serpa to d'Antas, 26 June 1883, forwarded to F.O., 7 July 1883 with translation.

CHAPTER VI

THE BRITISH OPPOSITION TO THE ANGLO-PORTUGUESE TREATY

THE emergence in England of some sort of opposition to a change in jurisdiction on the Congo was only to be expected. The merchants engaged in the trade of the river had become accustomed to a type of commercial intercourse whose rules and conventions they understood, occasionally lamented, and yet from which they on the whole profited. Lack of a civilized jurisdiction had the disadvantage of making possible extortion by native chiefs and occasional disputes with native tribes, sometimes involving the stoppage of trade and attacks on factories. But there were limits to such losses. Native as well as trader was injured by the cessation of trade—and knew it. He knew too that serious violence would eventually bring a warship to inquire into matters. For the trader there was also a positive attraction in the existing state of affairs, namely, the absence of a European administration for which in the last resort he would have to pay. Portuguese control of the Congo coast would, the traders thought, not even confer the doubtful benefits which European administration might ordinarily be expected to bring. The extortions of ill-paid officials, and high customs dues would cause far greater damage to trade than anything of which the native tribes were capable.

Nor was a treaty with Portugal likely to find favour in missionary and humanitarian circles. As a Roman Catholic country she was likely to hinder Protestant missionary activity, as the recent attempt of a Portuguese Catholic mission to influence the King and people of San Salvador against the Baptist Missionary Society implied, whilst as a suppressor of the slave trade Portugal's efforts had been characterized by half-heartedness and official corruption.

Intensity was lent both to the commercial and humanitarian opposition by the new-found realization of the importance of the Congo as an artery leading to the very centre of the continent, but it is none the less likely that this 'conventional' opposition would have been placated by the safeguards which were inserted into the treaty, had the leadership of the agitation not fallen into the hands of a distinct group. This group consisted of the British supporters of Leopold II who, convinced of the value of the Central African interior as a great new British market once it had been opened up by the International Association, were determined to prevent the possible hindrance of the mouth of the Congo falling into Portuguese hands.

The strength of this group lay in the appeal of Leopold's practical idealism, in the leading position which one of its members—Hutton—occupied in the conventional opposition, and in the influential position which another member—Mackinnon—enjoyed in the commercial and humanitarian world. They were thus able to harness the opposition, give it the impetus of their own enthusiasm, and make it a far more effective opposition to the treaty than it would ever have been of itself.

To the general oversight of the efforts of his British sympathizers Leopold directed considerable attention. Detailed direction of men of their standing was impossible—and was in any case unnecessary. Their plans and hopes for the Congo may eventually have proved incompatible with Leopold's own designs, but that was not apparent at this time and those sympathizers felt themselves to have as real an interest as Leopold in opposing the treaty. It is therefore misleading to take at face value such statements as Dilke's that 'the King of the Belgians *pulled the strings* of the Manchester Chamber of Commerce'[1] (in which, of course, Hutton was an influential director), or that of Serpa, the Portuguese Foreign minister, that the *Comité d'Etudes* was *behind* Manchester's opposition to the treaty[2] (my italics in each case). Dilke and Serpa both ignore—because they would not have known of it—the real identity of interest between Leopold and his British supporters at this time.

A paid agent, of course, was under closer supervision. When in England, General Goldsmid was made use of but otherwise there was only one paid British agent, E. F. Law, later to

[1] Quoted in Gwynn and Tuckwell, op. cit., I, 534.
[2] *M. des A.E., C. et D., Afrique, A.I.C. 1883*, Vol. 2, No. 25, Greindl to Minister of Foreign Affairs, 22 Mar. 1883.

achieve eminence, notably as Finance Member of the Government of India, but at this time merely a retired army officer and man of business.[1] He was mainly employed in drawing up propaganda against the treaty and had a hand in the insertion in various journals of matter of this kind.[2]

All the indications point to Hutton as the effective originator of the campaign against the treaty. As early as May 1881, on a mere report of a Portuguese intention to annex the Congo mouth, Hutton had approached the Foreign Office privately, expressing alarm, and, as he himself explained, seeking information for which Leopold had asked him in his capacity as a Belgian consul.[3] This had been followed—on Hutton's inspiration as an influential director, it can scarcely be doubted —by a fully-fledged memorial from the Manchester Chamber of Commerce in the same vein, begging Her Majesty's Government not to countenance any action which would interrupt trade, and singling out for mention the keen interest with which merchants were watching Leopold's pioneering work on the Congo.[4] The continuing interest of Hutton and Manchester in the matter was shown by a request of the Chamber of Commerce in June 1882 that the Loanda consul should visit Nokki on the Lower Congo to investigate a report that the Portuguese had established a station there.[5] The Chamber went on to express the hope that Portugal would not be permitted to establish herself on the Congo. In the autumn of 1882, with newspaper reports of the likely ratification of the de Brazza treaties, and rumours of the Portuguese intention to press her Congo claim on the Foreign Office (an official avowal that the Foreign Office was actually negotiating with Portugal was not made until 26 February 1883,[6] though it seems to have become widely suspected that it was doing so during November 1882),[7] the matter came decisively to the fore and an agitation was begun. In its early stages, with no firm knowledge of the

[1] *D.N.B., Second Supplement*, II, 421–3.
[2] *Strauch MSS.*, Nos. *171, 172, 174, 176, 177, 178*. Leopold to Strauch, 13 Mar. (two letters), 16 Mar., 27 Mar., 5 Apr. and 6 Apr. 1883.
[3] *FO84/1801*, Slagg to Dilke, 6 Mar. 1881 and Encl., Hutton to Slagg, 5 Mar. 1881.
[4] *FO84/1612*, Manch. Ch. Comm. to F.O., 30 May 1881.
[5] *FO84/1802*, Manch. Ch. Comm. to F.O., 15 June 1882.
[6] *Hansard*, CCLXXVI., H.C., 830, 26 Feb. 1883.
[7] *FO84/1802*, Hatton & Cookson to F.O., 17 Nov. 1882, Letter and Telegram. *Hansard*, CCLXXV., H.C., 207, 28 Nov. 1882.

British decision to negotiate with Portugal, the representations were against any change of jurisdiction in the Congo region. Of this character was the first shot in the campaign—a memorial from the Manchester Chamber of Commerce on 13 November. The freedom of trade and navigation on the Congo was threatened by the claims of both France and Portugal. To counter this a new consular post should be established on the river itself since it was impossible for the Loanda consul to pay adequate attention to this part of his district on account of the distances involved. The duty of the consul should be 'essentially that of watching over the interests and trade of Great Britain on the Congo, and on the neutral coast between the French and Portuguese possessions', and he should be provided with a 'steamer or gunboat'. But, it was implied, the problem could no longer be dealt with by such methods alone, and at the same time had become of more importance than formerly.

Through the important discoveries during recent years on the Congo and on its tributaries greater interests than those of the industry of Lancashire and of even the trade of Great Britain are becoming involved. Europe now seeks to promote the civilisation and the enlightenment of Central Africa and to extend peaceful intercourse with its vast populations. Great Britain stands among the first countries to reap the advantages of this development of trade. . . .

Your memorialists would therefore pray that the earnest endeavours of Her Majesty's Government may be directed towards promoting a friendly understanding with the respective Governments of Europe and the United States in order that the sovereign and territorial rights of the Congo and of the adjacent neutral territories may be respected and maintained, and that in future there shall be no interference on the part of any Power with the existing freedom of navigation and of commerce on that river and on its tributaries.[1]

Following the dispatch of this memorial a deputation from the Chamber had an interview with Dilke. A further indication of the importance now attached to the matter was the creation of a standing committee of the Chamber to watch over British trade in West Africa and especially on the Congo.[2]

The next four months saw the development of a considerable campaign of individual firms, trade associations and, especially latterly, Chambers of Commerce against any change in jurisdiction on the Congo. In the earlier part of this period fear of

[1] *FO84/1802*, Manch. Ch. Comm. to Granville, Memorial, 13 Nov. 1882.
[3] *Manch. Ch. Comm.*, Report for 1882, 9.

French protectionism on the Congo was commonly coupled with opposition to Portuguese claims, but by the turn of the year it was against Portugal that the main weight of hostility had come to be directed. This was natural enough. The ratification of de Brazza's Makoko treaty had been authorized by the French Chamber on 22 November 1882[1] and though that might be regrettable, nothing effective, it could be argued, could be done about it, and in any case it was no more than a foothold in an area to which British trade had not yet directly penetrated. Nor was France actively threatening the Congo mouth. Portugal, on the other hand, had 'pretensions' to an area where a thriving British trade was established. In the fact that it had become increasingly clear that negotiations with Portugal were actually in progress, and might be influenced, lay a third reason for the changed emphasis of the agitation. Consul Holmwood suggested what may have been an additional reason. For some of the merchants engaged in the African trade there was, he thought, a distinct reason for not emphasizing the French threat—they believed themselves to be insulated from the effects of French protectionism.

There are . . . several old established and wealthy firms in Liverpool, Manchester and London which have hitherto enjoyed almost a monopoly in supplying this demand for British goods through French houses, or through trade routes connected with French settlements on the West Coast, and these are naturally not anxious to see the vast districts bordering on the Upper Congo thrown open to general competition.

In discussing the question of the proposed Congo Treaty therefore, the disadvantages to our trade which have notoriously accompanied Portuguese Colonial Government have been fully brought forward by these parties, while a point which might become of equal importance, namely the effect of French rule being substituted for that of Portugal, has not perhaps received the attention it deserves. . . . The sympathies of those most opposed to the Congo Treaty are possibly, however, not so much with British commerce as a whole as with the special trade they are interested in; they do not therefore bring forward this point.[2]

If some of the merchants engaged in the West African trade had particular reasons for minimizing the French threat, Hutton and the other British supporters of the International Association had particular reasons for emphasizing the Portuguese. Writing to Mackinnon in July 1884, Hutton speaks of

[1] See p. 101 above.
[2] *FO84/1811*, Holmwood, Memo., 6 May 1884.

'the object we have in view, viz. of extending the action of the International to the Lower Congo',[1] an aim which clearly demanded outright resistance to the Portuguese claim. Whether at the beginning of the agitation Mackinnon and Hutton had this object in mind it is impossible to say, but without doubt their hopes of the International Association dictated opposition to the establishment of any European power across the mouth of the river so vital to its work, right from the start of the treaty negotiations. Nor was the mutual hostility of the International Association and Britain towards France a factor sufficient to modify this attitude. To support the British Foreign Office over a treaty which would only indirectly embarrass France would do nothing to remove the very direct and present threat of de Brazza on the Upper Congo. The Association's battle with France would have to be fought with other weapons.

The change towards emphasis of the Portuguese threat was not the only development in the form of the agitation. It was also phased in another sense. In November and December 1882 the memorials and other representations came mostly from Manchester and Liverpool, from firms and associations directly connected with the Congo trade. These were from Hatton & Cookson, dated 17 and 20 November; from the British & African Steam Navigation Co. on 28 November; from Jas. Irvine & Co. on 29 November; from the Liverpool African Association on 1 December; from the Liverpool Chamber of Commerce on 5 December; from John Holt on 11 December; from Hutton early in January. There were three exceptions—C. H. Aston, a Birmingham manufacturer, on 27 November; Sir J. Reed, M.P. for Cardiff, reporting feeling amongst his constituents, on 7 December; and the Glasgow Chamber of Commerce on 18 December. But of these Aston was directly interested in the Congo trade whilst Glasgow, traditionally involved in trade with western Africa, was the headquarters of at least two firms trading to the Congo.

Then, commencing in February, further representations were made by most of these same bodies, whilst in March and April other Chambers of Commerce joined in. Thus further submissions were made to the Foreign Office by the Liverpool African Association on 15 February followed by a deputation

[1] *M.P.*, Hutton to Mackinnon, 4 July 1884, Quite Private.

on the 21st; by Irvine & Co. on 14 February; by Aston on the 22nd; by Hutton on 3 March; by Hatton & Cookson on the 10th and 20th; by the British & African Steam Navigation Co. on the 17th; and by the African Steam Ship Co. (which, because it was the trading partner of the B. & A.S.N. Co., is in this context to be identified with it) on the same day, followed by a deputation a few days later. The Chamber of Commerce memorials came from Warrington on 5 March, London on the 14th, Dewsbury on the 22nd, Cardiff on the 29th, Greenock on the 30th, Bristol on the 31st, Sunderland on 12 April, and Huddersfield and Birmingham on the 23rd. The Manchester Chamber, moreover, sent further representations on 29 January and 12 March as well as indirectly supporting its case on 18 and 28 April by protests against Portuguese interference with mails on the Congo. In addition the Liverpool African Association petitioned both the House of Lords on 9 April and the House of Commons on 9 March, whilst on 30 March the Commons also received a petition from Bristol, probably sponsored by the city's Chamber of Commerce.[1]

In the activity of the Chambers of Commerce the hand of the Manchester Chamber is evident. Most of the memorials display a distinct debt to the Manchester memorial of 13 November 1882, although they also reflect the subsequent concentration on the Portuguese threat to the Congo. There is not only a general similarity of view, but in many cases identity of wording also. Even where the preamble is differently expressed, the prayer of the memorialists is almost always identically stated, whilst the memorials of Bristol, Huddersfield and Birmingham are identical in every respect.[2]

---

[1] To these should be added two representations from a certain Henry Jepson of Manchester who memorialized for the first time on 4 Apr. 1883 and made a second representation on the 19th. For the text—or, in the case of those to the Lords and Commons, the enumeration—of the various representations see under sender and date in *FO84/1631, 1654 and 1802–5*, and *P.P. 1883, Votes and Proceedings of the House of Commons*, I, and *P.P. 1883, Minutes of the House of Lords*, I.

[2] The following is the form of memorial used by the Bristol, Huddersfield and Birmingham Chambers. In other cases the final petition, only, was used verbatim, though often their preamble was an elaboration of the first paragraph.

That in the opinion of your Memorialists the important interests of Great Britain on the South West coast of Africa and more especially as they are connected with those countries threatened by the unfounded claims of certain European Powers, and by exclusive treaties that are being made with native chiefs by officers of those Powers, should have the immediate consideration of Her Majesty's Government, and your Memorialists earnestly trust that Her Majesty's

The London Chamber's representation alone broke new ground. Although Portugal and to a lesser extent France were the objects of alarm, although the abandonment of the treaty negotiations and the appointment of a British official on the Congo were urged, a new method of preserving the independence of the Congo was suggested. What was ultimately required was

> the establishment of a system of international regulations sufficiently concise to ensure law and order, which might be done by confederating and bestowing power upon the various stations already established on the Congo under a neutral flag.[1]

This proposal was clearly inspired by Brussels where, since 1879, great store had been set on the Confederation plan as a means of securing international recognition of the *A.I.C.* It was also the first instance of explicit Chamber of Commerce support for the International Association. Its inclusion in the memorial was probably due to Joseph Tritton, a member of the Chamber and Treasurer of the Baptist Missionary Society, which supported the Association,[2] and later active in an attempt to found a large British railway and concession company on the Congo.

Thus only the London Chamber's memorial showed significant independence of the Manchester line—and even then each served the same general aims. The phasing of the other commercial representations also suggests, though less certainly, the guiding hand of the Manchester Chamber of Commerce whilst such various sources as Dilke,[3] Baron Solvyns,[4] the Belgian minister in London, rumours circulating '*dans les*

> Government will on no account cede to Portugal any rights that will give to that country control over the mouth or any part of the River Congo.
> Your Memorialists therefore pray that the earnest endeavours of Her Majesty's Government will be directed to promote an amicable understanding with the respective Governments of Europe and the United States in order that the rights of the natives on the banks of the Congo and the adjacent neutral territories may be respected and maintained, so that in future there may be no interference on the part of any Power with the existing free navigation and commerce of that River and its tributaries.

[1] *FO84/1804*, London Chamber of Commerce to Granville, Memorial, 14 Mar. 1883.
[2] See p. 35 above and pp. 121–3 below.
[3] Gwynn and Tuckwell, op. cit., I, 534.
[4] *M. des A.E., C. et D. Afrique, A.I.C. 1883*, Vol. 2, No. 24, Solvyns to Minister of Foreign Affairs, 7 Mar. 1883.

coulisses' at Lisbon,[1] and Serpa himself,[2] join in implicitly or explicitly attesting its leading role.

Given Manchester's initiative, only Hutton can have been responsible for it. A director of the Chamber since 1877, he was sufficiently prominent to become its president in 1884. As a merchant engaged in the supply of goods to merchants trading to western Africa he had perfectly comprehensible grounds for opposing the treaty: a yet more commanding reason was his vision of the large opportunities for British industry and commerce which the development of the Congo region by the *A.I.C.* would make possible, a vision which made him more than ready to mobilize an agitation against the treaty. Anderson at the Foreign Office certainly saw Hutton's hand at work. At a later stage of the agitation, when the Manchester Chamber of Commerce made known to the Foreign Office its outright opposition to ratification of the treaty, Anderson had no doubt that Hutton was responsible.[3] Again, at Hutton's death the claim could be made that it was mainly owing to his influence that the treaty was never ratified.[4] Misleading as this claim was, it could not have been voiced had there not been something— a considerable activity against the treaty—on which to build. Moreover it will be seen that from the close of 1882 onwards Hutton was active in arousing an agitation in fields outside the commercial world. It can hardly be supposed that he would neglect the *milieu* with which he was most familiar and in which he was not uninfluential.

It was to the missionary world that Hutton first looked when he sought to broaden the base of the agitation. In mid-November 1882 he urged the two British missions working on the Congo, the Baptist Missionary Society and the Livingstone Inland Mission, to action. To the Rev. Alfred Baynes, Secretary of the B.M.S., Hutton wrote that the Manchester Chamber of Commerce had memorialized the Foreign Secretary expressing alarm both at the de Brazza treaty and at Portuguese

[1] *M. des A.E., C. et D. Afrique, A.I.C., 1883, Vol. 2, No. 23.* Greindl to Minister of Foreign Affairs, 4 Mar. 1883.
[2] *M. des A.E., C. et D. Afrique, A.I.C. 1883, Vol. 2, No. 25.* Greindl to Minister of Foreign Affairs, 22 Mar. 1883.
[3] *FO84/1809,* Anderson, Minute, n.d., on Manch. Ch. Comm. to F.O., 6 Mar. 1884.
[4] Obituary of J. F. Hutton. *Journal of the Manchester Geographical Society,* Vol. VII, Jan.–Mar. 1891, (kindly loaned to the author by the late J. Arthur Hutton).

pretensions on the Congo, and urging the British Government to take the initiative in persuading the powers to leave the Congo territories neutral. Dilke had replied, Hutton continued, that Britain did not herself want the Congo and, though she favoured its continued neutrality, would not go to war to stop other powers taking possession of it. Of the two claimants the Government favoured Portugal on account of France's attitude. Commenting on this, Hutton suggested that France and Portugal would reach a compromise, dividing the area between them at 5° 12' south latitude, France taking the territory to the north of this line and Portugal that to the south. This would give Portugal possession of the Lower Congo and France possession of the Upper Congo and Stanley Pool. Surely, Hutton adroitly commented, this would seriously prejudice the work of the two British Protestant missions—but they would doubtless take immediate action in the matter.[1] Hutton wrote twice more to Baynes in the same month. On the 24th he told him that there would shortly be a question in the Commons on Congo affairs, and also asked for reports of the work of the B.M.S. on the Congo. In his third letter, written on 27 November, Hutton expressed the hope that the Society's friends would support the forthcoming question in the Commons, which was to be put down by Jacob Bright, and offered a bale or two of goods to help with the expense of getting the B.M.S. steamer up the river. In conclusion he made a point of mentioning Leopold's friendly interest in the work of the Society.[2]

The Livingstone Inland Mission received a similar letter but, as Mrs. Fanny Guinness, a co-founder of the Mission, told Baynes, it was not prepared to join in the agitation against territorial changes on the Congo, believing that French annexation (on the Upper Congo, the field of the Mission's operations) was much to be preferred to the existing state of virtual anarchy.[3] The B.M.S., on the other hand, wanted neither Portugal nor France to establish itself on the Congo. In May 1882 a Portuguese Catholic Mission to San Salvador had sought to wean the king and his people away from the

[1] Hutton to Baynes, 18 Nov. 1882, cited in Slade, *English-speaking Missions*, 66-67.
[2] *B.M.S.* Archives, Hutton to Baynes, 24 and 27 Nov. 1882 (I am indebted to Miss R. Slade for summaries of these letters).
[3] Slade, *Bulletin*, 705. Slade, *English-speaking Missions*, 67-68.

Baptist Mission which was established there, an indication of the treatment likely to be accorded Protestant missions should Portugal become established on the Lower Congo. Such an extension of Portuguese sovereignty would also, the B.M.S. feared, lead to an increase of slave trading. The objection to France was a consequence both of the difficulties which a kindred mission had already experienced at the hands of her agents in the Gaboon, and of the amicable relations which the Society had established with the International Association. From 1877 onwards Leopold had shown a friendly interest in the Society's work whilst Stanley had on several occasions given assistance to Baptist missionaries. At the very time Hutton wrote, friendly negotiations for the cession to the B.M.S. of a tract of International Association land at Stanley Pool were in progress. Both Stanley in Africa, and Leopold and Strauch in Brussels, where the negotiations were continued, went out of their way to accommodate the B.M.S.[1]

Apart from these particular acts of goodwill, the Society appreciated the great advantages which it gained from the International Association doing much of the essential pioneering work on the Upper Congo. In Miss Ruth Slade's words,

After Livingstone, they had discovered that the missionary ought at one and the same time to be geographer, explorer and philanthropist, and they considered themselves fortunate to have found a secular body which seemed to relieve them of a part of this heavy burden.[2]

To respond to Hutton's suggestion was, therefore, a natural course for the B.M.S. to adopt. In the meantime the Portuguese threat had manifested itself as the most pressing; a memorial praying that Portuguese jurisdiction be not allowed to extend to the Congo was therefore sent to Granville on 21 March 1883.[3]

Hutton, certainly indirectly through his activity in the Manchester Chamber of Commerce and perhaps directly as well, also had something to do with the Anti-Slavery Society joining in the campaign against the treaty. The question of the proposed Congo treaty was first raised in the Society by Buxton, an influential member of its committee,[4] probably in the ordinary

---

[1] Slade, *English-speaking Missions*, 68–69. Slade, *Bulletin*, 689, 697, 702–6, 706.
[2] Slade, *Bulletin*, 699.
[3] *FO84/1804*, B.M.S. to Granville, Memorial, 21 Mar. 1883.
[4] *A/S Papers*, Buxton to Allen, 4 Mar. 1883.

course of the Society's activity, as a question with implications for the humanitarian cause. (Buxton had attended the 1876 Brussels Conference but had not subsequently entered into close relations with Leopold.) Two days after he had first drawn the attention of the Society's secretary to the matter, however, Buxton sent him an account of a discussion of the proposed treaty contained in the report of the Manchester Chamber of Commerce for 1882, a copy of which had been lent him.[1] This suggests that Buxton's view of the case may well have been influenced by what he had just read of the attitude of the Manchester Chamber of Commerce. The episode also suggests that the lender of the report was a member of the Chamber—who more likely than Hutton? And if not Hutton, then perhaps Mackinnon, into whose hands a copy of the report could easily have come, and who was a personal friend of Buxton's.

The Anti-Slavery Society's attitude was determined at a meeting of its committee early in March 1883 which Buxton had asked the secretary to arrange when he first raised the Congo question with him. The meeting decided that, owing to Portugal's poor reputation in the suppression of the slave trade, a treaty which placed more territory under her control must be opposed. On 9 March a memorial was therefore sent to Granville protesting against the proposal to admit Portugal to the Congo on humanitarian, and also commercial grounds,[2] and a campaign against the treaty was begun which the Rev. James Long, a member of the committee, was commissioned to direct.[3] There is no detailed evidence of his tactics but efforts were made to gain the support of Members of Parliament, the *Anti-Slavery Reporter* spoke out against the treaty, and there was collaboration with Chambers of Commerce, especially with the Manchester Chamber, and with the International Association.[4] A net of friendship and acquaintance facilitated this collaboration. Long, it was claimed, had 'great experience and influence with Chambers of Commerce and other public

---

[1] *A/S Papers*, Buxton to Allen, 6 Mar. 1883.
[2] *FO84/1804*, Anti-Slavery Society to Granville, Memorial, 9 Mar. 1883.
[3] *A/S Papers*, Minute Book. Vol. V, Minutes of Committee, 4 May 1883.
[4] *Anti-Slavery Reporter*, Series 4, Vol. III, No. 3, 19 Mar. 1883, 67–72; Series 4, Vol. III, No. 4, 16 Apr. 1883, 100–7; Series 4, Vol. IV, No. 7, 19 July 1884, 155–7. *A/S Papers*, Circular appealing for funds for purchase of annuity for Long, n.d.

bodies'[1] and, like Buxton, was well known to Mackinnon.[2] He was also well known in Brussels; indeed Strauch spoke of him in March 1884 as '*un de nos amis les plus zélés et les plus actifs*',[3] whilst the assertion was later made that, in his conduct of the agitation against the treaty, he acted '*under instructions from General Strauch*' (my italics).[4] As far as Parliament was concerned there was a natural link in W. E. Forster, a subscriber to the Anti-Slavery Society and a notable supporter of humanitarian causes. It seems probable that Long was the key figure on the purely humanitarian side of the agitation. At the same time, and despite the claims made concerning his close connexion with Strauch and the Brussels authorities, there is no evidence that he was a supporter of Leopold's Congo venture *per se*, or that he had particular hopes of it, as was the case with Hutton, Mackinnon and Kirk.[5]

This opposition of the Anti-Slavery Society and of the Baptist Missionary Society to the Anglo-Portuguese treaty was not unimportant. It strengthened the opposition in a crude quantitative sense but a more important consequence was, perhaps, that it gave moral strength to the representations of commercial men who might, even in an age which had a high conception of the moral value of commerce, be accused by some of merely seeking their own profit.

In Chambers of Commerce and the commercial world generally, in missionary and humanitarian societies, impressive support for the agitation could be found. Nor did Hutton neglect a more general means of influencing public opinion— the Press. On 26 February, in a letter to the *Manchester Guardian* he was at pains to point out that both the Manchester Chamber of Commerce and a number of Liverpool merchants had emphatically protested against the making over of the Congo to Portugal.[6] A month later he came forward with a long letter

[1] *Anti-Slavery Reporter*, Series 4, Vol. IV, No. 7, 19 July 1884, 155–6.
[2] *A/S Papers*, Allen to Chesson, 16 Dec. 1886.
[3] Strauch to Leopold, 27 Mar. 1884, quoted in J. Stengers, 'Rapport sur le dossier "Correspondance Léopold II—Strauch" ', *Bulletin des Séances de l'Institut Royal Colonial Belge*, XXIV–1953–4, 1204. *Anti-Slavery Reporter*, Series 4, Vol. IV, No. 7, 19 July 1884, 155–6.
[4] *A/S Papers*, Circular appealing for funds for purchase of annuity for Long, n.d. The quotation continues, 'and in conjunction with the late W. E. Forster, M.P., Jacob Bright, M.P., Sir William Mackinnon, Bart.'
[5] For biographical information, see *D.N.B.*, XII, 105–6.
[6] *Manchester Guardian*, 26 Feb. 1883, 7, letter from J. F. Hutton.

asserting the importance of the Congo for British trade, testifying to the good work of Leopold, and concluding with strong opposition to the admission of Portugal's Congo claim in view of her bad record in colonial administration.[1] This letter was paralleled by a letter to *The Times*, dated 28 March but actually published on 3 April,[2] the day of the important Commons debate on Congo policy.

The influence of Hutton's representations on public opinion generally can scarcely be assessed. *The Times* and *Manchester Guardian* did not, for their part, support Hutton, although they admitted the strength of his case (and although the *Guardian* believed, after the Government reverse in the Commons debate of April, that it would not be possible to continue with the treaty). In the policies they urged, *The Times* on 24 February and the *Manchester Guardian* on 31 March took much the same line. In the words of *The Times* the choice was between King Log and King Stork.

If, therefore, the choice really lies between recognising the dormant claims of Portugal and acknowledging the *de facto* position established for France by M. de Brazza, it will not be very difficult for the Government to show that the choice it has made is a wise one. The only alternative would be for England to claim the sovereignty for herself. That, however, is practically out of the question.[3]

One influential paper, however, did give some support to Hutton. In leaders of 3 and 4 April the *Manchester Examiner* opposed the admission of Portugal to the Congo on the grounds that she was too poor and because 'this vicarious mode of baffling the possible aims of a foreign Power' was unlikely to achieve its purpose.[4]

If Hutton was active in the agitation, Mackinnon was not less so, though his efforts were largely in a different sphere, were directed to a different end, and had a different emphasis. Mackinnon's distinctive role was to lobby the Foreign Office and various influential persons and in that way to try to obtain modifications in the treaty in the event of it being

---

[1] *Manchester Guardian*, 30 Mar. 1883, 4, letter from J. F. Hutton.
[2] *The Times*, 3 Apr. 1883, 4, letter from J. F. Hutton. See also *Manchester Guardian*, 6 Apr. 1883, 4, letter from J. F. Hutton.
[3] *The Times*, 24 Feb. 1883, 9, leader; 4 Apr. 1883, 11, leader. *Manchester Guardian*, 31 Mar. 1883, 7, leader; 3 Apr. 1883, 5, leader; 5 Apr. 1883, leader.
[4] *Manchester Examiner*, 3 Apr. 1883, 5, leader; 4 Apr. 1883, 5, leader.

passed. At the same time, whereas Hutton championed the cause of British commerce, Mackinnon emphasized the value of Leopold's work and the importance of not harming it. In the quite different approach of Mackinnon as compared with Hutton lies, perhaps, an indication of the co-ordinating hand of Leopold. There was particular opportunity for the exercise of co-ordination—it may even have been the object of his visit —when Strauch visited London at the end of November 1882.[1] Meetings between Leopold himself on the one hand, and Mackinnon, accompanied by Kirk, on the other, took place in Brussels early in February of the New Year.[2] As Kirk's participation in the visit to Brussels suggests, he was actively assisting in the agitation at this time for he chanced to be on leave in England.

Shortly after their return from Brussels Mackinnon and Kirk got to work. Mackinnon sent to the Foreign Office (and to Hartington and probably to other Cabinet ministers) a memorandum outlining the International Association's work on the Congo and urging that the freedom of the road and stations built by the Association be specifically provided for in any treaty with Portugal.[3] This was followed later the same month by two representations made by Kirk. These were far more likely to influence the Foreign Office for, by casting the International Association in the role of forestaller of France, they appealed to its primary intention in negotiating a treaty. Leopold, wrote Kirk in his first communication, a letter to Hill, the Senior Clerk,

will have soon he hopes 1,400[4] men occupying stations of which he is the owner by purchase all along the rapids from Vivi to Stanley Pool. His agents are now pushing up the river in a steam vessel to open up other stations and gain a first footing before de Brazza can arrive....

'Let me point out', he had said earlier in his letter, 'that the Congo will undoubtedly be the highway of the immediate future into Africa —France sees this and when I was staying with the King in Brussels I

---

[1] *M.P.*, Devaux to Mackinnon, 23 Nov. 1882, Telegram. Strauch to Mackinnon, 7 Dec. 1882.

[2] *FO84/1803*, Kirk to Hill, 18 Feb. 1883. Anderson, Minute, 1 Mar. 1883, on Leopold to Queen, 22 Feb. 1883. *Strauch MSS., No. 155*, Leopold to Strauch, 1 Feb. 1883.

[3] *FO84/1803*, Mackinnon to F.O., 13 Feb. 1883 and Encl., Strauch, Memo., 5 Feb. 1883. Strauch, Memo., 5 Feb. 1883, Copy, forwarded by Hartington to F.O., 27 Feb. 1883.

[4] Written as '14,000' but 1,400 is clearly meant.

heard on very good authority that one great object of the de Brazza treaty was to keep Great Britain out if possible of their new market.'

But the 'good result' of the king's work 'H.M. regards as in danger if Portugal gains a hold on the River.'

There would be no harm in Portugal having jurisdiction on the coast but the river, and the road built by the International Association to link the Upper and Lower Congo should be specifically excluded. The king was prepared to give the fullest guarantee that the road would be open and free to all. He, Kirk, hoped that it was not too late, especially in view of the considerable opposition to the treaty, to negotiate on a better basis or, failing that, to break off negotiations.[1]

Seven days later Kirk developed this theme. The present treaty did not touch the question of the French on the Upper Congo and their proposed road thence to the coast; it would compel British merchants to pay duties to Portugal with no compensating advantage; and it provided no guarantee that Portugal would not at some future date cede to France all the sovereign rights which the treaty would allow her. For all these reasons, he repeated, although Portuguese sovereignty might, on terms, be permitted on the coast up to 5° 12', it must not extend more than sixty miles inland, thus leaving Boma, Vivi and the International Association's road free. A clause specifically declaring the king's road and surrounding district free should be added to the treaty.[2]

In March Mackinnon again put himself in touch with the Foreign Office. In a representation of the 9th he asked once more for what had already been insistently requested—clauses in the treaty excluding the International Association's road and stations from Portuguese jurisdiction.[3]

In a memorandum submitted to Granville on 19 March, which 'You were good enough to say you would be ready to receive . . . from me regarding the conditions which would probably satisfy the commercial community of this country and at the same time meet the wishes of His Majesty the King of the Belgians', he was rather more elaborate. Let the West Africa squadron police the Lower Congo; 'Let any Convention

---

[1] *FO84/1803*, Kirk to Hill, 18 Feb. 1883.
[2] *FO84/1803*, Kirk, Memo., 25 Feb. 1883.
[3] *FO84/1804*, Strauch to Mackinnon, 1 Mar. 1883, communicated to F.O., 9 Mar. 1883.

with Portugal recognize Portuguese territorial sovereignty only as far as it has been practically exercised, but excluding any right to levy tolls or Customs dues on the river navigation'; let all ports on the river remain free ports; let any convention recognize the right of 'the Belgian Association' to free passage and to all lands and powers already possessed or to be obtained. These were minimum safeguards to be included in any treaty but, Mackinnon made clear in his accompanying letter, and in so doing clearly illustrated the two lines along which the opponents of the treaty were working,

'I believe I am right in saying that it would be still more in accordance with His Majesty's wishes if things were allowed to remain on their present footing and no treaty made.' He added, 'I am sure it is also the desire of the entire mercantile community in this country that no extension of Portuguese sovereignty should be permitted.'[1]

Written representations to the Foreign Office were not all. Mackinnon and Kirk were also active in putting the *A.I.C.*'s case to influential people. Mackinnon, for instance, put the Association's position to Gladstone through Lord Kinnaird,[2] an influential churchman and public figure, being guided at this time by advice from Brussels on what points to emphasize when in conversation on the treaty question.[3] He was also entrusted with the anonymous circulation of an anonymous pamphlet (it was in fact written by Emile Banning, one of Leopold's ablest collaborators at that period) against the treaty.

Devaux's English gave a delightful 'Cloak and Dagger' air to one particular instruction. 'You should send a copy of the pamphlet by book post and mysteriously (Devaux's

---

[1] *FO84/1804*, Mackinnon to Granville, 19 Mar. 1883, Private, and Encl., Memo., 14 Mar. 1883.
[2] *Strauch MSS.*, *No. 180*, Leopold to Strauch, 7 Apr. 1883. *M.P.*, Gladstone to Kinnaird, 16 Mar. 1883, Encl. in Devaux to Mackinnon, 20 Mar. 1883. Gladstone's Private Secretary to Kinnaird, 20 Mar. 1883, Encl. in Devaux to Mackinnon, 22 Mar. 1883.
[3] *M.P.*, Devaux to Mackinnon, 20 Mar. 1883. The points to emphasize were (i) The Association could itself police the mouth of the Congo [if H.M.G. thought otherwise that might constitute an inducement to entrust the task to Portugal]; (ii) In no case should Portuguese jurisdiction be recognized above Boma; (iii) Although the Association's work was not that of a 'Governmental Enterprise' it was 'perfectly legal'; (iv) Free trade and religious liberty were ensured in its sphere of operations; (v) Treaties with native chiefs must not be exposed 'to be discussed by foreign powers'. The Association would always 'make a liberal use of the rights we have obtained'.

underlining) to Lt.-General Sir Henry Ponsonby [the Queen's Private Secretary], Windsor Castle.'[1]

Leopold did not rely solely on Mackinnon and Kirk: he also went to some pains to put his case to the Foreign Office through semi-official and private channels. Between November 1882 and March 1883 he made his views known through, inter alia Devaux, Lambert and Lord Rosebery, Sir Saville Lumley, the British minister at his court, and by personal letter to the Queen and the Prince of Wales. The burden of all these representations was the same—that any treaty with Portugal must recognize the neutrality of the International Association's stations, for if Portugal were to be admitted to the Congo, the Association's work would be ruined.[2]

Mackinnon and Hutton, and Kirk and Long in subordinate roles, had worked along different lines in arousing an agitation. But whilst thus engaged, they had also combined to produce a further and very important manifestation of opposition to the treaty—a parliamentary campaign against it.

This campaign was compounded of a series of questions and, the climax of the agitation's first phase, the putting down of a motion against a treaty with Portugal. The campaign shows signs of careful organization. There was a steady flow of questions, starting just before the 1882 Christmas recess, which, though they differed in content, kept attention focused on the central issue. Moreover, the questioners and the speakers against the Government in the debate on the motion were members of standing and influence drawn from both of the parties. On the Liberal side both Jacob Bright, a member for Manchester, and W. E. Forster, a member for Bradford, had been members of the House since the sixties. Bright, by no means a nonentity himself, could scarcely avoid sharing the prestige which surrounded his brother, John Bright, who had only resigned from the Cabinet in July 1882. His membership of the Society of Friends, moreover, would bring him much

---

[1] *M.P.*, Devaux to Mackinnon, 26 Mar. 1883. See also Devaux to Mackinnon, 25 Mar. 1883. *Strauch MSS., No. 174*, Leopold to Strauch, 16 Mar. 1883. J. Stengers, *Textiles Inédits d'Emile Banning* (Brussels, 1955), 42.

[2] *FO84/1802*, Lumley to Granville, 6 Nov. 1882, Private. Lumley to Lister, 3 Dec. 1882, Private, and Encl. *FO84/1803*, Rosebery to F.O., 12 Feb. 1883 and Encl., Lambert to Rosebery, 9 Feb. 1883. Leopold to Queen, 22 Feb. 1883. *PRO30/29/156*, Lumley to Granville, 3 Dec. 1882, Private, and Encl., Memo., n.d. Devaux to Fitzmaurice(?), 1 Feb. 1883, Extracts. Lee, op. cit., I, 630–631.

Nonconformist and humanitarian support. Forster had resigned from the Cabinet only three months earlier, and had also been a member of Gladstone's first government. Still an influential Liberal he also enjoyed a reputation as a supporter of good causes and on both counts was likely to command support for the cause he favoured. On the Conservative side E. Whitley, a member for Liverpool, was merely an ordinary back-bencher but he represented Liverpool commercial opinion and his views would, therefore, command respect on that score. The same was true of Baron Henry de Worms, member for Greenwich, for he also was in close touch with Liverpool opinion. Another Conservative who took part in the campaign, R. Bourke, member for King's Lynn, was of some political eminence having been Parliamentary Under-Secretary for Foreign Affairs in Beaconsfield's last ministry.

If the fact and content of the series of questions concerning the treaty suggests careful organization, there is also some direct evidence. Bright's question of 28 November 1882 appears to have been specifically arranged with Brussels, for when it elicited from Dilke the very general assurance that the Government was most desirous that there should be complete liberty of navigation and commerce on all the great rivers of Africa,[1] this outcome was immediately telegraphed to Brussels, whereupon Leopold gave every indication that this was a vital assurance which he had been seeking. 'The King cannot express his gratitude and admiration', Devaux wired to Mackinnon, 'for the manner in which you have brought on the splendid result you telegraphed last night'[2]—somewhat fulsome praise for a very minor achievement, perhaps, but explicable on the grounds that Leopold must have been relieved to hear a public disavowal that Britain sought some exclusive settlement on the Congo.

The question of parliamentary action must have featured in the conversations between Kirk, Mackinnon and Leopold in Brussels early in February. Brussels had a hand in the question put down by Forster at the end of February in that Mackinnon was sent a substantiation of the Association's case for Forster

[1] *Hansard*, CCLXXV, H.C., 207, 28 Nov. 1882.
[2] *M.P.*, Devaux to Mackinnon, 29 Nov. 1882. See also telegram of same date.

to make use of in his question.¹ A good deal of lobbying of members must also have taken place—the outcome of the debate of 3 April on the motion against the treaty is in itself sufficient to suggest this.²

The idea of moving a parliamentary motion against the treaty appears to have been conceived by Hutton. He told Mackinnon at the end of February that if Slagg, a member of Parliament and prominent in the Manchester Chamber of Commerce, were available, he would 'get him to move that no treaty be concluded before the House having the opportunity of expressing their opinion upon it—or a direct negative to the Treaty, that none be concluded by which the present free navigation and Commerce will be interfered with'.³ It would seem, therefore, that it was from this that the very important motion put down by Bright, a member of the Chamber, on 3 April, emanated. Apart from these insights into the conduct of the campaign it can only be assumed that, as on one known occasion in March 1884 when Mackinnon, Bright and others met to discuss what line of action should be followed in Parliament,⁴ similar informal meetings were held as occasion demanded.

The first moves in the parliamentary campaign were made by Jacob Bright. On 27 November 1882, he drew attention to the Congo question by asking the Secretary to the Admiralty for particulars of the naval force stationed on the south-west coast of Africa, and of its duties.⁵ The next day he asked the Under-Secretary of State for Foreign Affairs if the Loanda consul could not be more frequently sent to the Congo and 'whether the Government can give any assurance that territorial changes which are said to be contemplated on the Congo River will leave unimpaired the freedom of commercial intercourse which has hitherto existed between this country and that part of Africa?'⁶

¹ *M.P.*, Strauch to Mackinnon, 23 and 25 Feb. 1883. Personal and Confidential (both). *M. des A.E., C. et D. Afrique, A.I.C., 1883, Vol. 2, No. 17 bis*, Solvyns to Lambermont, 19 Feb. 1883.
² See also *M.P.*, Strauch to Mackinnon, 29 Apr. 1883, 'His Majesty . . . begs of you to be so kind, in concert with Sir John Kirk, to explain to some of the influential members of Parliament the importance and the urgency of the neutrality of our stations being recognised.'
³ *M.P.*, Hutton to Mackinnon, 27 Feb. 1883.
⁴ *M.P.*, Mackinnon to Sanford, 3 Mar. 1884, Copy. See p. 151 below.
⁵ *Hansard*, CCLXXV., H.C., 108, 27 Nov. 1882.
⁶ Ibid., H.C., 207, 28 Nov. 1882.

TO THE ANGLO-PORTUGUESE TREATY 133

Parliament went into recess soon after Bright had put his questions, but a series of questions, expressing or implying concern at the possibility of Portugal extending her dominion over the Congo, was asked during February and March. Representative was the question of de Worms. Was it true that a Portuguese naval expedition was being fitted out to annex the coast between Ambriz and Landana, and, if so, would Her Majesty's Government instruct the Commander-in-Chief of the West Africa Squadron to prevent such a move? Furthermore, would the House be given an opportunity of expressing an opinion on any treaty sanctioning the annexation by any European Power of territory on or near the Congo, before the passage of such a treaty?[1] De Worms followed this up with a second question on 19 March,[2] others being put from the Conservative side by Bourke on the 5th and 8th of March,[3] and from the Liberal benches by Forster on 26 February,[4] and by Lord Mount Temple, a Liberal peer, in the Lords on 9 March.[5] During this time only one question—a second one put by Bourke on 8 March—was directed against the French threat.[6]

The high point of the parliamentary agitation in the first period of the treaty negotiations was the motion tabled by Bright on 3 April. He moved,

That in the interests of civilisation and commerce in South West Africa, this House is of opinion that no Treaty should be made by Her Majesty's Government that would sanction the annexation by any Power of territories on or adjacent to the Congo, or that would interfere with the freedom hitherto enjoyed by all civilising and commercial agencies at work in those regions.

In speaking to the motion Bright first affirmed the importance of the Congo as a waterway and then claimed that the treaty was everywhere opposed. 'This proposed Treaty has met with extraordinary resistance. Every class of persons, every individual who has had or has relations with the Congo country is in arms against it.' In consequence 'it does not seem that we should be wise in upsetting native rule on the Congo'. He went on to

[1] *Hansard*, CCLXXVI, H.C., 1724, 8 Mar. 1883.
[2] *Hansard*, CCLXXVII, H.C., 813-14, 19 Mar. 1883.
[3] *Hansard*, CCLXXVI, H.C., 1429, 5 Mar. 1883; H.C., 1724, 8 Mar. 1883.
[4] Ibid., H.C., 830, 26 Feb. 1883.
[5] Ibid., H.L., 1889, 9 Mar. 1883.
[6] Ibid., H.C., 1725, 8 Mar. 1883.

indicate some of the reasons for this opposition. He understood that the Foreign Office looked favourably on the Mozambique tariff but he would point out that in practice some articles carried duties as high as 25–35 per cent. Admittedly a treaty removing all grievances would be some gain, but the Portuguese were prone to make trade impossible by petty and illegal exactions, which a treaty could not prevent, and to levy injurious internal taxation. Moreover, the Congo trade was now a valuable one, having risen in thirty years from almost nothing to about £2,000,000 per annum. If Clarendon in 1853 had upheld the Government's determination 'to maintain the right of unrestricted intercourse with that part of Africa' in the interests of commerce, how much more important it now was, with trade immensely increased, that the Government should adhere to this policy.

It was not only on commercial grounds, Bright continued, that Portugal should be refused admittance to the Congo. In her colonial administration she was guilty of such practices as the veiled export of slaves from Loanda to San Thomé, and other forms of oppression and misgovernment. By contrast he extolled the work of 'what is ordinarily called the Belgian Association' which, he asserted, would in company with the Baptist Missionary Society, 'dread the possible approach of Portugal to the mouth of the Congo'.

Turning to an amendment to his motion tabled by E. R. Wodehouse, Liberal member for Bath, which would have approved the admission of Portugal to the Congo, subject to adequate guarantees, Bright contrasted opinion in the country generally with what appeared to be held in Bath.

Liverpool, Glasgow, Manchester, Bristol, Bradford and the City of London have all sent earnest memorials asking that this step may not be taken.... Let me ask the noble lord the Under-Secretary of State for Foreign Affairs, when he rises, to tell the House how many Memorials and representations of an earnest character from public bodies and eminent individuals, the Foreign Office has received in opposition to this Treaty.... The facts as to public opinion laid before the House would be such as to make any Government hesitate in going against it.

The French threat constituted by de Brazza's treaties may, Bright realized, have weighed with the Foreign Office, but he did not regard that threat as serious. Indeed, he added,

'Some of those who have communicated with me since this motion was put on the Paper ... think that there has been a great exaggeration with regard to this matter, and that it may only result in a salutary extension of French Commerce. ... But even if there should be annexation which comes down to the north bank of the Upper Congo, why', he pertinently observed, 'should we invite another Power to the Lower Congo?'

Lastly, Bright suggested an alternative to an agreement with Portugal.

'There is a widespread feeling ... that this subject is of sufficient importance for the different nations of Europe to come to some friendly understanding with regard to it. We have an International Commission for the Danube. It would seem a much easier thing to have an International Commission for the Congo. There are on the Congo every year', he added, not altogether accurately, 'national vessels from Austria, Germany, Italy, France, and England, which go there presumably to give protection to their subjects. Does not that point to the possibility of an international understanding?'[1]

Whitley seconded the motion. He cited the Government's disallowance of the Portuguese claim forty years since as sufficient argument that it could not now be admitted, for this policy had prompted British merchants to extend their trade in the area. He could only regard a treaty with Portugal as a serious blow to Free Trade and British commercial interests at a time of great difficulty for each, and urged the House 'to protect the interests of the English and of England, and not by an unfortunate Treaty put a hostile tariff on the struggling manufacturers and merchants of this country'.[2] The speeches of Bright and Whitley were the climax of the first stage of the agitation. The campaign of the preceding months had made the Foreign Office aware that there was feeling against the treaty, but not until the debate of 3 April did the Government realize its strength. When it did so it began to compromise. In the ponderous words of Gladstone, in confirmation of Fitzmaurice:

If we arrive at the conclusion that it is for the interest of the country ... that we should make a Treaty, that Treaty [will] be made known to Parliament before ratification in such a way, and with the intervention of such an interval, that Parliament shall be enabled to exercise an independent judgment upon it.[3]

---

[1] *Hansard*, CCLXXVII, H.C., 1284–96, 3 Apr. 1883.
[2] Ibid., H.C., 1296–1300, 3 Apr. 1883.
[3] Ibid., H.C., 1321–7, 3 Apr. 1883.

The measure of this concession to the opposition is that it was a near surrender of the Crown's treaty-making power.[1] Nor was it the only acknowledgement by the Government of the weakness of its position, for Gladstone also stated that he was prepared to accept Wodehouse's amendment. Gladstone did not make these concessions merely because he found that opinion against a settlement with Portugal was stronger than had been anticipated, but through sheer necessity. If the promise to refer the treaty to the House had not been made and the amendment not accepted, the Government would, in Dilke's view, have been defeated on a vote.[2] The treaty, Dilke added later, 'was virtually stopped by the House of Commons',[3] whilst early in May Austin Lee of the Foreign Office doubted if the treaty would ever get beyond the draft stage,[4] a view shared by the *Manchester Guardian*.[5] *The Times* and *Manchester Examiner* agreed that even if a treaty were eventually to be signed, Bright and the opponents of the Government had nevertheless substantially achieved their object by imposing a parliamentary scrutiny upon it.[6]

If the Government was conscious of a setback, the opponents of the treaty realized their success. In Forster's view, expressed towards the end of the debate, no treaty could now be made which would not be thrown out either by the *Cortes*, because the treaty demanded too many concessions of Portugal, or by Parliament, because it would regard the safeguards for British interests as insufficient.

I believe that this discussion has put an end to any Treaty; we shall hear nothing about it; or, if we do, it will be in a form that will enable us to put an end to it.[7]

Leopold too was well pleased. He was 'delighted', wrote Devaux to Mackinnon, thanking him for telegraphing an account of the debate,

at the excellent speeches of MM Bright, Forster and Bourke and at those of Lord Fitzmaurice and of Mr. Gladstone.... The King wishes me to

---

[1] Gwynn and Tuckwell, op. cit., I, 535.
[2] Ibid., op. cit., I, 534–5. [3] Ibid., op. cit., I, 418.
[4] *M.P.*, Lee to Mackinnon, 3 May 1883, Private.
[5] *Manchester Guardian*, 5 Apr. 1883, leader.
[6] *The Times*, 4 Apr. 1883, 11, leader. *Manchester Examiner*, 4 Apr. 1883, 5, Parliamentary correspondent.
[7] *Hansard*, CCLXXVII, H.C., 1330–2, 3 Apr. 1883.

say that he cannot express his thanks to you for what you have done to bring on such a satisfactory result. You have been simply *admirable*.[1]

That a Government with a majority of seventy-two over Conservatives and Irish nationalists combined could be compelled to trim its sails by the threat of an adverse vote is not as surprising as may at first sight appear. There was, of course, no monolithic Liberal party. The division between Whigs and Radicals, expressed in the Cabinet in the opposed poles of Hartington and Chamberlain, naturally had its counterpart in the Commons, and involved such a weakening of party unity that mutiny to the point of the division lobby was not infrequent even on matters unconnected with the Whig–Radical cleavage. Moreover the 1880 Parliament had already been racked, and feeling had been heightened, by contentious issues—Bradlaugh and the parliamentary oath, Majuba and the Transvaal, Egypt and above all Ireland.[2] In the words of R. C. K. Ensor,

A fever ran in the veins of that parliament, as in those of no other through the nineteenth century. The reason was not merely the continuing economic unrest outside, nor the new phenomenon of two oppositions—an Irish as well as a conservative. It was that, besides normal and open conflict between majority and minorities, there persisted a hidden one within the majority itself, which palsied the government's counsels and zigzagged its policy.[3]

If such was the situation, a part, at least, of the reason why formidable conservative *and* liberal support could be gained for a motion largely presented as a counter to a threat to British commercial interests is clear.

Hutton and Mackinnon, the principals behind the agitation had certainly secured a triumph. As late as 20 February Leopold had despondently written that he believed the Anglo-Portuguese treaty was about to be signed and that he hardly dared hope that the position of the *A.I.C.* would be safeguarded in it.[4] In the next six weeks the agitation, in its first phase, reached its peak—and the Government substantially yielded. But one can hardly account for the success of Leopold's British

---

[1] *M.P.*, Devaux to Mackinnon, 5 Apr. 1883.
[2] John Morley, *The Life of William Ewart Gladstone* (London, 1907 Ed.), 236–326 *passim*. R. C. K. Ensor, *England 1870–1914* (Oxford, 1936), 64–80 *passim*.
[3] Ensor, op. cit., 67.
[4] *Strauch MSS., No. 163*, Leopold to Strauch, 20 Feb. 1883.

sympathizers without postulating a readiness to respond to their initiative. Such a readiness there clearly was. In a time of trade depression a policy which appeared likely to be harmful to British commerce—and also to missionary and humanitarian work—by making them subject to the traditionally accepted vices of Portuguese colonial administration, was a ready butt for attack, especially when the emphasis put on the Portuguese threat by Leopold's British sympathizers is remembered. Nor was this reaction countered, it would seem, either by any widespread sense that the French threat to British interests in West Central Africa was the more serious and that the proposed treaty with Portugal was at least an attempt to meet it, or by any general conviction that a change in policy was necessary. *The Times* could point out that the Foreign Office motive probably was to counter de Brazza, and the *Manchester Guardian* and *Manchester Examiner* could remind their readers of the danger from France,[1] but the Government's case generally was not convincingly put and could not be convincingly put for this reason: no overt reference could be made to its anti-French purpose, the principal justification of the Foreign Office's policy,[2] because for the treaty to fulfil its purpose it must in due time be accepted, *inter alia*, by France. Thus Fitzmaurice, in the most public defence the proposed treaty ever received at this stage—his speech in the debate on Bright's motion—could not even mention the spectre which, if evoked, would have brought some, at least, to the side of the exorcist.

[1] *The Times*, 24 Feb. 1883, 9, leader; 4 Apr. 1883, 11, leader. *Manchester Guardian*, 31 Mar. 1883, 7, leader; 3 Apr. 1883, 5, leader. *Manchester Examiner*, 4 Apr. 1883, 5, leader.
[2] 'But it must not be forgotten, though Ministers could not with propriety dwell upon the fact last night, that the ambition of a great Power has been already directed to the Upper Congo.' *The Times*, 4 Apr. 1883, 11, leader.

CHAPTER VII

THE ANGLO-PORTUGUESE TREATY—
STIFFENING OF TERMS, SIGNATURE AND ABANDONMENT

By early April 1883 the treaty negotiations between Britain and Portugal, initially straightforward enough, had run into shoals. First had come Anderson's reappraisal of the British position and this was soon followed by the House of Commons debate. The result was a sharp stiffening of the British terms, expressed in a new and much more elaborate draft treaty. This new draft had its genesis in a meeting of Anderson, Hertslet, Lister and Kirk[1] at the Foreign Office on 20 April. After circulation in the Office and to other departments, emendation, and approval by the Cabinet, the new draft was submitted to d'Antas in 1 June. Much more comprehensive—it numbered fifteen articles as against seven—its terms were also more clearly defined.

Nine of the fifteen articles—II, III, IV, V, VII, VIII, X, XII, and XIV—introduced new conditions.[2] The new Article II, which concerned residential and commercial rights in the Congo lands to be recognized as Portuguese, was an advance both in that it claimed equality of treatment with Portuguese subjects not only for British subjects but for 'foreigners of all nationalities' also, and because the enumeration of the specific rights they were to enjoy was an assertion of commercial freedom for non-Portuguese.[3] This assertion was further amplified in Article III by the clear statement that there was to be freedom not only of navigation but also of trade by water— on the Congo itself, on other waterways of the teritory to be acknowledged as Portuguese, and along its coastline. Concluding

---
[1] *FO 84/1805*, Lister, Memo., 21 Apr. 1883. Kirk's presence at the meeting is on the surface surprising since in his official capacity as Consul at Zanzibar the matter was no affair of his. It is probable that his advice was wanted as that of an expert in African affairs and that he also attended because he could be relied on to give a temperate statement of the safeguards required by the International Association. If there was in the Foreign Office doubt about the permanence of the International Association's work, there was not at this time hostility towards it.
[2] See pp. 107–12 above for the earlier draft and the discussions upon it.
[3] For the terms of this article see Appendix A, 'The Anglo-Portuguese Treaty', for this particular article remained unchanged.

the third article was a permissive authorization for the appointment of a commission to draw up regulations for 'the navigation, police and supervision of the rivers . . . such commission to be composed of Delegates of such of the Powers interested in the trade of the Congo and other waterways of the territory specified . . . as shall be willing to send Representatives'. Article IV stipulated that 'no duties, direct or indirect, shall be levied on goods in transit, by land or water' through the Congo territories which were to be recognized as Portuguese, whilst Article V made it a condition that 'all roads in the territory specified . . . now open, or which may hereafter be opened, shall be kept free and open to all travellers and caravans, and for the passage of goods'. Under the terms of the seventh article Portugal engaged 'to respect and confirm all the rights of the native chiefs and of the inhabitants of the said territories', held by virtue of treaties concluded by Great Britain with those chiefs, as far as was compatible with Portuguese sovereignty. Portugal also undertook by the terms of this article 'to protect and maintain the said chiefs and inhabitants in the free possession . . . [of their] . . . lands and other property'. Article VIII demanded further fiscal concessions by its insistence on the application of the Mozambique tariff of 1877 to all Portugal's African colonies for a term of ten years, at the expiry of which the tariff could be revised, but only with the consent of the two contracting parties, and stipulated that, in the Congo districts, British goods should be in every respect on the same footing as Portuguese goods, whilst British vessels should not be liable to any higher duties, nor subject to any other restrictions than those imposed on Portuguese vessels. Article VIII also included the stipulation that 'no Bill of Health or other quarantine formality shall be required in any Portuguese port from British ships bound direct for British ports'. (The withholding of quarantine clearance was a powerful lever for obtaining bribes and was sometimes resorted to by ill-paid Portuguese colonial officials.) Article X was of little moment, merely providing for assistance to be given to vessels in difficulty, or wrecked, and for their exemption from dues and imposts, but Article XII might well have had an eventual importance, for the provisions of the treaty affecting the Congo districts were to be applied 'to all territories adjoining the same ... that may hereafter be brought under the sovereignty of ... Portugal'. Article XIV, which concerned Whydah, contained a new condition of a quite different kind. Whereas in December the outright cession of the fort at Whydah had been demanded, it was now stipulated merely that Britain should have the right of first refusal of it.

Not less important was the more precise drafting. The new Article I stated that the inland frontier of Portugal's proposed Congo acquisition 'shall coincide with the boundaries of the present possessions of the coast tribes', whilst Article III, which has already been seen to have broken new ground by its assertion of freedom of trade by water and its provision for a River Commission, also defined freedom of navigation more precisely (this being coupled, in the draft, with a definition of freedom of trade by water). In the question of missionary operations, Article IV of the original draft had merely guaranteed non-discriminatory treatment for British subjects as regards, *inter alia*, 'religious worship'. Article VI of the new draft was far more explicit. It stipulated that in the Congo territories there should be 'complete protection' for missionaries of any Christian denomination. 'They shall not be hindered or molested in their endeavours to teach the doctrines of Christianity', nor should their converts suffer molestation or other burden in consequence of accepting (Protestant) Christianity. Furthermore missionaries would be perfectly free to build churches, chapels and schools, and in the matter of taxation and other local charges there was to be no discrimination against any denomination.

Article III of the original draft had provided for most favoured third nation treatment for British subjects in all Portugal's African possessions, but this was more clearly defined in the new Article IX. Lastly, Article XIII, developing a part of the second article of the original draft, declared that 'the provisions of Article III (of the new draft) as to the freedom of trade and navigation on the Congo, and the regulations for securing the same, and the provisions of Article IV as to exemption from transit dues, shall apply in all respects to the River Zambesi'. The same article also contained an agreement that the 'jurisdiction of Portugal shall not extend to the River Shiré' (which connected Lake Nyasa, around which Scottish planters and missionaries were consolidating their hold, with the Zambesi).[1]

The effect, then, of Anderson's reappraisal and of the agitation against the treaty, and especially the debate in which it culminated, was a considerable stiffening of the British terms. There is no indication of the precise implications of Anderson's restatement of the British position, for the Congo debate supervened before that restatement could be put in draft treaty form, but it has been seen that, in general terms, he was responsible for the reversion to the original British position on inland boundaries, for a more stringent definition of freedom of navigation on the Congo, for the unequivocal claim to freedom of trade on that river, for the insistence that there be no transit dues, that the arrangements for commercial freedom be durable and that there be no discrimination between missionaries of different creeds. To the agitation may be ascribed, directly or indirectly, the proposal for a River Commission, the insistence that the Mozambique tariff be generally applied and that roads in the Congo territory be kept free and open, and the demands that the rights conferred on native chiefs by previous treaties be respected and that British ships be exempted from quarantine formalities. Serpa saw, or professed to see, the radical change in the British position in the draft of 29 May rather than in the dispatch of 15 March,[2] but speculation on the relative importance of the two factors is without point. The essential truth is that whilst Anderson was responsible for an important stiffening in the British position, the agitation against the treaty, especially in its climax of 4 April, made it absolutely indispensable that the Foreign Office should press for a quite exceptionally liberal treaty.

In the second period of the negotiations, lasting from the spring of 1883 to the signature of the treaty in February 1884, there were no sudden developments, no touch of drama as had earlier been given by the near defeat of the Government in Parliament. Opposition to the treaty was vigorously expressed only towards the end of the period but the strength of this hostile feeling was nevertheless the key factor throughout the

---

[1] *PRO30/29/267*, Draft Treaty, 29 May 1883, Encl. in F.O. to d'Antas, 1 June 1883 (Confidential Print).
[2] *FO84/1806*, Serpa to d'Antas, 26 June 1883, forwarded to F.O., 7 July 1883 with translation.

ten months, for during the negotiations on the new basis the Government knew in an unusually imminent sense that its actions were accountable to Parliament. Anderson, for instance, in minuting Serpa's reply to the new British proposals, in which Portugal had made appreciable concessions, commented, 'I think a Treaty even with the proposed amendments, would be rather an exceptionally liberal one, but it would not be good enough for us.' Lister's minute on the same dispatch likewise made clear his awareness of public opinion. He both stressed the importance of adhering to the clause ensuring the freedom of the coasting trade because British houses were engaged in it, and testified to his own belief that the River Commission—Serpa had opposed it—'would render the Treaty more acceptable to the British Parliament and people'. Fitzmaurice strongly endorsed Lister's second point. 'We cannot give up the Commission. It is the Commission which will carry the treaty here', a view which he repeated at least twice before the year was out. He also cited 'the opposition of the commercial world' as the ground for his view that it would be dangerous to accept certain of the commercial conditions desired by Portugal.[1] There was particular awareness, too, of the International Association's concern lest Portuguese jurisdiction stretch an illimitable distance up the Congo. In a minute of 30 July Anderson refers to 'what we are trying to get for the King of the Belgians Co.—a limit that will keep them outside Portuguese territory'.[2]

This constant awareness of the strength of the views held by the treaty's opponents kept the Foreign Office to a circumscribed course of action, for it knew that the treaty only stood a chance of ratification if it more than adequately met the objections which had been made to it. The Foreign Office was therefore reluctant to make concessions in the negotiations on the draft of 29 May, and the treaty would certainly have foundered had Portugal not been anxious to secure it[3] and correspondingly ready to make more than her share of concessions. On 26 June she accepted Article II (concerning

[1] *FO84/1806*, Anderson, 13 July 1883, Lister, 15 July 1883, Fitzmaurice, 18 July 1883, Minutes on Serpa to d'Antas, 26 June 1883, forwarded to F.O., 7 July 1883. *FO84/1807*, Fitzmaurice, Minute, 9 Oct. 1883. *FO84/1808*, Granville, Memo., 5 Dec. 1883.
[2] *FO84/1807*, Anderson, Minute, 30 July 1883.
[3] *FO84/1807*, Lister, Memo., 1 Aug. 1883.

domiciliary, commercial and other rights of foreigners in the Congo districts), Article V (guaranteeing freedom of roads in the Congo districts), Article VII (preserving the treaty rights of native tribes on the Congo), Article IX (guaranteeing most favoured nation treatment for British subjects in all Portugal's African colonies), Article X (promising assistance to wrecks), and Article XII (providing that conditions agreed for the Congo districts be applied to any adjoining territories subsequently annexed). In addition she accepted Article III (in respect of freedom of navigation only), Article VIII, to the extent of binding herself to the Mozambique tariff for the Congo alone, Article XI (facilities for British warships operating against the slave trade) in relation to the Mozambique coast only and for no more than three years, and went beyond the British demand expressed in Article XIV by offering the outright cession of the Whydah fort.[1]

Despite these concessions there were still, at the beginning of July, considerable differences to be bridged. The inland boundary on the Congo, freedom of trade by water, creation of a River Commission, the levy of transit duties by land and water in the Congo territories, the Portuguese boundary on the Shiré, the general application of the Mozambique tariff, the rights of British warships in Portuguese waters, exemption from quarantine requirements—all were in dispute, whilst the liberties and privileges of missionaries still remained to be defined in detail. At this stage Portugal sought to strengthen her hand by negotiating an overall West African boundary agreement with France which would include, as an initial assumption in the negotiations, explicit French recognition of Portugal's Congo claim. Such recognition France refused.[2] Portugal therefore turned back to Britain, where the fact of the Portuguese approach to France was not definitely known until early in the following year, and on 11 September made three more concessions, agreeing to the freedom of the riverain and coasting trade, accepting the British article defining the privileges of missionaries, and yielding over quarantine formalities.[3]

[1] *FO84/1806*, Serpa to d'Antas, 26 June 1883, forwarded to F.O., 7 July 1883 with translation.
[2] *D.D.F.*, 1st Series, Vol. V, pp. 86–87, No. 79, Serpa to Laboulaye, 13 Aug. 1883, Encl. in Laboulaye to Challemel-Lacour, 16 Aug. 1883, and f.n. 1, p. 87. Thomson, op. cit., 132–3.
[3] *FO84/1807*, d'Antas to F.O., 11 Sept. 1883.

THE ANGLO-PORTUGUESE TREATY

By mid-September Portugal had yielded on some ten points and it could scarcely be expected that Britain should make no concessions at all, if, after twelve months of negotiation, she still wanted agreement. Fitzmaurice, who was convinced of the necessity of a stiff treaty, was away from the Office at this time, and advantage was apparently taken of his absence to make a concession whereby Britain agreed to restrict her demand for freedom from transit dues to goods carried on the Congo and its affluents.[1] Portugal accepted this compromise in the following month.[2] After further consideration Britain made five more concessions in January. The Portuguese boundary on the Congo was conditionally extended from Punta da Lenha to Nokki, but not to Vivi as Portugal desired (in practice this extension was of little significance for the basic intention of keeping a port—Vivi—on the navigable portion of the Lower Congo outside Portuguese control was still fulfilled);[3] Portuguese dominion was allowed to extend sixty miles up the Shiré, provided Portugal accepted the Nokki limit; an urgent Portuguese request that an Anglo-Portuguese be substituted for an International Commission was reluctantly complied with, but at the same time made binding and not merely permissive; the limitation of the Mozambique tariff to the Congo districts was accepted (though still on condition that it should not be raised for ten years, and thereafter only with the consent of both parties), whilst a simple undertaking that duties should not be raised for ten years was all that was required in regard to Portugal's other African colonies; it was agreed that the right of British warships to operate in Portuguese waters be restricted to eastern Africa and that Portuguese warships be allowed a reciprocal right on the coast of British South Africa.[4] With Portuguese acceptance of this latest dispatch,[5] negotiations were virtually complete.

In the months that followed the Congo debate of 4 April no further general campaign against whatever form of treaty the

[1] *FO84/1807*, F.O. to d'Antas, 17 Sept. 1883. *M.P.*, Lee to Mackinnon, 2 Nov. 1883, Private.
[2] *FO84/1807*, d'Antas to F.O., 17 Oct. 1883.
[3] Leopold and his supporters differed from the Foreign Office over Vivi, however, constantly affirming that it was not accessible to ocean-going steamers.
[4] *FO84/1809*, F.O. to d'Antas, 7 Jan. 1884.
[5] *FO84/1809*, Du Bocage to d'Antas, 26 Jan. 1884, communicated to F.O. in English, 31 Jan. 1884.

Foreign Office might still be negotiating was launched. With its intentions not clearly known, none was possible, but Leopold's British supporters were active in putting the case of the International Association in influential circles. Mackinnon and Kirk concentrated on urging three points. Five days after the debate, Mackinnon submitted a memorandum to Granville in which, on his own initiative,[1] he took up the proposal for a River Commission and grafted on to it the suggestion that 'the King of the Belgians might be the first President'. Coupled with this was a renewed plea that the neutrality of the International Association's stations be recognized—this time by a 'common understanding . . . among all the powers'.[2] Such a recognition, with European attention drawn daily more and more to the Congo and interior of Central Africa, Leopold was increasingly anxious to obtain. In the early part of April, Kirk was asked to press this point[3] whilst at the end of the month Strauch asked Mackinnon to do the same.

His Majesty further begs of you to be so kind, in concert with Sir John Kirk to explain to some of the influential members of Parliament the importance and the urgency of the neutrality of our stations being acknowledged.[4]

It was to substantiate the plea for recognition of the International Association's stations that the third point was pressed. First put forward in Kirk's February memoranda,[5] the value of the Association as the forestaller of other powers and preserver of liberty of commerce was now, at Leopold's request, stressed. The argument was elaborated in the detailed instructions given by Leopold to Strauch for the letter to Kirk of early April. For the subjects of every state which recognized the independence and neutrality of the Association's stations there would be no legal or customs barriers; the Association was in possesion of the north and south banks of the Congo from Vivi to the western end of Stanley Pool and of the south shore of Stanley

[1] See *M.P.*, Devaux to Mackinnon of 16 and 20 Apr. 'The King wants me to say that he would see with great satisfaction the creation of an international commission for the Congo in which our Station should have a delegate.' (Letter of 20 Apr.)
[2] *FO 84/1805*, Mackinnon, Memo., 9 Apr. 1883, Private and Confidential.
[3] *Strauch MSS., No. 180*, Leopold to Strauch, 8 Apr. 1883.
[4] *M.P.*, Strauch to Mackinnon, 29 Apr. 1883. The importance which Leopold attached to this point was also made known to Granville in a private letter from Lumley, the British minister in Brussels, on 4 May (*PRO 30/29/156*).
[5] See pp. 127–8 above.

THE ANGLO-PORTUGUESE TREATY 147

Pool itself, whilst important stations had been founded along the river up to Stanley Falls; recognition of the neutrality of the stations would therefore assure the neutrality of the river itself; the Association had considerable resources, sufficient, if required, to found stations between Vivi and the mouth of the Congo and along the adjoining coast.[1] Mackinnon, for his part, made use of a variant of this argument. In June he forwarded to the Foreign Office a copy of a letter sent him by Leopold which cited the rumoured threat of an agreement between France and Portugal to divide between them the territory at the Congo mouth as, *inter alia*, an inducement to England to recognize the neutrality of the International Association's stations.[2] Mackinnon was certainly most active at this time. Leading Liberal members of Parliament, important Conservative members, Foreign Office officials including, notably, Anderson himself—all had the Association's case put to them, whilst Mackinnon also arranged a formal deputation to the Foreign Office. In Strauch's words, he was *'toujours admirable de dévouement et d'activité'*.[3] There is no reason to suppose that Kirk was not also busy.

During the summer Kirk returned to his post at Zanzibar whilst Mackinnon, perhaps reasoning that nothing further could be done until a decisive stage in the treaty negotiations was reached, was silent until the close of the year. The opponents of the treaty were nevertheless alert. In July questions about the progress of the negotiations were asked in the Commons[4] and in October the anonymous reviewer in *The Times* of *De Rebus Africanis*, a pamphlet containing the opinions on West Central African affairs of its author, Lord Mayo, who had recently returned from a hunting expedition there, took the opportunity to express strong opposition to a treaty with Portugal and to push the idea of an International River Commission for the Congo with Leopold as its president.[5]

In November attention was focused on the Congo question by the Portuguese occupation of Landana on the extreme

[1] *Strauch MSS., No. 180*, Leopold to Strauch, 7 Apr. 1883.
[2] *FO84/1806*, Leopold to Mackinnon, 4 June 1883, Copy.
[3] *Strauch MSS., No. 194*, Strauch to Leopold, 17 June 1883. *M.P.*, Devaux to Mackinnon, 8 May, 1883.
[4] *Hansard*, CCLXXXI, H.C., 791, 9 July 1883; H.C., 1888, 19 July 1883. *Hansard*, CCLXXXII, H.C., 301-2, 24 July 1883.
[5] *The Times*, 25 Oct. 1883, 3, review.

northern border of the disputed territory. This produced a flurry of protest from Liverpool and Manchester,[1] only quieted when Portugal undertook not to alter the fiscal conditions governing the trade there before the conclusion of treaty negotiations, without reference to the powers interested in that trade.[2]

With the turn of the year the relative quietness of Leopold's British sympathizers came to an end. On 28 December, at Devaux's request,[3] Mackinnon reiterated to the Foreign Office the importance of the neutralization in any treaty of the International Association's stations and surrounding territories, and repeated the assurance that they would be open to the commerce of all countries. He also promised that the subjects of those states which so requested, and, by implication, recognized the Association, would be exempted from the payment of customs duties.[4] In the new year, with negotiations on the treaty draft approaching a climax, Leopold concentrated his attention on the aspect of the settlement with most immediate bearing on the position of the International Association—the question of the interior limit of Portuguese authority on the Congo itself. To this end he emphasized to Mackinnon and to Goldsmid, now in his service and at that time in England, the importance of Boma and Nokki, where the Association had stations and which were embryonic deep-water ports, being kept out of Portugal's grasp.[5] Mackinnon's response was probably to make private and verbal approaches to the Foreign Office;[6] Goldsmid, for his part certainly had an interview with Granville in mid-January.[7] In February the attention of Hutton also was drawn to this same point.[8]

---

[1] See, for example, *FO84/1808*, Bright to Fitzmaurice, 13 Nov. 1883; British & African Steam Navigation Co. to F.O., 10, 16, 21, and 29 Nov. 1883.
[2] *FO84/1808*, Wyke (Lisbon) to F.O., 18 Dec. 1883, Telegram.
[3] *M.P.*, Devaux to Mackinnon, 11 Dec. 1883.
[4] *FO84/1808*, Mackinnon to Lister, 28 Dec. 1883, Private.
[5] *Strauch MSS.*, No. 244, Leopold to Strauch, 2 Feb. 1884. See also *M.P.*, Devaux to Mackinnon, 1 Feb. 1884.
[6] Mackinnon did not submit any written communication on this point to the Foreign Office. But there is his own testimony of 3 Mar. that 'the Congo has had a considerable share of my attention' (*M.P.*, Mackinnon to Sanford, 3 Mar. 1884, Copy), and H. Waller's 'I have been trying to lend a hand to thwarting the Portuguese on the Congo . . . Mr Mackinnon is tremendously active about it all and I think has got a spoke in their wheel.' (*A/S Papers*, H. Waller to C. H. Allen, 15 Feb. 1884.)
[7] *FO84/1809*, Goldsmid to Currie, 4 Jan. 1884 and Minutes thereon by Currie and Granville, n.d.
[8] *Strauch MSS.*, No. 244, Leopold to Strauch, 2 Feb. 1884.

THE ANGLO-PORTUGUESE TREATY 149

A little later, however, Leopold was obliged to modify his tactics, for on receiving, on 9 February, a copy of the draft treaty, sent to him privately by the Foreign Office,[1] he discovered both that the Portuguese boundary was as high up as Nokki and, what he deemed of great importance in view of this, that there was no provision for freedom from transit dues on land. He therefore decided to press for such freedom from transit dues and, in that way, to minimize the consequences of such an extension of Portuguese jurisdiction, but at the same time to continue to urge that the Portuguese frontier be kept below Boma. On 10 February Devaux wrote to Mackinnon urgently requesting him to take parliamentary action to secure the limitation of the Portuguese frontier to Boma, and freedom of transit by land, and later the same day wrote again to tell him that he had 'just received a cyphered telegram from Lisbon which shows that if the British Government makes a vigorous effort to obtain freedom of transit by land they will get it'. Mackinnon did not take parliamentary action but forwarded the second letter to an official, Austin Lee, Fitzmaurice's private secretary, who was able to reply that 'Between ourselves it *has* had some effect and I hope we shall obtain some addition to the Treaty in the sense you suggested.'[2] At the same time Leopold made a series of other representations. The Foreign Office was bombarded with notes putting the International Association's case—through Goldsmid on 9 February, through Malet, British minister in Brussels, on 10 and 21 February, through Baron Solvyns, the Belgian minister in London on the 15th ('*Encore Congo—Toujours Congo—Trop de Congo*', wrote Solvyns in his covering note!), and from Leopold himself on the 14th, 21st and 27th.[3]

The representations of Leopold and Mackinnon certainly had an effect. Full freedom from dues for goods in transit by land was not obtained, and Granville pointed out that the

[1] *PRO30/29/156*, Malet to Granville, 10 Feb. 1884, Private.
[2] *M.P.*, Devaux to Mackinnon, 10 Feb. 1884. Austin Lee to Mackinnon, 14 Feb. 1884 and Encl., Devaux to Mackinnon, 10 Feb. 1884 (a second letter of 10 Feb. from Devaux). See also *M.P.*, Strauch to Mackinnon, 10 Feb. 1884.
[3] *FO84/1809*, Encl. in Goldsmid to F.O., 9 Feb. 1884. *PRO30/29/156*, Malet to Granville, 10 and 21 Feb. 1884; Solvyns to Granville, 15 Feb. 1884; Leopold to Granville, 14, 21, and 27 Feb. 1884. At the same time Leopold looked to his second line of defence. Through Devaux he made detailed suggestions as to how amendments to the treaty might be obtained by Parliamentary action after the treaty had been signed (*M.P.*, Devaux to Mackinnon, 13 Feb. 1884).

Portuguese could hardly be expected to grant such freedom since no roads existed.[1] But a clause was inserted in Article V of the final draft (Article IV of the May 1883 draft), whereby goods in transit by land through Portuguese territory should pay only the import duties payable under the agreed tariff, i.e. no transit duties in addition. Moreover, by a further new clause, 'goods transhipped in course of transit, or landed in bond for further conveyance by water' secured complete exemption from all duties, save only for a charge to cover the expense of Portuguese supervision of transhipment. Granville hastened to inform Leopold of this concession on the 20th[2] (only to receive an immediate reiteration of the plea for entire freedom of land transit),[3] whilst five days later he wrote that he had insisted, in response to a last minute request from Brussels, on an exchange of notes stipulating that the International Association's station at Nokki should be outside the Portuguese frontier. 'It has been my earnest desire', Granville continued, 'to safeguard in every way the interests of the great institution which has been created by your Majesty.' To this he very reasonably added, 'It is a little discouraging to find how active some of your Majesty's friends in this country are in exciting opposition to the treaty.'[4]

The treaty was eventually signed on 26 February. Its opponents now had to consider their future course of action. On the very eve of news of the treaty's signature reaching Brussels, Devaux had reaffirmed that Leopold still favoured attempts to obtain modifications in the treaty rather than its rejection,[5] and Leopold held to this policy after news of the treaty's signature had arrived.

'H.M. thinks', wrote Devaux to Mackinnon on the 29th, 'that a desperate effort must be made to save the free port [i.e. the deep-water port of Boma which, by the terms of the treaty, was to be Portuguese]. He says that if we haven't got it we have nothing at all.'[6]

There is, nevertheless, no hint of a change of tactics, and

[1] *PRO30/29/198*, Granville to Leopold, 25 Feb. 1884, Draft.
[2] Appendix A, Terms of Treaty. *PRO30/29/198*, Granville to Leopold, 20 Feb. 1884, Draft.
[3] *PRO30/29/156*, Leopold to Granville, 21 Feb. 1884.
[4] *PRO30/29/198*, Granville to Leopold, 25 Feb. 1884, Draft. See also *FO84/1809*, Fitzmaurice, Minute, 23 Feb. 1884; Petre to F.O., 24 and 25 Feb. 1884, Telegrams.
[5] *M.P.*, Devaux to Mackinnon, 24 and 27 Feb. 1884.
[6] *M.P.*, Devaux to Mackinnon, 29 Feb. 1884.

THE ANGLO-PORTUGUESE TREATY

Mackinnon certainly understood Leopold still to be resolved on modifications rather than rejection.[1] This attitude Mackinnon doubtless made known at a meeting of the British opponents of the treaty held on 4 March in Jacob Bright's rooms, which meeting, Mackinnon had told Sanford on the previous day, he meant to attend.[2] At that meeting three alternatives were apparently considered. Mackinnon outlined them in his letter to Sanford.

1. Reject the treaty and maintain the *status quo*.
2. Modify treaty by permitting Portugal to occupy up to South Bank; Great Britain to occupy North Bank, and make it free to all nations or make it over on these conditions to the Brussels *Comité*.

or

3. Modify treaty by limiting Portuguese jurisdiction to a point west of Boma, and inland *northwards* to a straight line from such point. Restrict tariff to a uniform rate of 5 per cent. or at most of 10 per cent. Boma is accessible to Ocean going steamers, whereas Nokki is not.

It was the third of the alternatives that Brussels favoured.[3]

There is no record of the discussions in the meeting, or of what decisions were reached. It can be inferred, however, that it was decided to arrange for a series of parliamentary questions expressing or implying criticism of the treaty, at least as it stood, to be put down. Would the House be granted an opportunity to express its opinion on the treaty before ratification?—this anxiety about the fulfilment of Gladstone's promise was voiced more than once. Would not an international agreement amongst the Powers concerned be better than the proposed treaty? What portion of the territory to be recognized as Portuguese was at present under Portuguese occupation? Were there any stations of the International Association within this territory? Would the Congo chiefs with whom Great Britain had treaties be consulted before the treaty was signed? Had the Government received reports that excitement was growing amongst the Congo natives as a result of the news that they were to be handed over to Portugal? In view of the paralysis of trade caused by the prospect of a Congo treaty, when

---

[1] *M.P.*, Mackinnon to Sanford, 3 Mar. 1884, Copy. See also *PRO30/29/156*, Leopold to Granville, 6 Mar. 1884.
[2] *M.P.*, Mackinnon to Sanford, 3 Mar. 1884, Copy.
[3] Ibid.

could information be given that would end this state of tension? These are typical of the seventeen questions asked on the subject between March and June 1884. Bright was responsible for five,[1] Forster for two,[2] Bourke for two,[3] Sir Herbert Maxwell, Conservative Member for Co. Wigtown, for six,[4] and W. H. Houldsworth, Conservative Member for Manchester, for two,[5] whilst the Earl of Belmore, a Conservative peer, went to the lengths of proposing a resolution directed against ratification (subsequently withdrawn after objection on a point of order).[6]

If in Parliament the opponents of the treaty did not unequivocally press for its total rejection, outright rejection was certainly Hutton's attitude. 'We must get rid of this treaty firstly', he wrote to Mackinnon, 'and then come to a conclusion what steps to take.'[7] In the matter of the treaty, Hutton's influence in the Manchester Chamber of Commerce, of which he was now president, was supreme and within ten days of the treaty's signature the Chamber sent a letter to the Foreign Office unambiguously opposing ratification. 'Mr. Hutton', Anderson rightly commented, 'is beginning an active campaign.'[8] A fortnight later, on 17 March, a special General Meeting was arranged in order to emphasize the Chamber's opposition to ratification, and to encourage a similar attitude in other Chambers. The ground was prepared by letters in the Press and by the distribution of pamphlets. Sir Joseph Lee, the Government's principal supporter in Manchester, tried to stem the tide, and at the meeting itself introduced a nullifying amendment which received support from other speakers, but in a vote his amendment was decisively defeated, gaining only five votes. The way was thus clear for the passage of a motion

[1] *Hansard*, CCLXXXVI, H.C., 158, 18 Mar. 1883; H.C., 301, 20 Mar. 1884. *Hansard*, CCLXXXVII, H.C., 36, 8 Apr. 1884; H.C., 1700, 8 May, 1884. *Hansard*, CCLXXXVIII, H.C., 665–6, 19 May, 1884.
[2] *Hansard*, CCLXXXVI, H.C., 594, 24 Mar. 1884; H.C., 1804, 7 Apr. 1884.
[3] Ibid., H.C., 606, 24 Mar. 1884; H.C., 870, 27 Mar. 1884.
[4] Ibid., H.C., 1163, 1171, 31 Mar. 1884; H.C., 1507–8, 3 Apr. 1884. *Hansard*, CCLXXXVIII, H.C., 434, 15 May, 1884; H.C., 1310, 26 May 1884. *Hansard*, CCLXXXIX, H.C., 1395, 26 June 1884.
[5] *Hansard*, CCLXXXVII H.C., 1032, 1 May, 1884. *Hansard*, CCLXXXVIII, H.C., 438–9, 15 May, 1884.
[6] *Hansard*, CCLXXXVII, H.L., 1827–36, 9 May 1884.
[7] *M.P.*, Hutton to Mackinnon, 18 Mar. 1884.
[8] *FO84/1809*, Manch. Ch. Comm. to F.O., 6 Mar. 1884, and Anderson Minute thereon, n.d.

proposing that Parliament be petitioned not to ratify the treaty.[1]

The special General Meeting of the Chamber was followed not only by further Manchester representations against the treaty,[2] but also by an intensification of a general lobbying against ratification[3] which Hutton had begun at the same time as he made his first submission against ratification to the Foreign Office early in March. This had taken the form of a circular letter to all Chambers of Commerce and to members of Parliament and others, signed by Hutton as president, and setting out the case against the treaty. The notable new feature of the document was an *exposé* of the alleged harshness of the Mozambique tariff, to which the British Congo trade was now to be subject.

'I must respectfully request', ran the peroration, 'that you will without delay take such steps as will prevent the ratification of the treaty which Her Majesty's Government has concluded with Portugal, and which is so unjust to the natives of Africa, and so suicidal and so destructive to our commerce and to our industry.'[4]

As in the previous spring, the initiative of Hutton and Manchester met with a vigorous response, memorials and letters hostile to the treaty being sent to the Foreign Office by the Birmingham Fair Trade Union and the Morley Chamber of Commerce on 22 March, by a group of Liverpool merchants on 4 April, and by the Chambers of Commerce of Glasgow, on the 15th, Swansea on the 22nd, Wolverhampton on the 29th, and London on 12 May.[5] There were deputations also— from the London Chamber of Commerce on 7 April, introduced

---

[1] *Manch. Ch. Comm.*, Report for 1884, 6–7, and supplementary report of Special General Meeting, 1–31. *FO84/1809*, Lee to Fitzmaurice, 9 Mar. 1884. *Manchester Guardian*, 11 Mar. 1884, 4 and 8. *Manchester Guardian*, 12 Mar. 1884, 4, letter from Hutton. *The Times*, 30 Apr. 1884, 4, letter from Sir Joseph Lee.

[2] *FO84/1810*, Manch. Ch. Comm. to F.O., 26 Mar. 1884. *FO84/1811*, Manch. Ch. Comm. to F.O., 30 May 1884. *Manch. Ch. Comm.*, Report for 1884, 7, 98–100.

[3] *The Times*, 30 Apr. 1884, 4, letter from Sir Joseph Lee.

[4] *M. des A.E., C. et D. Afrique, A.I.C., 1884, Vol. 3, Jan.–May, No. 35*, Solvyns to Ministry of Foreign Affairs, 7 Mar. 1884 and Encl., Manch. Ch. Comm., Circular letter, 5 Mar. 1884. *The Times*, 11 Mar. 1884, 4.

[5] *FO84/1810*, Birmingham Fair Trade Union to F.O., 22 Mar. 1884. Morley Chamber of Commerce to F.O., 22 Mar. 1884. Group of Liverpool merchants to F.O. per S. Smith, M.P., 4 Apr. 1884. Glasgow Ch. Comm. to F.O., 15 Apr. 1884. Swansea Ch. Comm. to F.O., 23 Apr. 1884. Wolverhampton Ch. Comm. to F.O., 29 Apr. 1884. *FO84/1811*, London Ch. Comm. to F.O., 12 May 1884.

and probably inspired by Tritton,[1] from Liverpool at the end of the month,[2] and from Glasgow on 10 May.[3]

As in the previous year, the agitation was supported by religious and humanitarian bodies—and particularly by the Baptists. In April Congregations of Protestant Dissenters, who appear to have been Baptists under another name, at Clapton, Glasgow and Anstruther, submitted generally similar memorials, the final petition being worded identically with the Manchester Chamber of Commerce memorial of 13 November 1882, but with the addition of the now familiar plea that the neutralization and permanent freedom of the Congo be ensured by an International Commission.[4] Rejection was also formally urged by the Baptists of Middlesbrough and the Baptist Union,[5] whilst the Ladies' Negroes Friend Society and the Anti-Slavery Society also came out against ratification.[6]

Petitions to Parliament against ratification of the treaty were even more numerous. Those submitted to the Commons were from Dewsbury on 24 March, Liverpool on 27 March, 24 and 30 April and 6 June, the Liverpool African Association on 2 April, Birmingham on the 21st, Manchester on the 22nd, Halifax on the 23rd, Clapton and Hallamshire (near Sheffield) on the 24th, Sheffield on the 25th, Mountain Ash on the 28th, Glasgow on the 29th, Barnsley on the 30th, London on 1 May, Farsley on the 2nd, Rhos and Elgin on the 6th, Dundee and Hull on the 7th, Nantwich on the 8th, Bristol on the 12th, Redhill, Huddersfield and the Baptist Missionary Society on the 13th, Handsworth on the 16th, and Cardiff on 26 May.[7] Of these there is clear evidence that the petitions of Halifax, Hull, Bristol, Birmingham and Sheffield, and at least one of those from Liverpool, were in fact from their Chambers of

---

[1] *FO84/1810*, Fitzmaurice to Tritton, 24 Apr. 1884.
[2] *The Times*, 26 Apr. 1884, 11.
[3] *FO84/1811*, Statement of points made by Glasgow deputation, 10 May 1884.
[4] *FO84/1810*, Protestant Dissenters, Clapton, to F.O., 10 Apr. 1884. Prot. Dissenters, Anstruther, to F.O., 23 Apr. 1884. *FO84/1811*, Prot. Dissenters, Adelaide Place, Glasgow, Petition, 23 Apr. 1884, Encl. in Home Office to F.O., 3 May 1884. Slade, *English-speaking Missions*, 70–71.
[5] *FO84/1810*, Baptist Union to F.O., 28 Apr. 1884. *FO84/1811*, Middlesborough Baptists to F.O., 6 May 1884. Slade, *English-speaking Missions*, 71.
[6] *FO84/1810*, Anti-Slavery Society to F.O., 12 Apr. 1884. *FO84/1811*, Resolution of Ladies' Negroes Friend Society, 2 May 1884, Encl. in Rev. H. Bowlby to F.O., 16 May 1884.
[7] For petitions to the Commons see under name and date in *PP 1884, Votes and Proceedings of the House of Commons*, I and II.

Commerce,[1] whilst it seems likely that all or most of the other unspecified representations came from, or were inspired by Baptist congregations or alternatively, in the case of sizeable towns, their Chambers of Commerce. Petitions to the Lords were fewer and, apart from an unidentified representation on 27 March, came from the Birmingham Chamber of Commerce on 22 April, the Hallamshire Company of Cutlers and the Liverpool African Association on the 24th, and the Sheffield Chamber of Commerce on the 25th.[2]

Nor did the opponents of the treaty neglect the Press. The pen of Holman Bentley, the Congo missionary, who happened to be in England on furlough at the time, was active in the *Daily News* on 12 April, *The Times* on the 14th and the *Pall Mall Gazette* on 20 May,[3] W. T. Stead's acceptance of this last contribution being due to Forster's influence.[4] During this same period Goldsmid made an attack on the treaty in the *National Review*, coupling with it a plea that the International Association should be accorded 'the status of a distinct colonial power',[5] whilst Robert Capper, Lloyds agent on the Congo, who had probably been connected with the now bankrupt firm of John Capper & Co. (and who also took an anti-Portuguese line in an address to the Society of Arts), Forster and Bright, all, directly or by implication, opposed ratification in *The Times*.[6] *The Times* itself continued its support of the treaty[7] whilst the *Manchester Guardian*, which in April 1883 had reluctantly supposed the treaty to be done for, now reaffirmed support.[8] The *Manchester Examiner* persevered in its opposition[9] but was the exception, for the Press as a whole supported the Government.[10]

[1] *FO84/1811*, Lord Claud Hamilton to F.O., 26 May 1884. *The Times*, 23 and 24 Apr. 1884.
[2] For petitions to the Lords see under name and date in *PP 1884, Minutes of the House of Lords*, I.
[3] Slade, *English-speaking Missions*, 70–71.   [4] Stengers, *Bulletin*, 1206.
[5] Maj.-Gen. Sir F. J. Goldsmith, 'Portugal and the Congo', *National Review*, Vol. III, No. 15, 320–36, May 1884.
[6] *The Times*, 20 Mar. 1884, 8; 3 Apr. 1884, 4; 16 Apr. 1884, 8; 19 May 1884, 6.
[7] *The Times*, 4 Mar. 1884, 10, leader; 21 Mar. 1884, 9–10, leader; 16 Apr. 1884, 9, leader.
[8] *Manchester Guardian*, 5 Mar. 1884, 5, leader; 11 Mar. 1884, 5, leader; 13 Mar. 1884, 5, leader; 18 Mar. 1884, 4–5, leader; 31 Mar. 1884, 5, leader; 12 May 1884, 5, leader.
[9] *Manchester Examiner*, 8 Mar. 1884, 5, leader.
[10] *FO84/1811*, Report of Tariff Committee of Bradford Chamber of Commerce, 8 Apr. 1884, submitted to F.O., 1 May 1884.

The objections raised against the treaty after its signature were largely the same as those previously voiced, though Forster made an effective flank attack by suggesting that the treaty would prove useless since it was unlikely to secure that international recognition on which Granville had always insisted.

Hutton, for his part, did not stop at arousing a purely domestic opposition. During March he called on M. Waddington, the French ambassador in London, and Solvyns, the Belgian minister, and urged upon each that their Governments should oppose the treaty. From Waddington he received reassurance—France would not be bound by a treaty to which she was not a party and over which she had not been consulted. From Solvyns, on the other hand, he received a snub which, incidentally, was administered in a context which made unequivocally clear Solvyns' own lack of sympathy with his sovereign's African schemes. The Belgian minister replied, as he subsequently told C. M. Kennedy of the Foreign Office,

> that it was not usual for Englishmen to go to foreign ambassadors against their own government, that the African Association was the King's affair, not business with which the Belgian Government is connected, and that he as Belgian Minister, as far as he should express an opinion was favourable to the Treaty....[1]

There is no evidence to suggest that Hutton's approach to Waddington was the cause of the antagonistic attitude to the treaty which the French Government adopted at this time. There may, nevertheless, be some truth in Fitzmaurice's opinion that France was 'encouraged by the clamour in England' to refuse to recognize the treaty.[2] Nor did Hutton draw back from approaching the great Bismarck himself. On 7 March he sent to the German chancellor two copies of the Manchester Chamber of Commerce circular letter with a covering note which drew his attention to the fact that the treaty also affected the interests of the merchants of Hamburg, and to the point that the treaty could not take effect without the consent of other European Powers or of the British Parliament.[3]

Leopold, for his part, appears not to have abandoned his

[1] *FO84/1810*, Kennedy, Memo., 26 Mar. 1884.
[2] Fitzmaurice, op. cit., II, 346.   [3] Thomson, op. cit., 144.

THE ANGLO-PORTUGUESE TREATY 157

policy of placing his hopes on modifications in the treaty—modifications which now would have to be obtained by parliamentary action. On 5 April Strauch asked Mackinnon to bend all his energies to getting the limit of Portuguese territory as close as possible to Boma,[1] and whilst it is possible that Leopold was simultaneously using Hutton to work for a maximum aim of rejection of the treaty, it seems more likely that this was Hutton's own decision. Doubtless Leopold would have been glad to see the treaty rejected but two considerations suggest that he would not actively have urged this. One was a sense of decency, mixed with expediency. Overt action on behalf of rejection would be ungracious and would show up badly in the light of Granville's real attempt to safeguard the *A.I.C.*'s position. A skilfully conveyed warning by Granville may also have played a part. It emanated from a suggestion made by Anderson. Johnston, who had recently visited the Congo, told Anderson at the beginning of March that in his opinion the International Association was essentially a commercial company aiming at 'a gigantic . . . monopoly', the evidence being the commanding position which its agents had obtained on the Upper Congo and the exclusive nature of the treaties which they had made with native chiefs.[2] Anderson now urged that this knowledge could be used to advantage.

. . . I have a suggestion to make which is, I think, important. The King is, undoubtedly, getting up an opposition to the Treaty in the House.[3] We should break down the alliance between his friends and the genuine opponents if we show up the character of the Company's operations. I think we might do this by giving the Treaties and pointing to their exclusive character in contrast with the liberality of our Treaty and, while professing every respect for the Association, showing that, *if it became* a commercial enterprise, it would stifle our trade so far as it is not protected by our Treaty. This would not silence Mr. Hutton who

[1] *M.P.*, Strauch to Mackinnon, 5 Apr. 1884.
[2] *FO84/1809*, Anderson Memo., 'The Nature of the King of the Belgians Co.', 2 Mar. 1884. See also Memo. Encl. in Johnston to Austin Lee, 23 Feb. 1884.
[3] The sources of Anderson's information were Mackinnon himself and Goldsmid, but if Anderson understood them as meaning that Leopold hoped to obtain the rejection of the Treaty, he can only, if the argument of pp. 150–1, 156–9 is accepted, have misunderstood his informants. What Anderson understood is in any case not clear. He originally noted the information in as ambiguous terms as he used in this memorandum of 2 March—'. . . I hear from Sir F. Goldsmid and Mackinnon that the King is agitating to upset the treaty in the House, and Fitzmaurice tells me that he has similar information'. (*PRO30/29/156*, Anderson, Memo., 20 Feb. 1884, on Leopold to Granville, 14 Feb. 1884.)

has, if I am rightly informed, made a large sum of money from supplying the Belgian Co., but it would throw suspicion on the opposition from the Belgian quarter.[1]

As a public and open tactic Granville shelved this proposal[2] but Anderson's suggestion was utilized to inspire a private warning which, as a diplomatically expressed threat, is a tiny masterpiece.[3] Its occasion was the need to tell Leopold that no further modifications could be made in the treaty, and to cofirm that the *A.I.C.* station at Nokki would be outside Portuguese jurisdiction. Granville continued:

I cannot conclude this letter without expressing my absolute confidence in the objects of your Majesty being of a perfectly unselfish character, and that your Majesty's wishes are perfectly unselfish, animated by a desire to develop African commerce, in a manner perfectly fair to the whole world—*It will be unfortunate for the Association, if in the course of the debates which may arise on the Congo treaty, charges are made against some of your Majesty's agents, of acting on some important points, in direct contradiction to the spirit of Your Majesty's instructions.*[4] (My italics.)

Leopold's inactivity in England must also be explained by the fact that in the early part of 1884 he was busy with negotiations which, if successful—and towards the end of April they eventually were—would provide a far more effective guarantee of the International Association's position than could be won by any amount of tinkering with the Anglo-Portuguese treaty.[5] These comprised, firstly, a negotiation with France which resulted in the hoodwinking of Ferry and which was Leopold's diplomatic master-stroke. By an agreement of 23–24 April France recognized the flag of the Association in return for the pre-emptive right to its lands and stations if ever it should sell. Leopold's very concession, or rather 'concession', was a stroke of genius, for it meant that Britain would henceforth be bound to support the Association for fear of seeing the Congo basin fall to France.[6] His second negotiation was with

[1] *FO84/1809*, Anderson, Memo., 'Nature of the King of the Belgians Co.', 2 Mar. 1884.
[2] *FO84/1809*, Lister, Minute, 2 Mar. 1884, on Anderson, Memo., 2 Mar. 1884.
[3] *PRO30/29/198*, Anderson, Draft, n.d., of Granville to Leopold, 2 Mar. 1884.
[4] *Lambermont MSS.* (*Vol. 1876–84*), *No. 190.* Granville to Leopold, 2 Mar. 1884. (Copy in *PRO30/29/198*.)
[5] E. Banning, *Mémoires* (Paris–Brussels, 1927), 7. 'Pour conjurer le péril provenant de l'opposition de la France d'une part, du traité anglo-portugais de l'autre, le Roi . . . s'engagea dans une double négociation, l'une avec les Etats-Unis, l'autre avec le gouvernement français.'
[6] For the pre-emption agreement see Thomson, op. cit., 163–9.

the United States, and that, too, was successful. In the same month, the United States recognized the Association's flag as the 'flag of a friendly Government' in return for a promise of freedom of trade and navigation in the Congo basin for American citizens.[1]

Leopold, therefore, might be no problem to the Foreign Office, but the developing intransigeance of the domestic opposition clearly made some counter action necessary. The Foreign Office first tried to influence the Manchester Chamber of Commerce itself. In Hutton's words—and from his point of view—

The government took alarm and tried to bring influence on us to defer action—and begged us to go up at once to see Lord Granville, but it was too late, and I declined to entertain any more of their trifling work.[2]

The Foreign Office, however, continued to be placatory. A long justification of the treaty was sent to the Chamber in reply to its letter of 5 March, and at the same time printed and circulated to the Press and persons of influence.[3] At the same time the good offices of Sir J. C. Lee, the Government's principal supporter in the Chamber, were used in an attempt to change its attitude.[4] As a complement to this approach, an attempt was instituted to obtain from Portugal reductions in the Mozambique tariff.[5] But Lee's efforts were quite unsuccessful. By the end of April only one commercial body, the Manchester Cotton Spinners' Association, had come out in support of the treaty,[6] and this, as the opponents of the treaty did not fail to point out, at a meeting attended by only six members.[7] Despite the general support for the Government in the Press, Fitzmaurice concluded that the clear weight of opinion was against the treaty and that the Government's tactics must be changed.

[1] For the agreement with the U.S. see Thomson, op. cit., 147–62.
[2] *M.P.*, Hutton to Mackinnon, 18 Mar. 1884.
[3] *FO84/1810*, F.O. to Manch. Ch. Comm., 21 Mar. 1884 and Minute thereon by Kennedy, 21 Mar. 1884. See also *FO84/1811*, F.O. to Manch. Ch. Comm., 10 May 1884.
[4] *FO84/1809*, Lee to Fitzmaurice, 9 Mar. 1884. *The Times*, 30 Apr. 1884, 4, letter from Lee.
[5] *FO84/1809*, F.O. to d'Antas, 8 Mar. 1884, Draft. *FO84/1810*, F.O. to Petre, 31 Mar. 1884, No. 24a, Draft.
[6] *FO84/1810*, Manchester Cotton Spinners' Association to F.O. 25 Mar. 1884.
[7] *Hansard*, CCLXXXVIII, H.C., 438–9, 15 May 1884.

'It is I think beyond doubt', he wrote in a minute of 23 April, 'that H.M.G. may be beaten on the Congo question in the House of Commons, and I therefore consider that Lord Granville's attention should be called to the subject as soon as possible. . . . [Defeat] would be serious in the present condition of affairs and very serious at Manchester from the party point of view. I am inclined myself to think that the more time we can gain the better. Discussion will tend to strengthen our position. Our adversaries have had their say, our friends have hardly had time to assert themselves. Under the circumstances there is in my opinion a great deal to be said in favour of stating that negotiations with Portugal in regard to the Mozambique tariff . . . are still pending and that we think all things considered that it would be better not to take the judgment of Parliament till we can inform them more fully on the subject. We would inform the Portuguese Government that we had been reluctantly obliged to adopt this course from a conviction that if we proceeded now the Treaty would be thrown out. We would also state to the House that Lord Granville . . . having stated that "a merely dual arrangement between the two countries unrecognised by other Powers would be futile", it was desirable that the two Governments should have the opportunity of communicating with the other Powers and informing themselves as to their probable action, and that this information would be of importance to the House in forming a judgment.'[1]

This view was endorsed by Granville, Kimberley, Chamberlain, Dilke, and Fitzmaurice himself at a meeting at the Foreign Office on 26 April. It was agreed that ratification should be postponed, in view of the strength of the domestic opposition to the treaty, and that Britain and Portugal should jointly bend their efforts to obtaining international acceptance of the pact.[2] Fitzmaurice announced this decision in the Commons on 8 May.[3]

Shortly after this decision was taken two of the Government's supporters did 'assert themselves'. In a letter to *The Times* on 30 April, Lee offered an analysis of the Manchester-inspired opposition, suggesting that it was a quite artificial agitation which made clever use of a general ignorance of the case, that some four or five Liverpool and foreign firms were behind it, and that the value of the British Congo trade had been grossly overstated.[4] 'Cacimbo' followed in similar vein on the same day and went on to brand the International Association as

---

[1] *FO 84/1810*, Fitzmaurice, Minute, 23 Apr. 1884.
[2] *FO 84/1810*, F.O. to Petre, 23 Apr. 1884, Africa No. 35a, Draft. Gwynn and Tuckwell, op. cit., II, 84–85.
[3] *Hansard*, CCLXXXVII, H.C., 1700, 8 May 1884.
[4] *The Times*, 30 Apr. 1884, 4, letter from Lee.

THE ANGLO-PORTUGUESE TREATY 161

irresponsible.¹ Such representations might in time have had an effect, but domestic reactions to the treaty now became overshadowed by foreign.

France had been the first Power to protest against the treaty. In a note of 13 March she had made formal reservations regarding clauses in the treaty which affected French interests or which infringed a Franco-Portuguese agreement of 1786.² Nevertheless, and although the French reservations included a refusal to recognize the Portuguese claim to the coast between 5° 12′ and 8° south latitude, M. Ferry's protest was not such as to render vain any hope of winning France's acceptance by conciliation. France merely stipulated that Portugal must reach a direct understanding with France upon all the matters dealt with in the treaty. On 27 April the Foreign Office was informed that the Dutch Government considered that the interests of Netherlands commerce had not been taken into account in the treaty,³ whilst on 1 May, through Count Münster, its ambassador in London, the German Government protested against the application of the treaty to German subjects and expressed the hope that the agreement would not be proceeded with until its terms had been modified.⁴ From the United States, also, came a strong hint of hostility in the recognition of the flag of the *Association Internationale du Congo*—Portugal's rival—'as the flag of a friendly Government'.⁵ Certainly the American Press regarded this as tantamount to a protest against the treaty.⁶ Opposition also came from two Powers with no interests in the Congo region—Italy and Spain.⁷

The objections made by the Powers were real and would

---

¹ *The Times*, 30 Apr. 1884, 4, letter from 'Cacimbo'.
² *Yellow Book* (*Documents Diplomatiques, Affaires du Congo et de l'Afrique Occidentale, 1884*), Note, 13 Mar. 1884, Encl. in Ferry to Laboulaye, 14 Mar. 1884. *FO84/1810*, Petre to F.O., 23 Mar. 1884, Africa No. 23, Confidential. S. E. Crowe, *The Berlin West African Conference* (London, 1942), 24.
³ *FO84/1810*, Stuart to F.O., 27 Apr. 1884, Africa No. 1.
⁴ *FO84/1811*, F.O. to Ampthill, 1 May 1884, Africa No. 3, Draft. Crowe, op. cit., 28.
⁵ *FO84/1810*, West to F.O., 23 Apr. 1884, Africa No. 6, Telegram.
⁶ *D.D.F.*, 1st Series, Vol. V, 248, f.n. 1. See also *M.P.*, Sanford to Mackinnon, 8 Feb. 1884. In commenting on the information recently given to the American President by Queen Victoria, that the British Government proposed to recognize Portuguese sovereignty on the Lower Congo, Sanford wrote 'We don't anyway, and will not, and will, doubtless, be heard from on this subject.'
⁷ *White Book* (Aktenstücke betreffend der Congo–Frage, I Session, 6 Legislatur–Periode, Part III), 19–22, cited in Thomson, op. cit., 200.

have had to be met before international recognition could be obtained, but until early June no Power had refused outright to recognize the treaty—and both Britain and Portugal were prepared to admit modifications.[1] But on 7 June, in a note to Münster subsequently delivered by him to the Foreign Office, Bismarck refused to recognize the treaty in any form.[2] This categorical rejection was an action to which there was no counter—especially as Britain stood in particular need of Germany's support in Egypt—and Granville immediately accepted Bismarck's action. On 20 June, therefore, he showed d'Antas Bismarck's note and observed that it appeared to him to put an end to the treaty. The Portuguese Minister agreed.[3] The treaty, which had had to overcome unusual difficulties and strong opposition before it was signed, had finally foundered on unexpected opposition—the hostility of Bismarck.

From the viewpoint of this study Bismarck's rejection of the Anglo-Portuguese treaty appears an anti-climax. Mackinnon and Hutton had been to immense pains. They had inspired, and over a period of eighteen months sustained an unusually strong agitation by Chambers of Commerce, missionaries and humanitarians, all, it would seem, in retrospect, to no purpose. Bismarck had done in one diplomatic note (and for his own purposes) what they, with much expenditure of time and energy, had long striven for. But, against first appearances, the domestic agitation has a possible significance beyond what it can claim as a case study in organization, beyond its interest as a logical step towards the fulfilment of the Congo hopes of those who inspired it, and beyond its interest as an indication of the great importance they attached to these hopes. For whilst it was undoubtedly Bismarck who stopped the treaty in June 1884, it is arguable that the domestic opposition, by making obligatory the insistence on better terms first urged by Anderson, fatally delayed the conclusion of negotiations in the spring and summer of 1883 *when there was an appreciably greater chance of obtaining international recognition of the treaty.*

[1] *FO84/1810*, Petre to F.O., 27 Mar. 1884, Africa No. 24, Confidential. *FO84/1811*, Petre to F.O., 2 May 1884, Africa No. 37, Confidential. F.O. to Petre, 9 May 1884, Africa No. 40b. Crowe, op. cit., 23–24, 27–28.
[2] *FO84/1811*, Bismarck to Münster, 7 June 1884, Copy, and Translation. Crowe, op. cit., 32.
[3] *FO84/1811*, F.O. to Petre, 20 June 1884, Africa No. 65, Draft. Crowe, op. cit., 32.

THE ANGLO-PORTUGUESE TREATY

Both in the spring and summer of 1883, and a year later, Britain needed Germany more than Germany needed Britain. Since the rupture with France over the occupation of Egypt, Britain had stood in need of the support of the Triple Alliance, and especially of Germany, whereas Germany's international position was tolerably secure without a close alliance with Britain. In the interest of peace, which was also Germany's own interest, Bismarck was, however, prepared to give Britain reasonable support provided Britain gave Germany reciprocal treatment.[1] In the summer of 1883 this implied bargain held good and there is therefore no apparent reason why Germany should have refused to recognize the Anglo-Portuguese treaty had the British opposition allowed it to be signed and ratified at that time. But a year later the situation had changed. In the autumn of 1883 Bismarck had begun to draw closer to France and to encourage French colonial ventures in order to neutralize French hostility on the Rhine. By the early summer of 1884 this real if informal *entente* was fully in being and in view of Anglo-French colonial rivalry could only portend German hostility towards Britain in colonial affairs.[2] In the direct and immediate relations of Britain and Germany, grounds for a quarrel had also appeared. At the beginning of 1883 Bismarck had asked the British Government for British protection of a German settlement at Angra Pequena Bay, on the southwestern coast of Africa, clearly implying thereby that Germany had no intention of annexing it herself. The request for protection was formally repeated in December but the British Government kept Bismarck waiting six and a half months for an answer and in the meantime made vague assertions about their own still unsubstantiated claims to the whole district. This procrastination may well have annoyed the German Chancellor,[3] as Miss S. E. Crowe argues. By the early summer of 1884, therefore, there were in the realm of foreign policy two possible reasons why Bismarck should pick a quarrel with Britain. Whether it is believed, with A. J. P. Taylor, that Bismarck quarrelled with Britain in May and June 1884

[1] W. L. Langer, *European Alliances and Alignments, 1871–1890* (2nd ed., New York, 1950), 283.
[2] A. J. P. Taylor, *Germany's First Bid for Colonies* (London 1938), 20–21, 29–31.
[3] Crowe, op. cit., 39–41. For the Foreign Office view see Fitzmaurice, op. cit., II, 346–55. Taylor, *Germany's First Bid*, 23–29.

because a quarrel with Britain was a ready means of proving to France that he genuinely wanted to reach an understanding with her,[1] or whether it is believed, with Miss Crowe, that the quarrel resulted from a genuine annoyance at Britain's attitude over Angra Pequena,[2] or whether—as the third alternative—it is held that the quarrel arose as a consequence of both of these factors, is, in this context, immaterial. The central point is that there were grounds for a quarrel in the early summer of 1884; in the previous summer there were not. In Miss Crowe's words (though she was not concerned to prove this point),

Though the international situation, particularly in Egypt, was such as to facilitate the adoption of an anti-English policy by him [Bismarck], should he wish to embark on one, it was not necessarily such as to *cause* it, and there is no sign before 1884 of Bismarck's wishing to embark on such a policy, in spite of Great Britain's embarrassments in Egypt and his own predominant position on the Continent.[3]

There were possible domestic reasons also, reasons either inoperative or less urgent in 1883, why Bismarck should wish to pick a quarrel with Britain in 1884—the need to provoke a colonial conflict with Britain in order to be able to raise the cry, 'The *Reich* in danger', at the impending *Reichstag* elections, and the desirability of fomenting bad relations with Britain in order to cripple the anglophil liberalism of the Crown Prince, likely soon to succeed to the throne.[4]

Lastly, even if it be assumed that Bismarck was resolved to embark on a colonial policy as soon as Germany's European position permitted, it can still be argued that a European consideration—his desire for limited good relations with Britain—would not have permitted a colonial policy in the summer of 1883, had the protests of the Hamburg merchants been never so strong; and certainly they were vigorous enough in 1884.

The reaction of the other Powers, had the Anglo-Portuguese treaty been signed during the previous summer, is rather more speculative. But it is relevant to point out that Germany, a Power which, it has been argued, would have been most unlikely to have opposed the treaty in 1883, played some part in

---

[1] Taylor, *Germany's First Bid*, 32–40. A. J. P. Taylor, *The Struggle for Mastery in Europe, 1848–1918* (Oxford 1954), 294.
[2] Crowe, op. cit., 37, 48–49.   [3] Crowe, op. cit., 46.
[4] Taylor, *Struggle for Mastery*, 292–3.

evoking the hostility of Holland, Spain, Italy and the United States in 1884.¹ Spanish and Italian hostility was not in any case vitally important, whilst the Netherlands' attitude is scarcely likely to have been different from its opposed but not unyielding stance of 1884—eight days after the British minister at The Hague had reported Dutch non-acceptance of the treaty, he forwarded a report of a speech by the Netherlands Foreign Minister in which it was implied that his government hoped to safeguard Dutch interests by securing modifications in the treaty rather than by outright opposition.² The United States reaction is much less likely to have been favourable. Anglo-American relations were distinctly lukewarm at that time: on the other hand Leopold of the Belgians' diplomatic *démarche* and Sanford's mission to Washington to 'sell' the International Association, which together resulted in the U.S. recognition of the *A.I.C.* flag had not then taken place. Most important of all, what would France have done? A number of points may be made. Right up to the time of Bismarck's *nolle prosequi* in June she did not depart from her original position, one of distinct reserve but not outright opposition.³ Indeed in June 1884 Petre, the British minister in Lisbon, cited not only the opinion of the Portuguese Foreign Minister, but, more significantly, some remarks of the French minister also as indications that the French Government might be prevailed upon to accept the treaty 'if direct overtures are made to them for this purpose by the Portuguese Government'.⁴ It is scarcely conceivable that France could have taken a stronger line than this in the previous year, at a time when she did not enjoy German support. Most important of all—because most direct—is an actual statement by the French Foreign Minister of the French attitude to Portugal's Congo claim, made in May 1883. Lyons, the British ambassador, reported M. Challemel-Lacour thus:

M. Challemel-Lacour said that most certainly, as matters now stood, the French Government did not admit the claims put forward by Portugal to this portion of the coast. The French Government were well aware of the pretensions of Portugal, but this was a very different

---

¹ *White Book*, 19-22, cited in Thomson, op. cit., 200.
² *FO84/1811*, Translation of answer of Netherlands Foreign Minister to question in Second Chamber, 26 Apr. 1884, Encl. in Stuart to F.O., 5 May 1884, Africa No. 2. See also Petre to F.O., 14 June 1884, Africa No. 62.
³ *FO84/1811*, Petre to F.O., 2 June 1884, Africa No. 57, Confidential.
⁴ *FO84/1811*, Petre to F.O., 14 June 1884, Africa No. 62.

thing to agreeing that those pretensions were well founded. The question whether or no they were well founded might some day become a matter of discussion between France and Portugal, but the French Government did not feel called upon to express an opinion on that question at the present moment.[1]

This is very far from finally shutting the door on recognition of the Portuguese Congo claim and of an Anglo-Portuguese Congo treaty. Moreover, Challemel-Lacour was later to protest, when the Portuguese had got to hear of the interview, that 'the impressions which Lord Lyons gathered of our interview have evidently gone beyond on this particular point, the tenor of the language which I used (. . . *ont évidemment dépassé, sur ce point spécial, la portée du langage que je lui avais tenu*)'.[2]

(The truth of this disclaimer is difficult to assess. On the one hand Challemel-Lacour may well not have wished to disturb more than necessary the Portuguese belief that France recognized her Congo claim. On the other, he may have used stronger language to Lyons than the actual French attitude to that claim warranted, out of a reluctance to appear well-disposed to England in the matter.)

It only remains to add that in the abortive Franco-Portuguese discussions of July 1883, France's refusal to accept the Portuguese Congo claim was only a refusal to accept it *ab initio*, and that during 1883 (and most of 1884) France displayed little interest in the Lower Congo (as distinct from a certain interest in Stanley Pool and access to it from the coast north of the Congo mouth).[3]

On the other hand, the rancorous Anglo-French relations which followed unilateral British action in Egypt must not be lost sight of. It would seem therefore that, although the attitude of the various Powers to recognition of the treaty in the summer of 1883 must remain conjectural, the chances of a favourable response were markedly better. It might at least have been possible eventually to secure the recognition of a sufficient number of the Powers that mattered. The check which the negotiations suffered in the spring of 1883 was in part the result

[1] *FO84/1805*, Lyons to F.O., 23 May 1883, Africa No. 35.
[2] *D.D.F.*, 1st Series, Vol. V, 64, f.n. 1., Challemel-Lacour to da Silva Mendes Leal, 6 July 1883.
[3] See L. Jadin, 'Informations du lieutenant N. Cordier sur l'Association Internationale Africaine, tirées des Archives du Ministère de le Marine, 1883', *Bulletin des Séances de l'Académie Royale des Sciences d'Outre-Mer*, Brussels, V-1959-2, 288-316.

of Anderson's stiffening of the British terms, but more fundamentally a consequence of the flowering of a strong domestic opposition. It was mainly due, therefore, to this opposition that the British Government was unable to come to terms with Portugal in the summer of 1883 at a time when the treaty stood a better chance of obtaining international recognition.

The leading role of Leopold's British sympathizers, especially Hutton and Mackinnon, in arousing and directing this opposition has been emphasized. That is not to say that the opposition was a mere puppet show of their creation. The Congo merchants and the British commercial world at large feared the economic consequences of the admission of Portugal to the river, whilst missionaries and humanitarians were not less fearful that Portuguese legislation and maladministration would hinder their work. But the man with a clear and compulsive purpose is sometimes able to channel into a direction of his own choosing both the self-interest and the principles of others. He can do this because he takes the initiative, always being ready with a concrete proposal for action, because he is prepared to undertake the necessary work, because he can commonly lay claim to a certain idealism. This was precisely the role of Hutton and Mackinnon. They saw in the treaty a threat to a more ambitious purpose than any entertained by the conventional opposition—the realization of the immense potential of the Congo basin through the International Association, and for the benefit not least of British enterprise. Inspired by this vision they gave to the agitation by their leadership, co-ordination and enthusiasm an effectiveness which it would not otherwise have possessed.

CHAPTER VIII

BRITISH RECOGNITION OF THE *ASSOCIATION INTERNATIONALE DU CONGO*

As early as 1880 Gordon had discerned that the most fundamental of all the difficulties that confronted Leopold in his African projects was the lack of any international status either for the *A.I.A.* or the *A.I.C.* Without an accepted legal position, without a flag, these bodies could have no assurance that their jurisdiction would be respected, their treaties honoured, or that their work would survive the predatory interest of this or that European power. Stanley succinctly summarized the position in May 1884 (clearly before he had heard of American recognition and of the pre-emption agreement with France).

So long as we have not a character recognised by European nations, de Brazza with his walking stick, a French flag and a few words in the presence of the whites of Leopoldville, is really stronger than Stanley with his Krupps and all material of war, faithful adherents, aid of natives, etc.[1]

By the time Stanley wrote, Leopold had in fact already taken two important steps towards the solution of this problem. In November 1883 Sanford had been sent to the United States on a mission whose successful outcome was the only slightly qualified recognition by the United States of the *Association Internationale du Congo* on 22 April 1884. Even more important was the pre-emption agreement with France of 23–24 April, by which, in return for a promise that France should have first refusal of the Association's possessions if ever it was obliged to sell, France undertook to 'respect' the stations and territories of the Association. The task of securing some form of recognition from other Powers, including, not least, Britain, remained, and it was to the conversion of the British Government that Hutton and Mackinnon now addressed themselves. Their hopes for the Congo clearly demanded that they should now seek to bring on British recognition, just as those hopes had earlier dictated the mobilization of opposition to the Anglo-Portuguese treaty.

[1] *M.P.*, Extract of letter from Stanley, Vivi, 19 May 1884. Original addressee not named.

Nevertheless when the eight-year span 1876–84 is considered as a whole, the contrast between the scientific and philanthropic objects initially professed by Leopold and the state-building of the latter year is striking. Would not one expect that such a progression would have aroused suspicion? Is it not surprising that Mackinnon and Hutton should have unquestioningly believed that the creation of an independent state would serve their own and British interests?

In fact it would appear that neither suspicion nor doubts had any part in the minds of the two most notable of Leopold's British sympathizers. This was, quite simply, because they saw Leopold's ventures from the position of important debenture shareholders frequently admitted to the board-room. In this privileged position they had considerable knowledge of the inner workings of the Association and some ability to influence them, together with—a not unimportant factor—periodic contact with a reigning monarch of great charm. In consequence the gradual modification of the aims of 1876 so as to involve, first, participation in trade and second, the creation of a state, was seen from the inside and thereby made the more understandable. A principal aim of the *Comité d'Etudes du Haut Congo* was, in a more direct kind of way than had been envisaged for the *A.I.A.* in 1876, to pave the way for trade on the Upper Congo, whilst in 1879 Hutton and Mackinnon themselves urged—and successfully—that the *Comité* should as a matter of urgency begin to trade on its own account in order to prevent others moving into a market which the exertions of the *Comité* were opening up.[1] Why, after all, should involvement in trade be anything other than desirable? Men of the stamp of Hutton and Mackinnon are unlikely ever to have questioned that an extension of trade was to be commended, on moral no less than commercial grounds. Neither was there cause for doubt in the attempt to gain international recognition. Indeed, one can scarcely speak in such terms at all, for it would appear that Mackinnon, with Kirk, had actually advocated the creation of a state, or something essentially similar, in the early days of Leopold's African venture. 'You know the Association

[1] *Document Notte, Stanley au Congo, 1879–1884* (Ministère du Congo Belge, Private Circulation, n.d.), 15, 39. (I am indebted to Canon L. Jadin of Louvain for drawing my attention to this volume.) See also *M.P.*, Sanford to Mackinnon, 12 and 14 Apr. 1879 and 29 Apr. 1882.

are only acting as you and I advised long ago in building up a state', wrote Kirk to Mackinnon in December 1884,[1] probably in reply to some observations by Mackinnon on the Berlin Conference. Evidence of the compatibility of Leopold's evolving policy with the views of these two important British sympathizers, these words of Kirk are even more interesting as an indication of the form and scale which they advocated for Leopold's African venture at an early stage.

A further part of the explanation of why Leopold's state-building policy was no stumbling-block would appear to be that Mackinnon was vouchsafed the compliment of being given prior and confidential knowledge of at least one of its two main elements. 'The King's business requires haste. . . . You alone, save my wife, will know of the special business that I have undertaken', wrote Sanford conspiratorially[2] on the eve of his mission to Washington to obtain American recognition. Mackinnon may even have participated in the discussions in which the attempt to obtain United States recognition was decided upon—the wording of Sanford's letter does not exclude this possibility.

Even if Mackinnon and Hutton had had misgivings about the liberal intentions of the International Association, even if they had suspected that it might develop into a monopolistic trading state—and they never gave expression to any such feeling, even when they heard of the exclusive treaties made by agents of the Association—they still had the assurance of the promises made to them in 1879 when non-Belgian participation in the direction of the *Comité* was brought to an end. As subscribers they had been given a general promise of preferential consideration when concessions for the economic development of the Congo came to be awarded, and it is possible that a specific verbal undertaking of first refusal of a railway concession had been made to the two British subscribers.[3] With this

---

[1] *M.P.*, Kirk to Mackinnon, 16 Dec. 1884. This tantalizingly brief reference also bears the interpretation that Mackinnon had expressed doubts to Kirk about Leopold's state-building policy. But fundamentally the interpretation given above still stands for, assuming Kirk to have been right in his statement of what he and Mackinnon had advised 'long ago', Mackinnon could only have been jibbing at the form, having accepted, or rather advocated, the substance.

[2] *M.P.*, Sanford to Mackinnon, 24 Oct. 1883. See also the numerous letters from Sanford to Mackinnon between 2 Jan. and 22 Apr. 1884.

[3] See pp. 79–80 above.

assurance, or to represent their outlook more correctly, this vision, Mackinnon and Hutton had every reason to urge the British Government to recognize the International Association, and it was on an attempt to obtain such recognition that Hutton and Mackinnon, together with Stanley, concentrated in the second half of 1884.

But before there could be any hope that Britain would grant such recognition, an initial obstacle had to be removed. This was the strong feeling against Leopold and the International Association which had arisen in England when news of the pre-emption agreement reached London, and when the possibility—and to many the probability—that the possessions of the International Association would one day pass to France was realized.

'The reasons given by the King for the agreement with France', wrote Anderson, 'are the attacks of Portugal and the necessity of intimidating his adversaries. It is my conviction that the whole of these secret intrigues are directed more against England than Portugal.'[1]

The Times in a leader of 20 May was no less outspoken. There was an implicit duplicity in the International Association's agreements with France on the one hand and the United States on the other; notions about the Association's idealism must be discarded and it should be realized that 'we have to do with the simple exploitation of the Congo upon familiar commercial lines'; there was a very real threat to Britain in the possible transfer of the Association's possessions and rights to France who would thus come to control the whole interior.[2] Strauch himself, who visited London at the end of May, testified to a general feeling of hostility towards the Association. The pre-emption agreement, he wrote to Leopold, was considered 'as a desertion of England in favour of a country to whom just now she is strongly opposed'.[3]

---

[1] *PRO30/29/156*, Anderson, Memo., 18 May 1884, on Leopold to Granville, 15 May 1884, Private and Confidential, and Encls. See also Lister, Minute, 16 May 1884 on same letter; Anderson and Lister, Minutes, 29 May 1884, on Leopold to Granville, 22 May 1884, Private and Confidential; and *PRO30/29/198*, Lister, Minute, 20 May 1884, in which he refers to 'the shabby and mischievous trick which the King has played'.

[2] *The Times*, 20 May 1884, 9, leader.

[3] *Strauch MSS.*, Strauch to Leopold, London, 27 May 1884, quoted in J. Stengers, 'Rapport sur le Dossier "Correspondance Léopold II–Strauch"', Institut Royal Colonial Belge, *Bulletin des Séances*, XXIV–1953–4, 1203–7.

In trying to allay this widespread hostility Mackinnon was extremely active. Leopold had first sought to dispel this hostility by explaining the Association's intentions in two private letters to Granville, the essence of his argument being that the Association had no intention of ever disposing of its rights and possessions but that it was necessary to spike the guns of *'certains de nos adversaires'* by making it clear that attacks on the Association might well rebound on themselves by forcing the Association to sell out to France.[1] His second step was to send Strauch to London to repeat these reassurances both to officials of the Foreign Office and to British sympathizers of the International Association, some of whom had themselves been somewhat disturbed,[2] and it was in the fulfilment of this task that Mackinnon gave considerable help. It was through Mackinnon's good offices, where necessary, that Strauch saw Forster, Bourke, Long, Fowell Buxton, Sir John Kennaway, Sir Harry Verney, Jacob Bright and probably, though this is not entirely clear from Strauch's letters, Granville and Fitzmaurice as well. Mackinnon himself had twice put the Association's case to Anderson and, generally, had been immensely active in the whole affair.[3]

'M. Mackinnon', Strauch commented, 'has not said to me that he feared to incur the reproach of being lacking in patriotism by making himself the advocate of a cause which was regarded with such an unfavourable eye by all the English. But most certainly that was his feeling. Perhaps he has never given us such a proof of his devotion as by helping us in this affair. Although very busy, as always, he has spared neither time nor trouble.'[4]

The International Association's supporters did not neglect the Press. Goldsmid wrote to *The Times*, explaining the Association's case, at the beginning of June[5] whilst an article by Law on the same general lines appeared in the *Fortnightly Review* at the same time.[6]

[1] P. van Zuylen, *L'Echiquier Congolais* (Brussels, 1959), 86–88, quoting Leopold to Granville, Private, 15 May 1884, and n.d. but apparently shortly after 20 May 1884, from *Archives du Palais*.
[2] *Strauch MSS.*, Strauch to Leopold, London, 27 and 28 May 1884, quoted in Stengers, *Bulletin*, 1203–9.
[3] Ibid.
[4] *Strauch MSS.*, Strauch to Leopold, London, 27 May 1884, quoted in Stengers, *Bulletin*, 1203–7.
[5] *The Times*, 4 June 1884, 4, letter from Goldsmid.
[6] E. F. G. Law, 'International Rivalries in Central Africa', *Fortnightly Review*, Vol. XXXV, 819–28, 1 June 1884.

ASSOCIATION INTERNATIONALE DU CONGO

It does not appear that Hutton took much part in the justification, to British opinion, of the International Association's pre-emption agreement,[1] but from the end of May onwards he was extremely active in the Association's cause. Neither did he confine his activity to urging that the Association be recognized as a power having jurisdiction along the cataracts and on the Upper Congo, the main centres of its work. Against a background of some uncertainty that the Anglo-Portuguese treaty ever would come into operation, of its abandonment, and of the whole question of territorial jurisdiction in West Central Africa coming before the Powers, Hutton, no doubt at the request of Leopold, began to press that the International Association be recognized as the territorial authority for the Lower Congo and adjoining coast as well. As he put it in a letter to Mackinnon of early July,

... the object we have in view ... [is] ... extending the action of the International to the Lower Congo, and ... [getting] ... this administration ... recognised by our Government and by other Governments for the maintenance of future order on the whole of the river ... and the coastline between 5° 12' and 8°.[2]

Hutton hinted at such a solution in the somewhat vague peroration of a letter to the Foreign Office, written in his capacity as President of the Manchester Chamber of Commerce, at the end of May.[3] ('The last paragraph shows that the letter is from Mr. Hutton himself working for the King's new State' minuted Anderson.[4]) In a letter to *The Times* on 16 June he was a little more explicit. He urged that the Powers should consider:

whether all these native tribes in the whole Congo district cannot by international agreement be brought under, and their freedom secured through, the same or similar civilised administration and guarantees as are now being provided for the Upper river by the International Association.[5]

At this same time he was also busy with private approaches to the Dutch Company and the various British Houses trading on

[1] But he did send a memo. defending the Pre-Emption agreement to Fitzmaurice (*FO84/1811*, Hutton to Fitzmaurice, 22 May 1884, and Encl., Memo.)
[2] *M.P.*, Hutton to Mackinnon, 4 July 1884, Quite Private.
[3] *FO84/1811*, Manch. Ch. Comm. to F.O., 30 May 1884.
[4] *FO84/1811*, Anderson, Minute, 2 June 1884, on Manch. Ch. Comm. to F.O., 30 May 1884.
[5] *The Times*, 16 June 1884, 4, letter from Hutton.

the Lower Congo to obtain their approval of the Association exercising jurisdiction over the Lower Congo as well as the upper river, and over the adjoining coastline. These approaches came close to success but were then prejudiced by news reaching Britain of the exclusive terms of a treaty recently concluded with a chief on the Lower Congo by an agent of the Association.[1]

On 29 July came a parliamentary representation in favour of recognition of the International Association, albeit on the Upper Congo only, in the form of a question put down by Jacob Bright.[2] A campaign proper to secure British recognition, and approval of the Association exercising jurisdiction over the Lower Congo originated only in August in an instruction Leopold sent to Strauch.

> I should like the Manchester Chamber of Commerce and the others to begin a campaign for the recognition of the new independent state and the entrusting of the Lower Congo to its protection on a *Free Trade* basis.

In support of this campaign Stanley would give a number of lectures, in which it would be emphasized that the new state would have no customs barriers. Attempts would be made to give the lectures the widest publicity in the British Press.[3] Stanley, equipped with a letter of introduction from Leopold, put the ball in play by a visit to Granville at the end of August. He urged that the International Association be recognized as 'undertaking the non-commercial superintendence of the whole Congo'. Its income would be a recurrent grant of £50,000 per annum from Leopold. Stanley pressed Granville to define his attitude to the Association but the Foreign Secretary continued to be completely non-committal.[4]

Stanley's first public lecture was to a distinguished audience called together by the London Chamber of Commerce on 18 September. He spoke warmly of the International Association's past activities, emphasizing how they had opened up the way for Free Trade, and went on to describe the scheme for building up a confederation of Free States through which the whole of

---

[1] *M.P.*, Hutton to Mackinnon, 4 July 1884, Quite Private.
[2] *Hansard*, CCXCI, H.C., 850, 29 July 1884.
[3] *Strauch MSS.*, *No. 289*, Leopold to Strauch, 5 Aug. 1884.
[4] *FO 84/1812*, Granville, Memo., 29 Aug. 1884.

ASSOCIATION INTERNATIONALE DU CONGO

the Congo basin could be governed and preserved for Free Trade. The prospects of that trade he painted in the most lavish terms, and the whole address was enthusiastically received.¹ It was at Manchester, however, that Stanley received the warmest welcome. On 21 October he addressed, in the Town Hall, a meeting of its Chamber of Commerce attended by some 300 members. In it he laid the same stress on the International Association as the guardian of Free Trade as he had laid in London, but went into a good deal more detail about the commercial potentialities of the Congo basin, engaging in much proportional arithmetic. Beginning with the amount of cotton cloth that would be sold if each inhabitant of the region had one garment only, he progressed proportionally, not omitting to allow for the somewhat ambitious use of cloth in winding-sheets which local custom dictated! Bradshaw, he concluded, a Manchester man who in 1878 had unsuccessfully tried to interest the Chamber in Africa, had called that continent a second India: he, Stanley, could assure them that the African trade could be made to yield even more than India. Sustained applause welcomed this rosy prospect, and in such an atmosphere it was not difficult for Hutton to secure the unanimous adoption of a resolution that:

> The Chamber of Commerce of Manchester hereby expresses its warm sympathy with the earnest efforts of His Majesty the King of the Belgians to establish civilisation and free trade on the Upper Congo; it also trusts that the independent state or states proposed to be founded there may be recognised by all nations, and that the beneficent work now inaugurated may be ultimately extended throughout the whole of that river from its sources to its mouth.

The resolution was transmitted to the Foreign Office two days later.² Subsequently the Board of Directors also passed a resolution which certainly confirms the Free Trade emphasis in Stanley's address, and probably does much to explain why it received such a welcome. Stanley was to be thanked for the assurance he had given that it was the aim and intention of the International Association to secure 'for all nations in perpetuity

---

¹ *The Times*, 19 Sept. 1884, 6.
² *Manch. Ch. Comm.* Report for 1884, 6, and Appendix, 103–4. *The Times*, 22 Oct. 1884, 10. *FO84/1814*, Manch. Ch. Comm. to F.O., 23 Oct. 1884. *M. des A.E., C. et D. Afrique*, A.I.C., *Jan.–Dec. 1884, Vol. IV, No. 103 bis.*, Steinthal to Daumas, 22 Oct. 1884, Copy.

entire freedom of navigation and of trade in the territories on or adjacent to the Congo'.[1]

Stanley himself was well pleased at the outcome of the meeting. He had been, he told Hutton, 'rather afraid Manchester had drifted into old fogiism and senility. Her loud manifestations and eager expressions of gratification at the prospect of a *new market* prove the reverse.'[2] Stanley appears to have given only two further public lectures, both in Scotland, and those not until December.[3] Back in Manchester, however, Hutton got to work. The heads of several Liverpool firms interested in the Congo trade were invited over to Manchester towards the end of October and their agreement with the view already expressed by the Chamber of Commerce obtained.[4] Then on 5 November came a further representation to the Foreign Office from thirty-six Manchester merchants and manufacturers in which the signatories declared that their

> commercial interests and the freedom of trade and navigation in that district [the Congo] will be best secured by its entire jurisdiction being entrusted in perpetuity to the free and independent State now being founded by the International Association, under the auspices of His Majesty the King of the Belgians.

Hutton's covering letter, written as President of the Manchester Chamber of Commerce, went on to express the hope that the British delegates at the Berlin West Africa Conference, which had by this time been arranged, would be instructed to act in accordance with the petition.[5]

Representations to the Foreign Office did not cease after the British Government, at the end of November, had accepted the necessity of recognizing the Association.[6] On 12 December the Chamber urged that, in view of the possible reversion of the Congo basin to France, the condition recently agreed to by the Conference whereby the guarantee of freedom from import

---

[1] *Manch. Ch. Comm.*, Report for 1884, 6.
[2] Stanley to Hutton, 24 Oct. 1884 (kindly communicated by the late J. Arthur Hutton).
[3] *The Times*, 4 Dec. 1884, 6, and 8 Dec. 1884, 6.
[4] *M. des A.E., C. et D. Afrique, A.I.C., Jan.–Dec. 1884, Vol. IV*, Hutton to (?) Strauch or (?) Béraud, Oct. 1884, n.d., Confidential, Copy, and Encl., Draft of Petition. But no petition seems to have been sent to the F.O. from Liverpool.
[5] *FO84/1814*, Manch. Ch. Comm. to F.O., 5 Nov. 1884, and Encl., Petition, 31 Oct. 1884. *Manch. Ch. Comm.*, Report for 1884, 10, and Appendix, 108–9.
[6] See pp. 183–4 below.

duties was limited to twenty years, be removed. The opportunity was also taken to press that the International Association be given control of both banks of the Lower Congo.[1] Three days later Hutton, as president, and Elijah Helm, a director, represented the Chamber in an interview with Granville at Walmer. They attached especial importance to the need to delimit the boundaries of the new state before the Conference broke up. Otherwise there was a danger of a general scramble for territory. Specifically, they urged that the Association be given jurisdiction over both banks of the Congo to its mouth, and backed their case by producing extracts of letters from Stanley and others concerned in the Berlin Conference.[2]

Mackinnon, for his part, approached the Foreign Office, through Austin Lee, at the end of June, making a sounding as to whether the British Government would agree to the International Association taking the north bank of the Lower Congo in return for a British right of pre-emption—a proposal clearly on the pattern of the Association's earlier agreement with France. Lee's reply was that there was no possibility of such an arrangement if only because the strong views of the Foreign Office on the pre-emption agreement were so well known.[3] Furthermore, in September, Mackinnon visited Brussels, probably to discuss tactics with Leopold.[4] But his main energies were directed to a number of visits to the Foreign Office—to which he claimed, and appears to have had 'easy access'[5]—in December and the New Year. Mackinnon's advocacy, in close collaboration with Stanley, who was sent over especially from Berlin, and on similar, but more precise lines to Hutton, was on behalf of the Association's territorial claims. They sought to obtain British support for the claim that the Association's jurisdiction should extend, on the left bank of the Congo, down to Nokki, whilst to the north of the river France, on payment of compensation, should take over

[1] *FO84/1817*, Manch. Ch. Comm. to F.O., 12 Dec. 1884.
[2] *FO84/1817*, Granville, Memo., 15 Dec. 1884. Extracts of various letters submitted to Granville by Hutton, 12 Dec. *Manch. Ch. Comm.*, Report for 1884, 10, and Appendix, 110, Manch. Ch. Comm. to F.O., 19 Jan. 1883.
[3] *M.P.*, A. Lee to Mackinnon, 1 July 1884.
[4] *Strauch MSS., No. 306*, Leopold to Strauch, 4 Sept. 1884.
[5] Mackinnon to Sanford, n.d., but from textual and other evidence almost certainly 15 Dec. 1884, quoted in R. S. Thomson, 'Léopold II et la Conférence de Berlin', *Congo*, 1931, II, 339. See also the A. Lee–Mackinnon correspondence (*M.P.*).

from the Association both banks of the Niari-Kwilu but should otherwise be kept north of a diagonal line linking Massabé, where the 5° 12' south latitude line intersected the coast, with the western end of Stanley Pool. The territory between this line and the north bank of the Congo would thus fall to the Association.[1] Their representations, as will be seen, had a limited success.

Great occasion as was Stanley's Manchester address, active as the Manchester Chamber of Commerce continued to be, there was, in the autumn of 1884 a notable absence of any general agitation in favour of the International Association. Immediately after Stanley's address to the Manchester Chamber of Commerce, emissaries of the Chamber had been sent to London, Liverpool, Glasgow and other cities with the object of persuading their Chambers to make representations similar to that of Manchester.[2] But these approaches appear to have been unsuccessful. Only the Oldham Chamber made any sort of representation in favour of the International Association and that was to urge the necessity of deciding the Association's boundaries before the Conference broke up, rather than recognition.[3] If Hutton tried to persuade the Anti-Slavery Society to submit a representation in favour of the International Association, he was unsuccessful. In fact, amongst missionary and humanitarian circles, only the International Arbitration and Peace Association sent in a memorial on the *A.I.C.*'s behalf.[4] The Baptist Missionary Society, however, though it did not make a representation, gave Leopold's cause considerable support, being the more ready to do so no doubt, as a result of further kindnesses the king had recently shown to the Society. Stanley's addresses were favourably reported in the

---

[1] *Lambermont MSS.*, Vol. *1876–84*, No. *563*, *Annexe*, Extracts in translation of Mackinnon to Leopold, 11 Dec. 1884, Encl. in Leopold to Lambermont, 12 Dec. 1884. Mackinnon to Sanford, n.d., but from textual evidence almost certainly 15 Dec. 1884; Mackinnon to Sanford, 12, 15 and 20 Dec. 1884; Sanford to Mackinnon, 24 Dec. 1884; Stanley to Sanford, 4, 24 and 29 Dec. 1884 in Thomson, *Congo*, 1931, II, 336–46. Crowe, op. cit., 157, 160. See also *FO84/1692*, Sanford to Mackinnon, 25 Nov. 1884, Copy, communicated by Mackinnon to F.O., 28 Nov. 1884.

[2] *M. des A.E., C. et D. Afrique, A.I.C., Jan.–Dec. 1884*, Vol. IV, No. *103 bis.*, Béraud to Strauch, 25 Oct. 1884, Copy. See also *FO84/1814*, Lee to Fitzmaurice, 31 Oct. 1884.

[3] *FO84/1818*, Oldham Chamber of Commerce to F.O., 26 Dec. 1884.

[4] *FO84/1814*, International Arbitration and Peace Association to F.O., 15 Nov. 1884.

Freeman, one of the Society's missionary journals, and an outright plea made for British recognition of the Association's flag. The *Missionary Herald* took much the same line, whilst at the Berlin Conference itself, Baynes, the Society's General Secretary, and Bentley, were very ready to lend assistance to the Association.[1]

In Parliament there was no campaign. There were isolated, weighted questions from Bright on the 20th,[2] and Houldsworth, also a prominent member of the Manchester Chamber of Commerce, on 21 November,[3] but that was all.

A significant exception to this general picture is the activity of a trade association formed in July 1884 for the defence of the interests of British merchants trading to the Congo—The Congo District Defence Association.[4] Its members, who came mainly from Liverpool, were Hatton & Cookson, Stuart & Douglas, the Congo & Central Africa Co., Taylor Laughland, the British & African Steam Navigation Co., the African Steamship Co., John Holt & Co., and Edwards Bros.[5] In a Liverpool deputation to the Foreign Office on 1 November, in which members of the Congo Association preponderated, it was urged that the International Association should become the territorial power on the Congo and over the whole coast from Gaboon to Angola,[6] a plea which was formally reiterated in a memorial submitted in mid-December.[7] Moreover the Congo Association was sufficiently concerned about the outcome of the Berlin Conference to send four of its members —F. W. Bond, A. L. Jones, E. H. Cookson and John Holt —to Berlin as a lobby.[8]

But against first appearances, the formation and activities of the Congo Association were probably not the result of Hutton's initiative. It is highly significant that when the deputation from the Association went to the Foreign Office they

---

[1] Slade, *English-speaking Missions*, 72–74. Slade, *Bulletin*, 717–19.
[2] *Hansard*, CCXCIV, H.C., 57, 20 Nov. 1884.
[3] Ibid., H.C., 136, 21 Nov. 1884.
[4] *FO84/1812*, Congo District Defence Association to F.O., 21 July 1884.
[5] *FO84/1812*, Congo District Defence Association to F.O., 7 Aug. 1884.
[6] *FO84/1814*, Anderson, Memo., 1 Nov. 1884, and accompanying list of members of deputation.
[7] *FO84/1817*, Congo District Defence Association to F.O., 10 Dec. 1884, and Encl., Memorial, 25 Oct. 1884.
[8] *FO84/1814*, Jacob Bright to Fitzmaurice, 11 Nov. 1884. Crowe, op. cit., 99–100.

privately expressed to Anderson considerable doubts about the lengths to which Hutton went in his attempt to inspire petitions in favour of the International Association. The apprehension which the delegation expressed at the International Association's pre-emption agreement with France is a pointer to the reasons for the reserve with which they now regarded Hutton, the champion of the International Association.[1] A further pointer is the alarm which, as has been seen, the Congo merchants expressed on receiving news of the conclusion of an exclusive treaty by an agent of the International Association.[2] This was at the beginning of July. It is perhaps significant that it was during the course of that month that the Congo District Defence Association was formed. It has been seen that, despite the widespread resentment which followed the conclusion of the pre-emption arrangement, Hutton, at the beginning of July, was in a fair way to securing the agreement of the British (and Dutch) Congo Houses to the International Association exercising jurisdiction over the whole of the Congo, and the adjoining coast.[3] It may well be that the news of the exclusive treaty re-kindled a latent distrust and decided the Congo merchants to form an organization quite independent of Hutton to safeguard their interests. When, with the reference of the whole question to the Powers in the Berlin West Africa Conference, a decision had to be made, those merchants resolved to support the claims of the International Association. But it is difficult to avoid the conclusion that they did so only because France and Portugal inspired even less confidence, in spite of some mistrust of the new state's likely fiscal policy, and in the not completely confident hope that France would never succeed to that state's heritage.

All the indications are that opinion in the country generally over the recognition of the International Association and the extent of its jurisdiction reflected that of the Congo merchants. In the sanctuary—the Manchester Chamber of Commerce—itself, according to Lee, Hutton's line had begun to be questioned by some members as early as April 1884.[4] News of the pre-emption agreement had been something of a shock there, as it

---

[1] *FO84/1814*, Anderson, Memo., 1 Nov. 1884.
[2] See pp. 173-4 above.   [3] Ibid.
[4] *The Times*, 30 Apr. 1884, 4, letter from Lee.

has been seen to have been generally, a shock which Hutton was not altogether successful in treating. Stanley's reputation and Hutton's careful management had been sufficient to ensure a unanimous vote in favour of the resolution put at the end of Stanley's address, but doubts persisted.

'The arrangement with France', wrote R. C. Richards, a Government supporter influential in the Chamber, to Fitzmaurice at the end of November, 'has opened the eyes of some of our commercial men to the possible drift; and they are beginning to realise that Portugal with all her faults may be more easy to deal with than France.'[1]

It is understandable that doubts about the International Association should have been more pronounced beyond the circle of Hutton's immediate influence. (The more so since the Manchester Chamber of Commerce was a somewhat unpopular body owing, according to a well-informed contemporary, 'to their setting themselves up on a pedestal as regards Free Trade'.[2] After the Chamber had twice initiated an agitation by other Chambers of Commerce, this chicken was perhaps coming home to roost.) The *Manchester Guardian*, for instance, in a leader at the close of September, expressed some apprehension at the recent report that agents of the International Association had been buying up the sovereign rights of native tribes on the Lower Congo,[3] and four days later urged that the business community ought 'to weigh the possible advantages offered by Portugal against the still undefined conditions proffered by her Belgian rival'.[4] After Stanley's Manchester address the paper spoke more favourably of the International Association's claim to the Congo but even so with reservations and reluctance. France's right of first refusal was still termed a 'black shadow' and the conclusion that 'in any case the best way to keep France out would apparently be by maintaining the Association',[5] is scarcely enthusiastic. That Hutton had overplayed his hand is suggested by the strong criticism made of him in a leader early in November. His role as the 'known and accredited champion of the Association in Manchester' had its advantages, but these were outweighed by its disadvantages in that he had been able to persuade the

[1] *FO84/1816*, Richards to Fitzmaurice, 28 Nov. 1884.
[2] M.P., A. Lee to Mackinnon, 23 Mar. 1884.
[3] *Manchester Guardian*, 27 Sept. 1884, 7, leader. See also 26 Sept. 1884, 5.
[4] Ibid., 1 Oct. 1884, 5, leader.   [5] Ibid., 22 Oct. 1884, leader.

Chamber of Commerce to advocate recognition of the International Association without sufficient knowledge, 'inconsiderately and prematurely'.[1] When the *Guardian* eventually endorsed British recognition of the Association it was still with reservations.[2]

The attitude of the *Manchester Examiner*[3] and *The Times*[4] was generally similar—an eventual qualified endorsement of recognition of the International Association. That it should be established in the Lower Congo as well, was also accepted.[5] This, indeed, would appear to have been the generally held view of the case. That there was little positive enthusiasm for the International Association is made comprehensible by the widespread fears aroused by the Association's exclusive treaties and by its pre-emption agreement with France, and is made clear beyond reasonable doubt by Hutton's complete failure to arouse a general agitation in favour of recognition. That commercial opinion and public opinion generally, as far as can be judged, wanted the International Association to be recognized is no less comprehensible. To work for the establishment of France on the Congo was unthinkable; and despite second thoughts by some, there was still too much prejudice against Portugal for her claim to the Lower Congo to be supported. Some still refused to admit that there was no other course but recognition of the International Association; hence the latter part of 1884 saw such improbable proposals as that of Mr. J. Dodds, Liberal M.P. for Stockton, that the Lower Congo be placed under an International European Protectorate.[6] But most saw that, though there were grounds for misgivings and distrust, the International Association's claims must be supported. Fundamentally there was no other choice.

The Foreign Office was perfectly aware that British commercial opinion as well as Leopold's British supporters, wanted Britain to recognize the International Association.[7] But

---

[1] *Manchester Guardian*, 4 Nov. 1884, 5, leader.
[2] Ibid., 22 Nov. 1884, 7, leader; 4 Dec. 1884, 5, leader; 20 Dec. 1884, 7, leader.
[3] *Manchester Examiner*, 22 Oct. 1884, 4–5, leader; 19 Dec. 1884, 5, leader; 23 Dec. 1884, 4–5, leader.
[4] *The Times*, 10 Dec. 1884, 9, leader; 18 Feb. 1885, 9, leader.
[5] See, e.g. *The Times*, 18 Feb. 1885, 9, leader.
[6] *Hansard*, CCXCIII, H.C., 1849, 17 Nov. 1884.
[7] *FO84/1816*, Pauncefote, Memo., 2 Dec. 1884, on Malet to F.O., 1 Dec. 1884, Telegraphic, No. 40.

the expression of this view played no essential part in formulating the British decision on recognition. For, for the Foreign Office also, there was no other practicable choice beyond recognition. The Foreign Office was reluctant to realize this,[1] for the part Leopold had played in the agitation against the Anglo-Portuguese treaty, the discovery of the monopolistic nature of the International Association's treaties, and particularly the pre-emption agreement with France had induced in the Office a considerable distrust of the Association.[2] But the grant of German, as well as American and French recognition of the International Association's flag, Bismarck's support of Leopold, the growing realization that England needed to be on good terms with Germany and that her interests on the Niger would best be maintained by collaboration with Germany at the Conference, a deterioration in relations with Portugal,[3] and a basic awareness that to act against the International Association would be to help France to take its place, combined to show the Foreign Office where Britain's interests lay. Her first step was still hesitant and taken before Bismarck had fully shown his hand. In his instructions, dated 15 November, Sir Edward Malet, the British ambassador in Berlin and chief British plenipotentiary at the Conference, was told that in the view of the British Government the International Association was not yet a state. But it clearly had in it the possibility of becoming one and Britain would watch sympathetically her efforts to do so.[4] Only a fortnight later Bismarck both emphasized the danger and undesirability of the Association's lands falling into the hands of France, and implied that he would make things unpleasant for Britain on the Niger if she did not recognize the Association. This was sufficient. Granville immediately told Malet to negotiate a treaty with the Association and this was signed on 16 December.[5] By it Britain recognized the Association's flag as the flag of a friendly government. For its part, the Association undertook not to levy import or transit duties on the merchandise of British subjects, to grant to British subjects full rights of entry and establishment, and most favoured nation treatment. In addition the Association accepted the continuance of consular jurisdiction over

---

[1] Crowe, op. cit., 89. [2] Crowe, op. cit., 86–87. [3] Crowe, op. cit., 90–91, 144–7.
[4] Crowe, op. cit., 90. [5] Crowe, op. cit., 146–7.

British subjects in its territory. An article was also included which stipulated that the residential and fiscal rights granted to British subjects should continue in force in the event of the Association ceding her territories to another Power.[1]

If the representations of the British Congo merchants and of Leopold's British sympathizers played no significant part in the British Government's decision to recognize the Association, the lobbying of Mackinnon, Hutton and Stanley in regard to the territorial negotiations did have a limited effect. The lobbying was efficacious in the sense that Mackinnon and Stanley were able to prevent the dispatch to Malet of instructions which would have allowed France to come a very long way south of the Massabé–Stanley Pool line (see p. 178 above), which the Association wanted as a boundary, and, indeed, in the sense that they were able to gain the Foreign Office's general acceptance of the Association's proposition concerning its boundary with France.[2] But their achievement was very severely qualified by the British Government's insistence, despite further approaches by Mackinnon in February 1885,[3] on receiving German assent and co-operation in pressing such a settlement on France and Portugal, and this assent was only forthcoming to a very limited extent. The approach which Bismarck eventually made to France, did, however, elicit from her a statement that she was quite prepared for a triple partition of the Congo between herself, Portugal and the Association. This, in turn, made possible the negotiations which led eventually to that final territorial settlement which was not unfavourable to the Association.[4] Two other expressions of British opinion also had some effect. The local knowledge of Holman Bentley, the Baptist missionary who was in Berlin during the Conference, was of value to the International Association in enabling it to moderate some of the extensive claims put forward by France on the basis of de Brazza's Makoko and other

[1] Crowe, op. cit., 148.
[2] *Lambermont MSS.*, Vol. *1876–84*, *No. 563, Annexe*, Extracts in translation of Mackinnon to Leopold, 11 Dec. 1884, Encl. in Leopold to Lambermont, 12 Dec. 1884. Mackinnon to Sanford, 12, 15 and 20 Dec. 1884; Sanford to Mackinnon, 24 Dec. 1884; Stanley to Sanford, 4 and 29 Dec. 1884 in Thomson, *Congo*, 1931, II, 336–46. *FO84/1818*, Hill, Memo., 22 Dec. 1884 on Malet to F.O., 20 Dec. 1884, Africa No. 261, Confidential. Crowe, op. cit., 157, 160.
[3] *M.P.*, A. Lee to Mackinnon, 4 Feb. 1885, Private, and 14 Feb. 1885, Confidential.
[4] Crowe, op. cit., 160–75.

treaties.[1] The opinions of the four British merchants sent to Berlin by the Congo District Defence Association also had some effect—in a different field. Their advice on various fiscal and commercial matters was sought by the British delegation,[2] whilst their experience of the Congo trade was apparently of constant general value.[3]

As a result of the Berlin Conference and supplementary agreements, and principally because Germany and Britain acted together in its support, the International Association came away from Berlin in the new garb of the internationally recognized Congo Free State and with by far the greatest share of the Congo basin. Her territory comprised both banks of the river and a vast hinterland to the north, south and east of its inverted U-shaped course, with the exception of the left bank from Nokki to the sea, which went to Portugal, and a deep belt of territory on the right bank, extending from Manyanga to the basin of the River Likona (close to the Equator), which was secured by France. In addition to this the new state was specifically permitted by Portugal to construct a railway round the cataracts, and from Nokki to the sea.[4] With the political security of his African venture assured, Leopold, with the encouragement and co-operation notably of his British sympathizers, could turn to the promotion of its economic development. Those British sympathizers, for their part, must now have felt that, after long striving, the promised land was within their grasp.

[1] Slade, *English-speaking Missions*, 73–74. Slade, *Bulletin*, 718–19.
[2] *FO84/1815*, Malet to F.O., 25 Nov. 1884, Telegram, Africa No. 24. Anderson, Memo., undated, Copy, Encl. in Malet to F.O., 26 Nov. 1884, Africa No. 130.
[3] Crowe, op. cit., 100.
[4] Crowe, op cit., 169, 173–5.

CHAPTER IX

THE CONGO RAILWAY CONCESSION

EVEN before political security for Leopold's Congo venture had been obtained, attempts had been made to begin the economic development of the river basin. In response to an initiative of Leopold's in February 1883, following discussion during Mackinnon's visit at the end of January, Strauch told Mackinnon on 23 February that Leopold believed the time had come to form an Anglo-French-Belgian Company to exploit the river's resources, French participation being invited, Strauch explained, in order to disarm French suspicions of the *A.I.C.* Would Mackinnon approach Hutton and ask him to sound commercial opinion in Manchester, and to inquire of Hatton & Cookson (the most substantial British Congo company) whether they would consider a merger with the new company?[1]

Hutton was encouraging.

If such a company could be formed in England and obtain a Royal Charter, it would be one of the best modes of defeating the ambition of Portugal and France [this, of course, was the time when the agitation against the Anglo-Portuguese negotiations was getting under way] and would meet with the support of the principal African merchants.[2]

On these conditions Hatton & Cookson were quite disposed to join, and the other Congo firms would probably follow their example.[3] Within three days of Mackinnon's report of the success of Hutton's soundings, a visit of Lambert to London to see Mackinnon and Hutton was arranged[4]—but the project progressed no further, at least not in the form originally proposed. This was probably because both Hutton and Hatton & Cookson had emphasized that the company should obtain a royal charter and in consequence be a British company, a condition which might lead to the Congo becoming a British

[1] *M.P.*, Strauch to Mackinnon, 23 Feb. 1883 and 30 Nov. 1883.
[2] *M.P.*, Hutton to Mackinnon, 1 Mar. 1883.
[3] *M.P.*, Hutton to Mackinnon, 3 Mar. 1883.
[4] *M.P.*, Mackinnon to Strauch, 6 Mar. 1883, Telegram, Draft. Strauch to Mackinnon, 9 Mar. 1883.

preserve. Certainly Lister noted, shortly after the original approach to Mackinnon had been made, that he had heard that the International Association was likely to become a British company[1]—probably a confused reference to the views of Hatton & Cookson, Hutton and, it would seem, Mackinnon himself in regard to the Brussels proposal. The principal grounds for the belief that Mackinnon shared the Liverpool-Manchester view are the same as those for the view that the project came to nothing because Leopold feared a British predominance in it, namely a note from Leopold to Strauch of 2 March: 'I will reply myself to Mackinnon on the subject of his memorandum which is perfectly impossible. Between ourselves it put us under English domination.'[2] There is additional ground for the view that the reason why Leopold went no further with the proposal in its original form was his fear of British domination, in the eventual outcome of the matter. When the basis of a Congo company again came to be considered by Leopold some months later, the British contribution was to be much smaller, and the combined Belgian and French share almost as large as the British.[3] In other words Leopold, alarmed at the drift of things in March, drew off for a while, albeit without damage to the smooth tenor of his relations with his British sympathizers. When he again spoke to them of the matter it was in such a way as to make clear that the proposed company could be neither British dominated nor British registered.[4]

This company was still-born—as was a railway scheme also conceived by Leopold at this time and which was probably intended to be complementary. Leopold had hoped to persuade a French financier, M. Joubert, to f r a a French company to

[1] *FO84/1803*, Lister, Memo., 28 Feb. 1883.
[2] *Strauch MSS.*, No. *169*, Leopold to Strauch, 2 Mar. 1883. Whilst, in view of the date of the note, the likelihood is that Mackinnon's memorandum and Leopold's reaction referred to the proposal for a Congo company, the evidence is not conclusive. It is possible that Mackinnon's memorandum proposed a political countermove to the threatened Anglo-Portuguese Treaty—the suggestion, perhaps, that Britain might herself take possession of the Lower Congo, a variant of which Mackinnon was at least prepared to consider in March of the following year, and a course which Stanley was to recommend in July 1883. *M.P.*, Mackinnon to Sanford, 3 Mar. 1884, Copy. *FO84/1807*, Stanley to Hutton, 11 July 1883, forwarded to F.O., 25 Sept. 1883. *Johnston Papers*, Stanley to Johnston, 23 July 1883 (published in *The Times*, 25 Sept. 1883). See also p. 204 below.
[3] *Strauch MSS.*, No. *201*, Leopold to Strauch, 1 Aug. 1883.
[4] *M.P.*, Strauch to Mackinnon, 30 Nov. 1883.

build a double track line inland from the Congo mouth, and running on French or International Association territory as geography dictated, and to obtain from the French Government a $3\frac{1}{2}$ per cent. guarantee of its 400 million francs capital.[1] Neither failure is surprising for in 1883 conditions were not yet ripe for enterprises of this kind. Stanley's work was still incomplete and the Association's international position precarious. A sound political basis was as necessary for economic development as it was to ensure the permanence of the Association's work in general, and was only secured by the Berlin Act and the various related agreements concluded at that time.

During 1884, of course, Leopold's energies were concentrated on securing such a basis and, whilst hopes for a future railway and large trading company were cherished,[2] no further steps were taken to realize them. At the Berlin Conference measures were taken to ensure that there should be no obstacle to the construction of a railway round the cataracts. Sanford, nominally an American representative, but in practice the advocate of the International Association, proposed at the third meeting of the Conference that whatever state came to control the greatest part of the Congo should be authorized either itself to build a railway round the cataracts or to grant a monopoly to a company for this purpose. His proposal met strong opposition from France and Portugal and was eventually withdrawn—but only after the Association had achieved its purpose by the alternative means of incorporating such permission in the treaty which the Association eventually and laboriously made with Portugal for the delimitation of their frontiers.[3]

Whilst the Conference was still in session Sanford was turning his attention to a general plan of economic development. He had told Leopold, he wrote to Mackinnon in February 1885, that the time had come for the formation of 'another East India Company'. Certain of the existing stations of the Association should be turned over to this trading company and all new ones would be founded by it. Mackinnon, Sanford

---

[1] *Strauch MSS.*, *No. 206*, Leopold to Strauch, 14 Sept. 1883.
[2] *Strauch MSS.*, *No. 244*, Leopold to Strauch, 2 Feb. 1884. *M.P.*, Devaux to Mackinnon, 10 Feb. 1884. *The Times*, 19 Sept. 1884, 6, Report of Stanley's address to London Chamber of Commerce.
[3] Crowe, op. cit., 130–1.

urged, should devote attention to the working out of such a project.[1] In the weeks that followed, Sanford continued to press his particular scheme on Mackinnon's attention and no doubt advocated it in Brussels also.[2]

Meanwhile Stanley had been authorized by Leopold to make inquiries in London as to the financing of a railway round the cataracts from Vivi to Stanley Pool. The response was encouraging, one firm, Stanley reported to Borchgrave in June, offering to purchase £600,000 worth of debenture shares.[3] Hutton also, even before the end of the Berlin Conference, began to move in the matter of a Congo company,[4] seeing in it, there can be no doubt, the consummation of, and reward for his assistance to Leopold and exertions against the Anglo-Portuguese treaty. An important emphasis in his scheme was on actual trading and in June 1885, possibly after an audience with Leopold, he discussed some draft proposals with Mackinnon.[5] At the end of the month the head of the Dutch Congo company visited Hutton and appeared disposed to join in the scheme, subject to his company's assets being taken into account and valued.[6] A day or two later Hutton had a meeting with Stanley and discussed the whole matter with him.

'He thinks', Hutton reported to Mackinnon, 'that, if a few men of position and means will now go into this, and lay their views before the King, certain valuable concessions may be obtained and the basis of a company formed—I told him I should be willing to join with you and take my part, and in addition do my share of the work, provided you would take the lead and that Stanley also cast in his lot.'[7]

Such threefold collaboration now in fact began and the hitherto distinct schemes of Hutton and Stanley were merged in one body of proposals, which was seemingly sent off to Brussels at the end of July.[8]

No reply came from Brussels for two months. Already at the beginning of July Hutton had let go a possible hint that he felt Brussels was dragging its feet[9] whilst Stanley, since early June, had felt that he was not being kept fully informed of the king's

[1] M.P., Sanford to Mackinnon, 10 Feb. 1885.
[2] M.P., Sanford to Mackinnon, 15 and 25 Feb., and 10 May 1885.
[3] Hird, op. cit., 205–6.   [4] M.P., Stanley to Mackinnon, 17 Dec. 1884.
[5] M.P., Hutton to Mackinnon, 3 July and 29 Sept. 1885. *Strauch MSS., No. 420,* Leopold to Strauch, 29 May 1885.
[6] M.P., Hutton to Mackinnon, 3 July 1885.   [7] Ibid.
[8] M.P., Hutton to Mackinnon, 24 July 1885.
[9] M.P., Hutton to Mackinnon, 3 July 1885.

intentions.¹ Stanley, at least, regarded the delay as serious and was only reassured by a meeting with Leopold in September when the king explained that he felt the matter could go no further until the report of a survey team (led by a Belgian engineer, M. Petit-Bois)² was received, and passed on to Stanley and his two associates. Moreover, there was also an element of misunderstanding, each side expecting the next move to be made by the other.³ Whether Leopold's explanation was a complete one is open to question, for a letter he wrote to Strauch in May indicates that he was then trying to raise a bank loan of 8,000,000 francs specifically for the construction of a railway.⁴ This sum (£320,000) might have been deemed enough to build a railway round the cataracts: alternatively Leopold may have been negotiating for the loan in order that the Free State itself might be able to come forward with a substantial contribution to the railway company and thus have a greater share in its control. In any case it would appear that the negotiations were unsuccessful. But whatever the real cause of the Free State's slowness in replying to the July proposals, Leopold does not appear to have waited for the survey report once he had heard from Stanley how uneasy he and his associates were. Only a week after Stanley's meeting with Leopold, Van Eetvelde, Administrator-General of Foreign Affairs in the Free State Government, wrote to Hutton, informing him that his Government had decided 'to make a concession to a Company for the construction of a narrow gauge railway from the Lower Congo near Vivi to Stanley Pool. . . . The Free State would be glad', Van Eetvelde added, 'if the Company undertaking the building and working of the railway would also enter into commercial transactions with the natives.' If Hutton could see his way to helping in the formation of such a company, would he sound his friends and get into touch with the state authorities again?⁵

This was just what Hutton and his two associates needed. In forwarding to Mackinnon a translation of Van Eetvelde's

[1] Hird, op. cit., 204–7.
[2] A. J. Wauters, *L'Etat Indépendant du Congo* (Brussels, 1899), 66.
[3] *M.P.*, Stanley to Mackinnon, 16 Sept. 1885.
[4] *Strauch MSS.*, *No. 412*, Leopold to Strauch, 15 May 1885.
[5] *M.P.*, Van Eetvelde to Hutton, 24 Sept. 1885, Encl. in Horace Hutton to Mackinnon, 28 Sept. 1885. A similar letter was apparently sent to Stanley (Hird, op. cit., 207).

letter, Hutton wrote that he was prepared to do everything in his power to make a success of the project[1], and in the next three months Hutton, Mackinnon and Stanley appear to have devoted considerable attention to developing it.[2] Early in December, for example, Hutton collected an audience of about thirty of Manchester's leading business men to hear Stanley speak on the scheme,[3] whilst a few days later Stanley was busy trying to arouse interest in London.[4] The efforts of the group were moderately successful for they secured promises of participation amounting to £400,000 without making a public appeal for subscriptions.[5] After further intensive work[6] definite proposals for a railway and other concessions were drawn up and dispatched on about 12 December to Brussels,[7] and a syndicate formed in England[8] as a preliminary to the formation of a company, and to do whatever else might be necessary to obtain the concessions.

The Congo Railway Syndicate had twenty-six shareholders of whom fourteen came from the Manchester district and eight from London.[9] The directors were Lord Egerton of Tatton, a prominent Mancunian, Jacob Bright, H. M. Steinthal, a Manchester merchant and prominent in the affairs of its Chamber of Commerce, Sir James Fergusson, M.P., who was to become Parliamentary Under-Secretary for Foreign Affairs in 1886, Houldsworth, Daniel Adamson, a Manchester iron-master and influential member of the Chamber of Commerce, Hutton, Mackinnon and Stanley.[10]

The primary object of the company which the syndicate hoped to found was 'to establish direct and regular communication between the Upper and Lower Congo by the construction of a railway and placing light-draught steamers on the river'. In the first instance the line was to run from Vivi to Isangila, a distance of 50 miles, and from Manyanga to Stanley Pool, a further 100 miles. The intervening stretch of 88 miles from Isangila to Manyanga would be built last and pending its completion traffic would be carried by three river

---

[1] *M.P.*, Hutton to Mackinnon, 29 Sept. 1885.   [2] Hird, op. cit., 207–8.
[3] *M.P.*, Hutton to Mackinnon, 4 Dec. 1885.
[4] *M.P.*, Hutton to Mackinnon, 10 Dec. 1885.   [5] Hird, op. cit., 207–8.
[6] *M.P.*, Hutton to Mackinnon, 11 Dec. 1885.
[7] *Strauch, MSS., No. 504*, Leopold to Strauch, 13 Dec. 1885.
[8] *BT31/3579/21948. (B.o.T. records in P.R.O.)*   [9] Ibid., Form E.
[10] Ibid., Articles of Association.

steamers, whilst steamers would also be built to tap trade above Stanley Pool and to connect Vivi with Banana. The line was to be constructed to a gauge of two feet only and 'on the plan of the Ffestiniog line'. (The Ffestiniog Railway had been built to carry slate from Blaenau Ffestiniog to Portmadoc in North Wales. Although under twenty miles long and of narrow gauge it achieved world wide renown in the later nineteenth century by virtue of its general efficiency and the heavy traffic which a unique design of double-boilered locomotive enabled it to carry.)[1] It was estimated that the line could be constructed for £3,000 per mile, and that the whole line of communication from Banana to Stanley Pool and above, including stations, jetties, stores, steamers and barges, and the railway itself could be built for £1,000,000.

The promoters of the company not only hoped to profit, as carriers, from the trade that the railway would open up, but also proposed actively to participate in the economic development of the Congo. For this purpose they sought powers to develop land, 'to acquire the assets of any trading concern, to open trading stations and to carry on trade at any place within the territories of the State or elsewhere, and to carry on mining, banking, or any industrial enterprise, including transport by road, rail or water, and any other commercial undertaking which might be of advantage to the enterprise. . . .' For these purposes an additional £1,000,000 capital would be required.

For the carrying out of these objects the syndicate demanded far-reaching concessions from the Free State Government. It was to provide the lands necessary for the construction of stations and landing places free of all payments and taxes, a strip of land one mile in depth on the south bank of the river from Leopoldville to the upper end of Stanley Pool and not less than 10,000 acres of land for every mile of railway completed and open to traffic. This land was to include all mineral rights and to be free from royalties and taxes. 5,000 out of each 10,000 acres was to adjoin the railway whilst the remainder could be selected by the company at any place or places within the frontiers of the Congo State. In addition the company was to have the first option of occupying or purchasing any other piece of land within the State in the event of its disposal. A transport monopoly

[1] Charles E. Lee, *Narrow Gauge Railways in North Wales* (London, 1945), 6, 51–58, 108–15.

was also stipulated. The company was to have 'the first option of acquiring or undertaking any railway, canal, or road projected or to be made' whilst the State Government was to undertake that the company should carry the whole of its traffic between Vivi and Stanley Pool, and pay for this service a minimum of £10,000 per annum during the first ten years of operation. The octopus-like nature of the company's activities is made especially clear in the right of customs collection it was to be given over the whole length of the river. Moreover, the company would retain 50 per cent. of such revenue after the expenses of collection had been deducted. The Congo State authorities were to lend the company every protection and assistance but in the event of the State being unable adequately to maintain its authority, the company would be empowered to exercise authority and jurisdiction in its own territories.

Leopold was to be honorary president of the company, to be credited with shares to the value of one-twentieth of the paid-up capital, and, with his heirs and successors, to have the right to appoint one director, but it was specifically stated in the prospectus that the company was to be British.[1]

Shortly after this memorandum, or proposals based upon it, had been sent to Brussels, Hutton, Stanley and probably Mackinnon themselves crossed to Brussels for further discussions with Leopold and the authorities of the Free State.[2] The outcome was the signature of a provisional agreement on Christmas Eve, 1885, whereby the syndicate was to form a company for the construction of a line of communication. The company—The Royal Congo State Railway and Navigation Co.—would receive concessions by royal charter, concessions which were based on the syndicate's memorandum but amongst which were a number of changes in the Free State's favour. The company to be formed was to enjoy the first option to construct or acquire any other line of communication for fifty years only; in regard to customs duties the company would receive 40 per cent. and not 50 per cent. and only in respect of export duties if such ever came to be levied, and only to the

[1] *M.P.*, Memorandum of the Congo Railway Syndicate Ltd., n.d. but almost certainly Dec. 1885. It is printed as Appendix B.
[2] *M.P.*, Hutton to Mackinnon, 10 Dec. 1885. *Strauch MSS., Nos. 498 and 512*, Leopold, Minute, n.d., on Strauch to Leopold, 6 Dec. 1885; Leopold to Strauch, 24 Dec. 1885.

extent necessary to make possible a dividend of 6 per cent. on the capital of the line of communication; nothing was said about the collection of customs duties by the company; no mention was made of the clause in the memorandum which stipulated that the Free State should give redress to the company for 'any neglect or maladministration affecting the company by the officials of the Congo State or any person over whom the State shall have jurisdiction'; the State would appoint two directors instead of one; there was no reference to the memorandum's concluding paragraph with its proposal for an agreement between the Congo State and the British Government which would reserve the right of that Government to intervene for the protection of the company in the event of interference by a third Power. Finally two clauses were added, the more important of which stated that no clause of the agreement was to be interpreted in a sense contrary to the Berlin Act, the formal and immediate outcome of the Berlin West Africa Conference. A note appended to the provisional agreement played down the pronounced British emphasis which the scheme had hitherto had, if only by the probably intentional ambiguity of the note's statement on the nationality of the company.[1] The stipulation, also contained in the note, that subscriptions to the £1 million capital up to an amount of £50,000 in each country must first be sought in the fourteen states represented at the Berlin Conference, unsubscribed shares only then being offered in London,[2] would not appear to

[1] One of the four sources for the December agreement, the Van Eetvelde memoranda (f.n. 2 below), speaks of the company being incorporated as a Congo company in the sense, it would appear, of being registered in the Congo State but with (the use of the indefinite article is significant), 'un siège d'administration à Londres comme Société Anglaise'. A second source, a summary of a Free State Government memorandum on the negotiation with the British syndicate (f.n. 2 below), says that the company 'pourrait notamment se constituer d'après les formes de la loi anglaise, quitte à faire approuver ses statuts par le gouvernement congolais.' A third source, the British syndicate's own history of the affair (f.n. 2 below), claims that the agreement stipulated 'that the Company should be empowered by Charter to be established and administered in accordance with the laws of Great Britain'. A fourth source, a German translation of a memorandum by Lambermont (f.n. 2 below), speaks of a 'foreign company'.

[2] *FO84/1753*, Van Eetvelde, Memoranda, n.d., Copies, Encls. in Vivian to F.O., 2 Jan. 1886, Africa No. 2. *M. des A.E.*, A.F. 1–39, Bassompierre, Résumé du Dossier 'Chemin de Fer du Congo', Négociations avec le Syndicat Anglais, Feb. 1900, n.d. *M.P.*, Hutton to Mackinnon, 16 Sept. 1886, Confidential Circular. Lambermont, Memo. on the origin of the Congo Railway, n.d., published in translation in *Aus den Archiven des belgischen Kolonialministeriums*, II (Berlin, 1918), 45–47.

have constituted a material concession by the syndicate—the bulk of the capital could probably have been found only on the London market.

The key to Leopold's reserve towards the syndicate, to his unreadiness to sign any binding undertaking, is not so much the exacting terms propounded by the syndicate—hence, nevertheless, the modifications which he secured—as the fact that he had another iron in the fire. This was the hope, similar to the hope of the previous May, that he might yet raise the money for the Congo railway himself. From mid-November onwards he had been sounding out the possibilities of raising Congo State loans on the Continental money market. The strongest hopes were centred on a French lottery loan and with this project de Brazza was to be associated. He was apparently asked, in Leopold's words, if he would become the 'Lesseps of the Congo railway'. (If successful in this, Leopold told Strauch, de Brazza would be offered an important position in the administration of the Free State which, in turn, would oblige the French Government to make him Governor of the Gaboon.)[1] As the idea of raising money in this way matured in Leopold's mind, he broadened it to include loans in Germany, Austria and Belgium also.[2]

At Christmas 1885 the hope that he might obtain the money for the railway in this way, and thus avoid subjecting himself to the conditions of the syndicate and incipient British domination, was still very much alive. He therefore resolved to reach an agreement with the syndicate, yes, for he could not afford to alienate it in case, in the event, he needed it, but in principle only. As he put the matter in a letter to Strauch of 20 December:

I think that the English will want to sign something tomorrow. We must try to satisfy them (they are our friends), whilst remaining prudent. Perhaps one could sign that one is in agreement in principle, if agreement is in fact established, to give a provisional concession to the syndicate which could be converted, within twelve months, into a concession to a company which we would have to approve.[3]

In fact, discussions delayed the signature of an agreement

[1] *Strauch MSS., Nos. 476, 497, 501, 540*, Leopold to Strauch, 20 Nov., 6 and 11 Dec. 1885, 25 Jan. 1886.
[2] *Strauch MSS., Nos. 475–614*, Leopold–Strauch letters, 20 Nov. 1885–14 July 1886 *passim*.
[3] *Strauch MSS., No. 510*, Leopold to Strauch, 20 Dec. 1885.

until 24 December, and it would appear that Leopold's resolve to temporize was strengthened by the advice of Lambermont and Banning who freely pointed out the disadvantages of certain of the British proposals at a dinner party given by Leopold on the very eve of the day appointed for signature.[1]

For its part, the syndicate approved the Brussels agreement early in January[2] and, according to one of the syndicate's members, at least, 'never for a moment believed that any further serious difficulty would arise'.[3]

By this time a second British consortium had become interested in the building of a Congo railway. This consortium appears to have consisted of manufacturers of railway material and Yorkshire ironmasters who were prepared to unite in an effort to open up the Congo 'by the construction of railway works and other industries'. As early as January 1884 the group had approached Brussels and had been told by Strauch that the *A.I.C.* proposed eventually to build a railway and that he would communicate with the consortium again when the Association was ready to proceed in the matter. With the formation of the syndicate, the consortium entered into full discussions with it, apparently with the aim of obtaining the contract for the actual construction of the line and the provision of locomotives, rolling-stock and other material, but after a number of meetings it was decided that nothing definite could be agreed until the railway company had been formed and had obtained the necessary concessions.[4]

Before the syndicate could proceed further with this task a serious obstacle had to be removed. Not only did Stanley believe, as has been seen, that he no longer enjoyed Leopold's full confidence, but this had also been widely rumoured in the

---

[1] This would seem to be the purport of a portion of Lambermont's memorandum, printed in the original French as a footnote in *Aus den Archiven*, II, 47. It reads: 'Dans une réunion tenue chez le Roi à la suite d'un dîner offert par S.M. la veille du jour fixé pour la signature du contrat, le Baron Lambermont et M. Banning firent resortir les graves inconvénients que ce dernier présentait à leurs yeux. Leurs objections furent longuement discutées et l'on décida finalement que le contrat ne serait pas ratifié. Les négociations entre l'Administration du Congo et le syndicat anglais furent rompues et l'affaire définitivement abandonnée'.

A possible confusion lies in the fact that Lambermont, in this portion of his memorandum, is summarizing the whole course of negotiations from December 1885 to September 1886.

[2] *Strauch MSS., No. 526*, Leopold to Strauch, 8 Jan. 1886. *The Times*, 6 Jan. 1886, 6.
[3] *The Times*, 6 Oct. 1886, 10, letter from W. Towers Smith.
[4] *FO 84/1793*, Baker to F.O., 1 Nov. 1886, and Encl., Nelson to Baker, 30 Oct. 1886.

Press. The consequences of this were not only hurtful to himself personally, Stanley informed Leopold, but were also vitally endangering the syndicate's prospects.

> The principal promoters of it [the railway] are holding aloof and withdrawing their promises. Mr. Hutton is despairing, and urges me to appeal once more to your Majesty to resolve all doubts upon the subject of my present and future relations with the Congo State. Finally, I implore your Majesty to respond to this request in clear and definite language that I may satisfy intending investors in this matter. For the information of your Majesty, I may state that I am expected to declare at the meeting on Wednesday next, how many shares in the railway I would take to demonstrate my confidence in the enterprise. If the answer is at all ambiguous, I must abstain from the meeting, lest I should be involved in loss and litigation.[1]

Reassurance came by return of post in an assertion that Stanley's services were no less esteemed than ever; in the extension of his engagement with the Free State until 1895; and in the conferring of the Grand Cross of the Order of Leopold. The syndicate—and Stanley—were satisfied.[2]

A lesser problem to worry Hutton and Stanley in mid-January was Mackinnon's absence from London and inactivity in the syndicate's business. The explanation was probably indifferent health and other commitments, but Hutton and Stanley were alarmed lest others conclude that he thought less well of the project than formerly.[3]

This last difficulty also appears to have been resolved for, at a meeting of the syndicate on 20 January, Mackinnon accepted appointment to a committee, whose other members were Hutton and Stanley, charged with the preparation of drafts of the prospectus, rules, articles of association and charter of the company. After submission to Sir Travers Twiss, the eminent international lawyer, the draft documents were sent to Brussels at the end of February or beginning of March.[4]

Difficulties then arose. The Congo Government replied on 14 April proposing certain amendments to the drafts, the most important of which alterations concerned the question of

---

[1] Stanley to Leopold, Jan 1886, n.d., quoted in Hird, op. cit., 208–9.
[2] *Strauch MSS.*, *No. 539*, Leopold to Strauch, 25 Jan. 1886. Hird, op. cit., 212–13.
[3] *M.P.*, Stanley to Mackinnon, 14 Jan. 1886.
[4] *M. des A.E.*, *A.F. 1–39*, Bassompierre, Résumé du Dossier 'Ch. de Fer du Congo', Feb. 1900, n.d. *M.P.*, Hutton to Mackinnon, 16 Sept. 1886, Confidential Circular. *The Times*, 21 Jan. 1886, 6, and 25 Sept. 1886, 10, Reports of Syndicate meetings.

the jurisdiction under which the company was to operate. The State Government demanded that any disputes which might arise between it and the company should be settled according to Belgian law until such time as a code of Congo legislation was promulgated. To this proposal the committee of the syndicate returned a firm insistence both that any actions between the Congo State and the company should be brought before British courts, and that the company should be unequivocally regarded as a British registered and based company (*'fût censée exclusivement domiciliée en Angleterre'*—Bassompierre, *Résumé*). In an attempt to resolve this serious difference, and other subsidiary divergences, an English solicitor, Thomas Barclay, was sent to London by the Free State Government in May for further discussions. According to Stanley, Barclay's method of negotiation was to see Hutton and himself separately and say to each—of a contentious clause—'Mr. [the other] agrees to it, and sees no objections', when in fact objections did exist. By the beginning of June, according to the syndicate's statement of the case, Barclay's views were met and a revised form of charter was settled. By Barclay's account, and by the account of *The Times* Brussels correspondent, who appears to have derived his information from official Congo State sources, the revised form of charter represented only the furthest limit of the concessions which the syndicate was prepared to make. In the second half of August the committee of the syndicate agreed to certain minor modifications and also, at the request of Barclay, obtained the endorsement of the syndicate as a whole of the position it had taken up. But the negotiations ended in failure. On 12 September 1886 the Free State authorities informed the syndicate that acceptance of the draft charter proposed by the syndicate would compromise the sovereignty of the Congo State, whilst certain of the terms infringed the Berlin Act. This infringement lay in the fact that they constituted a veritable monopoly.

It only remained for the syndicate to go into liquidation.[1] What had gone wrong?

[1] *M. des A.E., A.F. 1–39*, Bassompierre, Résumé du Dossier 'Ch. de Fer du Congo', Feb. 1900, n.d., *M.P.*, Hutton to Mackinnon, 16 Sept. 1886, Confidential Circular. Stanley to Mackinnon, 21 May 1886. *The Times*, 25 Sept. 1886, 10, Report of Syndicate meeting; 2 Oct. 1886, 7, letter from Barclay; 4 Oct. 1886, 6, Brussels Correspondent.

Dr. Towers Smith, one of the syndicate, immediately alleged bad faith in a letter to *The Times* of 6 October,[1] and his imputation might appear to be justified by the immediate sequel to the rupture of the negotiations in the formation in October by Captain Thys, a Belgian Army officer, of a Belgian syndicate which eventually obtained the concession to build the Congo railway.[2] The existence of this alternative may have influenced the Free State Government, but only in the closing stages of the negotiations. On 25 August, Sanford specifically told Mackinnon that Leopold did not then know of Thys' scheme, though he understood that it would be submitted to the king in the following week.[3] Moreover by this time the negotiations were already in difficulties and Leopold, in a note of mid-July, had already signified his intention of making clear to Mackinnon that it would be very difficult for the Free State to accept the syndicate's conditions.[4] There was not, therefore, double-dealing, as Towers Smith, and subsequently others, alleged, whereby negotiations with the syndicate were continued whilst an agreement with the Thys group was perfected.

On the other hand, Belgian opposition to such potentially important concessions going to foreigners, which was also the mainspring of Thys' scheme, played a larger part in the breakdown. On 10 July Van Eetvelde told Vivian, the British minister, that if the negotiations with the syndicate failed, the concessions would be offered to Belgian capitalists who had lately shown jealousy at the offer of them to foreigners.[5] Vivian himself, after the breakdown of negotiations and the inception of Thys' scheme, commented:

... it is possible that when the Congo Administration became aware of the jealousy which the concession of the construction of the railway to foreigners had aroused here, they were glad of a reasonable pretext to offer it to a Belgian Company.[6]

[1] *The Times*, 6 Oct. 1886, 10, letter from Towers Smith. See also *The Times*, 15 Oct., 6, and 29 Oct., 4, letters from Towers Smith.
[2] For this matter see R. J. Cornet, *La Bataille du Rail* (Brussels, 1947).
[3] *M.P.*, Sanford to Mackinnon, 25 Aug. 1886. Lambermont, in his rather general memorandum on the origins of the Congo railway, after speaking of the breaking off of negotiations with the British syndicate, insists: 'Nunmehr erst dachte man an die Gründung einer belgischen Gesellschaft zum Bau der geplanten Verbindung.' (Lambermont, *Aus den Archiven*, II, 47).
[4] *Strauch MSS.*, No. 616, Leopold, note, n.d. but clearly mid-July, on Strauch to Leopold, 15 July 1886.
[5] *FO84/1753*, Vivian to F.O., 10 July 1886, Africa No. 17.
[6] *FO84/1753*, Vivian to F.O., 14 Oct. 1886, Africa No. 31.

It is, however, significant that it is in July, only after the negotiations had run into serious difficulties, that there is talk of offering the concessions to Belgian capitalists, whereas as early as December 1885 Leopold was aware of—indeed had expected—a Belgian outcry against dealings with a foreign syndicate, had not then been deflected by it,[1] and had asserted in a private note at the end of March that it was the clear interest of the Free State that the negotiations with the British syndicate should be successful (*'notre intérêt évident est de faire réussir la compagnie anglaise'*).[2] The effect of the Belgian opposition appears to have been this. In order to meet it, Leopold, through Barclay during the May discussions, asked as a personal favour that the railway company engage to buy the rails for the line in Belgium. To this the committee replied that it was a matter for the contractors.[3] At this reply, in Stanley's words, 'Barclay seemed to be stunned.' There would appear to be much truth in Stanley's further comment in the same letter: 'I fancy this was the last straw that broke the Camel's back.'[4]

If it is true that Belgian opposition had such an influence, and that the rejection of Leopold's request was decisive, the very metaphor which Stanley used conveys a yet deeper truth, though he did not intend it in quite this sense. It was at bottom the sheer weight, the sheer comprehensiveness of the syndicate's demands that was the cause of failure.

One need not treat too seriously the Free State's citation of the obligations of the Berlin Act as a ground for rejecting the syndicate's terms. After all, although Travers Twiss had not given a written opinion as such on the compatibility of the syndicate's February draft with the Berlin Act, that draft, in Hutton's words, 'actually went to Sir Travers Twiss and was settled by him'[5]—and Twiss was one of the leading authorities of his day on international law. On the other hand, the openly stated objection of the Free State that the privileged legal position which the syndicate claimed for the future company would be incompatible with the State's sovereign rights was as real a ground for the termination of negotiations as the fear

---

[1] *Strauch MSS., Nos. 518 and 522*, Leopold to Strauch, 28 and 30 Dec. 1885.
[2] *Strauch MSS., No. 578*, Leopold to Strauch, 26 Mar. 1886.
[3] *M.P.*, Stanley to Mackinnon, 21 May and 18 Sept. 1886.
[4] *M.P.*, Stanley to Mackinnon, 18 Sept. 1886.
[5] *The Times*, 25 Sept. 1886, 10, Report of Syndicate meeting.

of a British monopoly of the commerce and industry of the new state. The memoranda both of Bassompierre and Lambermont,[1] and a private letter of Sanford to Mackinnon make this abundantly clear. Sanford's letter, written back in June 1886, put the point succinctly. Sanford was reporting a conversation he had had with Leopold earlier that same day.

He said it was quite impossible that the State, as a State, submitted itself to the British courts, and it would be a precedent for other States, already likely to be jealous of this quasi (if not real) monopoly in favour of British subjects.[2]

The Congo Administration's case is entirely understandable. The minimum terms on which the syndicate was prepared to settle by the summer of 1886 included, as far as can be gathered: the registration of the proposed company as a British company; its proceedings to be subject to British law; very considerable land and mineral concessions, and pre-emptive rights; virtual immunity from taxes and royalties; a virtual transport monopoly and guaranteed minimum revenue; a guaranteed dividend.

It is significant that the terms later agreed with the Thys group were much less generous—the concession was to last ninety-nine years only, the grant of land per length of completed line was smaller, the company was to have no monopoly of Free State traffic and no preferential right to build other lines of communication, to name but some differences.[3] In short, if the syndicate's proposals had been accepted, the proposed company would have enjoyed such powers and immunities that the Congo Free State would certainly have become a British sphere of influence, and might well have become a British possession in everything but name.

With the final rejection of the syndicate's proposals, the consortium which had hoped to act through the syndicate made a direct offer to Brussels to survey a route, free of charge, in return for a first option to build the line,[4] but by that time

[1] *M. des A.E., A.F. 1–39*, Bassompierre, Résumé du Dossier 'Ch. de Fer du Congo', Feb. 1900, n.d. *Aus den Archiven*, II, 47. See also *FO84/1753*, Vivian to F.O., 30 Oct. 1886, Africa No. 33.
[2] *M.P.*, Sanford to Mackinnon, 4 June 1886.
[3] *FO84/1830*, Vivian to F.O., 8 Jan. 1887, Africa No. 4 and Encl, *Moniteur Belge*, 4 Jan. 1887, Supplement. See also *The Times*, 19 Oct. 1886, 7.
[4] *FO84/1793*, Baker to F.O., 1 Nov. 1886 and Encls., Baker to Strauch, 2 Oct. 1886, Copy, and Baker to Administrator-General of Finance Dept. of Free State Govt., 29 Oct. 1886, Copy.

Thys' scheme had been put up to Leopold and accepted.

The attempt of Mackinnon, Hutton and Stanley to make the Congo British through the promotion of a monopolistic railway and trading company had failed. In the light of this attempt the activities of Mackinnon and Hutton between 1879 and 1886 stand out as necessary steps towards a final goal. The assistance to Leopold in his pioneering work on the Congo, the energies devoted to arousing an agitation against the Anglo-Portuguese treaty, the subsequent campaign to procure British recognition of the International Association—all stemmed from the hope, given point by the promises of 1879, of making the Congo a large new sphere for British commercial and industrial enterprise, and all pointed to a railway and trading concession as the consummation of this hope.

That in 1878 Stanley also entertained such a hope is well known. That he never lost sight of it may appear more surprising, but there is evidence which, in the present writer's view, suggests just this. After he had first traced the course of the Congo to the sea, Stanley, with that strong streak of idealism which was an important element in his character, sought to bring civilization to the interior of Africa. 'The prime force to which he looked', says Dorothy Stanley, 'was the natural, legitimate desire for gain, by ways of traffic; the African and the European both eager for the exchanges which should be for the good of both. With this, he counted on the scientific curiosity, and the philanthropic zeal, of the civilized world to assist the work.' It was to England and Englishmen that he looked to take the lead.[1]

In the spring of 1878, as numerous entries in his Journal apparently show, he had lost no opportunity, in a period of crowded engagements, of pressing on men of influence in the world of finance, the Press, philanthropy and science the opportunity which the Congo offered to the enterprise of Great Britain. But although he secured the promise of wholehearted support from a number of influential people, including the Duke of Sutherland, the Baron Ferdinand de Rothschild and the Baroness Burdett-Coutts, it became clear by early summer that he was making little real headway. In consequence, in July, whilst in Paris, he had further discussions

[1] H. M. Stanley, *Autobiography* (London, 1909), 333-4.

with Baron Greindl, Leopold's representative, Leopold having already, as soon as he had set foot in Europe, invited him to take command of a great venture for the opening up of Africa under the aegis of the *A.I.A*. But before committing himself to service under Leopold, so strongly did Stanley feel, that he made one further attempt to arouse Englishmen to what he conceived to be their destiny. This time he concentrated on the commercial world, giving thirty lectures in important centres of commerce and industry, and devoting special attention to Liverpool and Manchester, trying to rouse his audience 'to adopt early means to secure the Congo basin for England'. But again he met failure. It was only then that he threw in his lot with Leopold and assisted in the formation of the *Comité d'Etudes du Haut Congo*.[1]

But this step is not to be taken as the assumption of the position of a mere executive in an organization, nor did it indicate that thenceforth Stanley was to be the unqualified supporter of Leopold's African work regardless of the direction it took. His own assessment of the relationship is highly significant:

I am devoured with a desire to do something for Africa, and have found in King Leopold one who not only possesses the means but the will to assist . . . Leopold's unmeasured munificence, his resolution and tenacity of purpose to prosecute our project—strikes me as a marvellous providential interposition. If my wishes had been prayers that God would raise such a man to assist me in the development of Africa, I could not be more secretly surprised at having found him. While coming down the Congo I dreamed of some Rothschild undertaking the civilisation of the Congo basin and entrusting me with the task . . . saying, 'There is the money you need. Go and fulfil your wish.'[2]

These are the words of a man who saw in Leopold a munificent benefactor, the provider of the means required for

---

[1] Hird, op. cit., 169–71. Stanley, *Autobiography*, 333–4. The scanty Press references to Stanley's campaign need not lead to the conclusion that Stanley did not conduct it with great energy. The private approaches would naturally not command Press notices, and *The Times*, at any rate, showed itself perfectly familiar with Stanley's advocacy that England should possess herself of the Congo. It is perhaps a little surprising that his lecture tour in the autumn of 1878 did not command more attention in the Press. Nevertheless a correspondent writing to the *Manchester Guardian* in October 1884 could recall Stanley's unsuccessful visit to Manchester in 1878. (*The Times*, 30 Nov. 1877, 9, leader and 31 Jan. 1878, 3–4, leader. *Manchester Guardian*, 23 Oct. 1884, 4, letter from Herbert Birch.)

[2] Stanley, Extract from Journal(?), Winter, 1882, n.d., quoted in Hird, op. cit., 187–8.

Stanley to fulfil his consuming desire 'to do something for Africa', a collaborator rather than a master. To serve Leopold —and he served him as no other man did—was not to debar Stanley from cherishing the hope that the Congo venture would provide, above all, large openings for British commerce and influence.

Viewed in the light of these attitudes, Stanley's controversial letter to Johnston of July 1883 in which he proposed not only that Britain herself should take possession of the Lower Congo rather than allow it to pass to Portugal, but also envisaged some future extension of British sovereignty to the Upper Congo, becomes more comprehensible. At a time when the work and very existence of the *A.I.C.* were threatened by France and Portugal, what more natural than that he should revive his hopes of Britain, not, indeed, as a usurper of the *A.I.C.* but, as Professor Stengers has argued, as the power which would save everything, which would save Leopold himself and which would enable his plans to develop henceforth on non-political lines and protected from the greed of others.[1] A marginal influence on Stanley at this time may well have been a pessissism about the *A.I.C.*'s prospects born of a generally unfavourable impression of the Belgian officers seconded to the Congo—unfavourable, that is, as far as their suitability for the work in hand was concerned.[2]

Such an interpretation of Stanley's atitude in 1883 is quite

[1] *Johnston Papers*, Stanley to Johnston, 23 July 1883. J. Stengers, 'Stanley, Léopold II et l'Angleterre', *Le Flambeau*, No. 4, 1954, 383–5. For a discussion of this episode see also Roland Oliver, *Sir Harry Johnston and the Scramble for Africa* (London, 1957), 42–45. For further evidence that Stanley envisaged the Inner Congo coming under British protection, see H. H. Johnston, *The Story of My Life* (London, 1923), 117, 123. Johnston had visited Stanley on the Congo earlier in 1883 and, on the latter page, he wrote, 'I certainly derived the impression from our intercourse that Stanley intended the Inner Congo basin to come under British Protection'. He added, 'What role he mentally assigned to King Leopold, I cannot say.' See also *FO84/1807*, Stanley to Hutton, 11 July 1883, forwarded to F.O., 25 Sept. 1883. Extracts from the letter to Johnston are printed as Appendix C. It is also printed in Oliver, op. cit., 42–45. It is possible that it is to this episode that some enigmatic words written by Strauch to A. J. Wauters in 1911 refer: 'Je devrais aussi vous parler des tentatives de trahison de Stanley, tentatives qui n'echouèrent que par le refus des Etats-Unis et de l'Angleterre' (*Strauch MSS.*, No. 769, Strauch to Wauters, 1 May, 1911). What was treason from the Free State's, or at least, Strauch's point of view, was no such thing from Stanley's. The reference to the United States is obscure. Does it suggest that Stanley, possibly some time in 1883, also cast the U.S. in the role of protector of the *A.I.C.* and Upper Congo?

[2] For indications of this unfavourable impression see *Document Notte, Stanley au Congo 1879–1884*, passim, and A. Maurice, *Stanley, Lettres Inédites* (Brussels, 1955), passim.

compatible with the considerable exertions he made on behalf of international recognition of the *A.I.C.* before and during the Berlin Conference. By the summer of 1884 Leopold had already secured the recognition of France and the United States and had the assurance of Germany's support. There was thus a good chance of completing that international recognition of the *A.I.C.*, the absence of which had been the essential cause of his advocacy of a British Protectorate over the Inner Congo in his conversations with, and letter to Johnston.

After the Conference it appears to have been Stanley who took the initiative in urging an early start on the construction of the railway round the cataracts[1] which he had long regarded as vital. What, finally, could be more expected, what more natural, than that Stanley should have played a prominent part in seeking to obtain through the railway syndicate a large new field for British enterprise? That it was not to be secured through the extension of British sovereignty was not vital: it might still be obtained through exclusive concessions.

In short, Stanley's relationship with Leopold was never one of complete subordination, and could scarcely be expected to be. As the pioneer who traced the course of the Congo to the sea, as the engineer who linked the lower and upper rivers, as the political agent who established the International Association on the banks of the Congo as far up as Stanley Pool, he would naturally have a proprietary interest in the work. Leopold, Stanley valued as a munificent benefactor: he was too much involved in the king's Congo venture to be a mere unquestioning servant. His English affections, no less, prevented a complete subordination to Leopold. Confronted with a refusal to take in hand his child, the Congo, Stanley never lost sight of the hope that Britain might still profit from it. On one notable occasion, when the whole future of the Association looked insecure, he expressed the hope that she would eventually intervene more openly. When encouragement came for the flotation of a Congo railway company, which he had always regarded as the key to the riches of Central Africa, he worked heart and soul to obtain this prize for British enterprise.

It may be that Stanley's exertions on behalf of the Congo Railway Syndicate were the stronger because of a simultaneous

[1] Hird, op. cit., 205.

cooling of his relations with Leopold. It has already been noticed that during the early summer of 1885 Stanley had begun to feel that he no longer enjoyed the king's full confidence. This feeling had first taken root at the end of May or in early June 1885 and was the result of Leopold's complete silence on the question of Stanley's return to Africa. Stanley had supposed that a further spell of work on the Congo would begin on, or shortly after 1 June for that had been the substance of the new contract he had signed with Leopold in November 1884. But no instructions came, and when Stanley raised the matter he received only vague and indefinite replies. Moreover the previous flow of letters from Brussels dried up for a time, at least, whilst reports appeared in certain Continental newspapers that he had incurred Leopold's disfavour.[1] It has been seen, also, that this was the very time when Brussels appeared to be dragging its feet in the preliminary discussions about the railway.[2] Matters improved a little in September when Leopold's British sympathizers were told to go ahead with their proposal for a railway whilst at the same time Stanley's opinion again came to be asked on matters of Congo administration.[3] But in November Stanley, in the privacy of a note to Mackinnon, is found expressing the fear that the king would discard him on account, he feared, of the 'weak-stomached' of his own people[4]—presumably a reference to the various allegations of Stanley's harsh and brutal treatment of Africans which had from time to time been made. The hope which Stanley appears to have entertained that an interview with the king would set everything right was disappointed when, at the time of the Brussels discussions on the syndicate's proposals in December, no mention was made of Stanley's personal position.[5] It has been seen that in January 1886 Stanley had to demand some clear manifestation of Leopold's continued confidence. When this was given, Stanley expressed himself to the king, at least, as completely satisfied[6] and in the following April, though he laments the continued ignorance about his future in which he is kept, his complaint is in a minor key.[7]

[1] Hird, op. cit., 199, 204–7.   [2] See pp. 189–90 above.
[3] Hird, op. cit., 207.   [4] M.P., Stanley to Mackinnon, 4 Nov. 1885.
[5] Strauch MSS., No. 512, Leopold to Strauch, 24 Dec. 1885.
[6] Strauch MSS., No. 539, Leopold to Strauch, 25 Jan. 1886.
[7] M.P., Stanley to Mackinnon, 6 Apr. 1886.

But through the summer of 1886 still no word came of future employment. Understandably, therefore, the news of the final rejection of the syndicate's proposals brought all Stanley's smouldering resentment to a head. His first comment to Mackinnon, however, was restrained. He contented himself with the observation that 'every day the King is closing the Congo against the English and seems resolved to make it more and more Belgian'. 'This is another fine scheme of mine which has become exploded', he added, and went on to paint a gloomy picture of the immediate commercial prospects of the Congo.[1] Five days later his resentment boiled over. Leopold had kept him 'on the quiver of expectation' for sixteen months and for a part of this time he had been made doubly unhappy by a difficult passage in his relations with his future wife. After elaborating on these themes, Stanley broke out:

It has not been his money I wanted [he was receiving £1,000 a year from Leopold, a not ungenerous sum], but simply fair treatment, common honesty between man and man.

I have been thus frank with you that you may understand the relief I feel that all this is now at an end. I propose to use my life to more purpose if I can than to be waiting for the good will or the decision of another. If the King needs me he can telegraph to me. If not I propose to go on indifferent to what he does until he shall be pleased to think it necessary to remind me that he has authority over me.[2]

This was no passing explosion—three and a half years later Stanley could dwell upon Leopold's ingratitude, as he termed it, in 1885–6.[3] For Stanley, September 1886 was a watershed in his relations with Leopold, and the influence of the new, more distant relationship was to be felt within a matter of months. At the close of 1886 Stanley's last African expedition was set on foot. On it, he was required to serve two masters, Leopold and Mackinnon, and Stanley was in no doubt where his first loyalty lay.

In Hutton's case, September 1886 by no means brought a

[1] *M.P.*, Stanley to Mackinnon, 18 Sept. 1886. The writer went on to add, 'This is what I was afraid of and would put no money in it.' This remark indicates that fears had been growing for some time, and the attitude it expressed perhaps constitutes the element of truth in the view, expressed once by Leopold and once by Sanford, that the Syndicate by June–July 1886 had become lukewarm. (*M.P.*, Sanford to Mackinnon, 4 June 1886. *Strauch MSS.*, *No. 616*, Strauch to Leopold, 15 July 1886.)
[2] *M.P.*, Stanley to Mackinnon, 23 Sept. 1886.
[3] *M.P.*, Stanley to Mackinnon, 19 Jan. 1890.

rupture, though one senses that a certain reserve was thenceforth present in his attitude to the Free State. When accepting, with regret, the Free State's termination of negotiations in September 1886, he had gone on to express his readiness to share in any future combination formed for the construction of the Congo railway.[1] But when, a few months later, Strauch and Thys invited Hutton both to sound out the other members of the syndicate and himself to subscribe to the new company which it was proposed to form, he told Mackinnon that he declined to call a meeting but would only circularize the members and would not himself subscribe more than five or six thousand francs (£200–£240). For a man of his means this was little more than a token subscription. Moreover, it is significant that he went on to remind Mackinnon that under the terms under which foreign participation in the *Comité d'Etudes du Haut Congo* had been terminated in 1879, they were each entitled to 20,000 francs worth of fully paid-up shares in the company now being formed.[2]

Despite the strain on Mackinnon's relationship with Leopold, caused by the breakdown of the concession negotiations, its even tenor was not disturbed. The volume of the communications Mackinnon received from Strauch, Sanford and Lambert, his main Brussels correspondents—as they survive in the *Mackinnon Papers*—certainly diminished markedly after this date, but in content they remained more than cordial, whilst in the summer of 1888 there is elsewhere a record of the king being about to embark for a two to three week trip on Mackinnon's yacht.[3] Mackinnon did not content himself with the maintenance of good relations with Leopold and the Congo Free State; he also made a significant contribution to the economic development of the new state. When the *Compagnie du Chemin de Fer du Congo* eventually came to be formed in 1889, the British contribution of 5,000,000 francs (£200,000) was in the name of 'MM. William Mackinnon and consorts'. Moreover, the Mackinnon group's holding was the largest single block of shares, save for the Belgian Government's holding of 10,000,000 francs, of the 25,000,000 francs capital. This

[1] *M. des A.E., A.F. 1–39*, Bassompierre, Résumé du Dossier 'Ch. de Fer du Congo', Feb. 1900, n.d.
[2] *M.P.*, Hutton to Mackinnon, 14 Feb. 1887.
[3] *Lambermont MSS., Vol. 1885–8, No. 316*, Leopold to Lambermont, 5 Aug. 1888.

contribution carried Mackinnon and another share-holder and business associate, the bank chairman Robert Ryrie, to seats on the Board of Directors.[1] Mackinnon also subscribed 20,000 francs (£800) to the Katanga Company, a company of whose capital British investors subscribed about 28·5 per cent.,[2] and of whose Board of Directors another of Leopold's British sympathizers, Kirk, became a member in 1891.[3] It is clear that an important slice of British investment in the Congo Free State between 1886 and 1908 was initially made, or inspired by Mackinnon. The only other significant British contribution was that of Robert Williams and Tanganyika Concessions Ltd. which came to have important interests, mainly in Katanga.[4]

But despite its importance, investment of this kind was of a different order to that of which Leopold's British sympathizers must have been thinking in the years after 1878-9, and to that envisaged by the Congo Railway Syndicate. The hope that the vast basin of the Congo would become a new preserve for British industry, British capital and British enterprise died with the receipt of the Free State Government's letter to Hutton of 12 September 1886.

*   *   *

It only remains to speak of two notable cases of co-operation between Mackinnon and Leopold—the Emin Pasha Relief Expedition of 1886-9 and the Mackinnon treaty of 1890.

[1] H. Waltz, *Das Konzessionswesen im Belgischen Congo* (Jena, 1917), I, 526, II, 812. *FO84/1946, Mouvement Géographique*, 11 Aug. 1889, Encl. in Vivian to F.O., 12 Aug. 1889, Africa No. 66.
[2] Waltz, op. cit., II, 128.
[3] *L'Etoile Belge*, 17 Apr. 1891.
[4] Waltz, op. cit., I, 442 ff., 528 ff. *passim* and II, 646 ff. The British interest in A.B.I.R. (Anglo-Belgian India Rubber Co.) was more apparent than real. Though founded by Colonel North, an Englishman, in 1892, and though almost all its capital was held in his name, he was a 'dummy' for Leopold himself. (Waltz, op. cit., I, 40, 54.)

CHAPTER X

AFTERMATH AND CONCLUSIONS

It has been noticed that during the second half of 1879 Mackinnon's interest turned from East Africa to the Congo. Did Mackinnon, then, display no independent interest in East Africa in the period when he was so closely involved with Leopold?

A minimal interest there always was; the British India Company continued to enjoy the Zanzibar mail contract and subsidy, and Mackinnon could not but be interested in the progress of East African trade and in the political and other considerations which influenced its development. But for East Africa 1879–84 were quiet years and with the disappointments of 1878 and 1879 still in his mind, and with his energies much engaged over the Congo, not to mention his numerous other activities, it is scarcely surprising that there is no evidence of active interest in the affairs of East Africa in this period. Hutton, similarly involved in Congo and other matters, took the same negative attitude. A radical change in the situation at Zanzibar came towards the close of 1884, and brought to an end the period when Great Britain could assert her paramountcy on the East African coast through the Sultan. With the German irruption into East Africa came the possibility of the closure to Britain of a territory to which she had traditionally claimed a pre-emptive right of access. Here, surely, was cause for alarm and occasion of positive action.

Hutton now showed himself aware of what was at stake and, after initial coldness[1] and for some time with less enthusiasm, so did Mackinnon. They took up a scheme of Holmwood, the Zanzibar vice-consul and an enthusiast for empire, which would serve as a check on the more extreme German ambitions. The scheme provided for the creation of a British company which would, on the broad lines of the 1877–8 attempt, obtain the concessions necessary for the construction of a port at Tanga and the building of a railway inland to Mt. Kilimanjaro,

[1] Johnston, *Life*, 149.

and thus counteract German activities in that area. A subsequent phase might see the extension of the railway so as to link up with steamers on the Lakes and Upper Nile. For this project Hutton and Mackinnon asked official support in April 1885.[1] Discussions at the Foreign Office followed but it soon became clear that the promoters wanted their concession to be ' "guaranteed by the British Government" '.[2] When the generally accepted canons governing African policy, and the Foreign Office's reluctance to antagonize Germany at this time are remembered, it is scarcely surprising that official support of this kind was not forthcoming.[3] Moreover by July, Hutton reported, Mackinnon had become lukewarm about the whole affair.[4]

When Salisbury took office in June 1885 he was prepared to adopt a slightly more positive policy. He obtained German acceptance of a proposal that rival Anglo-German claims in East Africa be submitted to a boundary commission and, when German treaty-making continued unabated, he approved Anderson's 'private' advice to Johnston, on whose treaties with native chiefs the British claims in the Kilimanjaro area rested, that he should cede those claims to Hutton. Then in March 1886 the Foreign Office sanctioned an expedition by the agents of Hutton and Mackinnon to Kilimanjaro to confirm and reinforce the British claim.[5]

In this last stage, Mackinnon's role was probably to place at Hutton's disposal the facilities which Smith, Mackenzie & Co. could command at Zanzibar, rather than to take the initiative. Timidity on Mackinnon's part is also seen in another means he adopted at this time to protect British interests in East Africa—private negotiations with Dr. Karl Peters, the initiator of German colonial enterprise in East Africa, himself. Mackinnon's aim in these talks was to obtain Peters' recognition of British claims over some part of East Africa. Alternatively, the possibility of a merger of Anglo-German interests in East Africa was discussed. But the only merger which Peters seems to have been ready to consider involved the subordination of

[1] Coupland, 425–7. De Kiewiet, op. cit., 66–68.
[2] Quoted in Coupland, op. cit., 428.
[3] Coupland, op. cit., 428. De Kiewiet, op. cit., 68.
[4] Coupland, op. cit., 428–9.
[5] De Kiewiet, op. cit., 69–71. See also Coupland, op. cit., 469–70.

British interests to those of the German East Africa Company, and the discussions came to nothing.[1]

From being stone-cold about East Africa in the early spring of 1885, Mackinnon had become mildly interested, but no more. The essential characteristic of his attitude was insistence that there be a firm basis for any East African project before he would embark upon it. Hence the demand in the spring and early summer of 1885 that the concessionaires' intended activities in the Kilimanjaro area be guaranteed by the British Government; hence the conversations with Peters and the attempt to obtain German recognition of a belt of British territory. In the event Mackinnon never did move in East Africa without what he regarded as reasonable assurances for the security of his operations, but his interest was quickened, early in October 1886, by news of the position of Emin Pasha in Equatorial Africa.

Emin Pasha, born in Silesia as Edouard Schnitzer, had been one of Gordon's lieutenants. When Egyptian power in the Sudan collapsed with the fall of Khartoum, he alone had successfully defended himself against the Mahdi. Withdrawing to the southern portion of the Equatorial Province he was beyond the Mahdi's reach and, with a miscellaneous following of Egyptian and Sudanese troops, their wives and dependents, existed quite tolerably on the natural resources of the region. Whether he could continue to do so indefinitely was another matter and, indeed, news that he was increasingly short of certain supplies from time to time filtered through to Europe.

When more urgent news of Emin's plight reached England at the beginning of October 1886, his case attracted a certain amount of public interest—the last of Gordon's lieutenants must not be left to the same fate as had overtaken Gordon himself—and largely for this reason, no doubt, the Government considered whether official action should be taken to carry

[1] *FO84/1783*, Mackinnon to F.O., 9 Apr. 1886. *FO84/1790*, Peters, Report on exchange of views with Mackinnon, 14 Aug. 1886, and Mackinnon's revisions, n.d., communicated to F.O., 18 Sept. 1886. *FO84/1794*, Mackinnon to Peters, n.d., Draft, Encl. 3 in Mackinnon to Anderson, 22 Nov. 1886. De Kiewiet, op. cit., 72. A factor in the termination of negotiations was undoubtedly the conclusion of the Anglo-German East African boundary agreement with gave Mackinnon the security for which he had been negotiating with Peters. See *M.P.*, Kirk to Mackinnon, 30 Oct. 1886: 'It is important for you on meeting Peters to know that a definite settlement has been come to and he cannot modify it now. . . .'

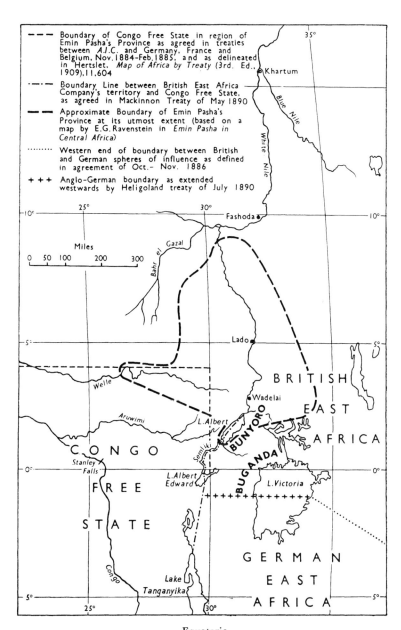

Equatoria

AFTERMATH AND CONCLUSIONS 213

relief to Emin. Decisive was a minute of Salisbury's. An armed expedition was out of the question. It would be too expensive and would involve a close alliance with the Sultan of Zanzibar (which would offend Bismarck). A diplomatic mission, on the other hand, might run into trouble in faction-torn Uganda and might therefore have to be rescued or avenged. Salisbury's conclusion—and it must be remembered that the decision to remain permanently in Egypt had not yet been taken—was against official action. Rather did he express the view that 'the Germans should be placed in possession of our information. It is really their business if Emin is a German.'[1]

Mackinnon and Hutton certainly took a more positive line than Salisbury. Early in October they sounded Stanley on the possibility of conveying relief to Emin, and Stanley had agreed in principle to lead an expedition.[2] At this stage, according to Stanley, Mackinnon and Hutton envisaged only the carriage of ammunition to Emin, believing that this would enable him to maintain himself in Equatoria.[3] What seems to have been lacking was much sense of urgency.[4] Indeed, in Mackinnon's mind, a desire to send relief to Emin and perhaps to use the opportunity to further the creation of a politico-commercial enterprise in East Africa ran counter to a reluctance to engage in an East African scheme. 'I quite understand *your unwillingness* (my italics) to embark on an East African concern. There is little to encourage you. . . .' wrote Kirk on 11 October.[5] This unwillingness stemmed, Mackinnon's attitude over the previous eighteen months suggests, from an unreadiness to act without reasonable security. It is therefore significant that at the end of October a development took place which gave, or appeared to give, the desired security, whilst at the same time a yet more urgent request for help was received from Emin.[6] In the weeks that followed, Mackinnon, with the partial backing of Hutton, acted with much more urgency, and

[1] *FO84/1775*, Salisbury, Minute, Oct. 1886, n.d.
[2] H. M. Stanley, *Darkest Africa* (London, 1890), I, 31–33.
[3] Stanley, *Darkest Africa*, I, 31.
[4] Stanley, *Darkest Africa*, I, 32. In a telegram to Mackinnon of 13 Dec. 1886, accepting the call to return from America to lead the expedition, Stanley said, 'It is only one months delay after all' (ibid., I, 34), thereby implying that the expedition only came to be seriously contemplated in mid-November.
[5] *M.P.*, Kirk to Mackinnon, 11 Oct. 1886.
[6] G. Schweitzer, *Life and Work of Emin Pasha* (London, 1898), I, xxii.

it seems probable that the events of this period—the preparation of an Emin Pasha Relief Expedition, the decision to use it to undertake important preliminary work for a concession company, and the simultaneous re-opening with the Sultan of Zanzibar, through the leader of the expedition, of negotiations for concessions—were all sparked off by Emin's plea, and fundamentally inspired by the sense of security conferred by the Anglo-German boundary agreement of October–November 1886. By this agreement, the fruit of the Salisbury-inspired boundary commission, the authority of the Sultan of Zanzibar was confirmed over the islands, along the coast to a depth of ten miles and over five ports on the Benadir coast to the north. The country between the Rovuma River to the south and, roughly, the Tana River to the north was, apart from the Sultan's coastal strip, to be divided into British and German spheres of influence by a line running from Vanga, some fifty miles south of Mombasa, to the point where the first degree of south latitude intersects the eastern shore of Lake Victoria Nyanza, but skirting the northern base of Mt. Kilimanjaro. Germany's was the southern sphere, Britain's the northern.[1]

Mackinnon received early news of the agreement from his friend Kirk who, as an authority on Eastern Africa, had participated in the discussions on the boundary commission's report. The manner of Kirk's portrayal of the agreement is important for he presented it not only as conferring the security of tenure on which Mackinnon had been so insistent, but also as nothing less than a golden opportunity, provided Mackinnon did not delay.

... we are to have the free run so far as Germany is concerned between that [Vanga] and the River Tana. Germany will give no protectorates inside that zone, which strikes north-west.

Thus we have Mombasa under the Sultan and a free run inland to the Lake, etc., but not Kilimanjaro. We have the best of any line for a rail if ever one is made. We also have the Equatorial Province now held by the brave Emin Bey well governed and quiet to this day. Germany will rent Dar Salam from the Sultan which arrangement we may make at Mombasa. This is the outline of the scheme and you will see we have an opening as good as any.[2]

Again seven days later:

[1] E. Hertslet, *The Map of Africa by Treaty* (London, 1894), II, 615–21, No. 123. Coupland, op. cit., 474–5.
[2] *M.P.*, Kirk to Mackinnon, 30 Oct. 1886.

Our hands are free and we hold the situation if we act at once [probably a reference to the fact that the western boundaries of the two spheres of influence were in the air, thus leaving the position of the lakes region undetermined]. . . . Stanley will be the best agent. . . .[1]

And at about the same time:

[The Germans] now fully understand they have lost what is undoubtedly the best route to the Lake and the Upper Nile and also the most promising district as well as the best shore line with the port of Mombasa.[2]

Kirk then, who as late as 11 October had approved Mackinnon's unwillingness 'to embark on an East African concern', was now convinced that the events of the end of October had provided a new opportunity. This was, it would seem, the carrying of relief to Emin and at the same time the opening up of a permanent route to Lake Victoria and the Upper Nile, free, for the moment at least, of fear of German interference. It is not difficult to believe that the eventual aim of this activity was to be the opening up of the region to British commercial enterprise.

That Mackinnon shared Kirk's vision is strongly suggested by the fact that from November onwards he applied himself with great energy to the preparation of a relief expedition whose purpose was to be something more than the fulfilment of a humanitarian desire to carry help to Emin. From the early or middle part of the month, Mackinnon, with Hutton, urged upon the Foreign Office that the British Government countenance and give unofficial support to a relief expedition.[3] The Cabinet was still not prepared to assume responsibility for an expedition,[4] nor was it asked to do so, but the British Government prevailed upon the Egyptian Government to grant £10,000 in order finally to discharge its responsibility to Emin.[5] It was not difficult to raise another £11,500,[6] and by the end of

[1] *M.P.*, Kirk to Mackinnon, 6 Nov. 1886, Private.
[2] *M.P.*, Kirk to Mackinnon, n.d., but by internal evidence early Nov. 1886.
[3] *FO84/1793*, Anderson, Minute, 12 Nov. 1886 on Anti-Slavery Soc. to F.O., 8 Nov. 1886, and Encls. Mackinnon to Ferguson, 15 Nov. 1886 and Encl., Stanley to Mackinnon, 15 Nov. 1886, Copy. *FO84/1794*, Ferguson, Memo., 20 Nov. 1886. Mackinnon to Iddesleigh, 27 Nov. 1886, and Encl., Memo on relief of Emin Bey, n.d.
[4] *FO84/1794*, Iddesleigh, Memo., 25 Nov. 1886.
[5] *FO84/1795*, F.O. to War Office, 8 Dec. 1886, Draft.
[6] Stanley, *Darkest Africa*, I, 35.

the year preparations were well advanced. An Emin Pasha Relief Expedition Committee had been formed under Mackinnon's presidency;[1] it had been agreed that the expedition should start from the east coast (though it was to pass through the German sphere on the outward journey) in order to avoid complications with the Congo Free State;[2] and Stanley had been recalled from a lecture tour in the United States to take over the command.[3]

What, more precisely, was Mackinnon planning beyond the sending of relief to Emin—which in itself, owing to the strategic and potential economic importance of his province and of the adjoining territories, could not avoid serving a political as well as a humanitarian object? Mackinnon originally proposed to find £10,000 for the establishment of trading posts along the expedition's route,[4] though this proposal seems to have been abandoned when it was decided that the expedition should traverse the British sphere only on the return journey. That his ultimate aim remained the same, however, is shown by a request to Stanley to sign treaties with chiefs between Equatoria and the sea on that return journey.[5] What Mackinnon was not prepared to do was to back Hutton in the immediate foundation of 'a large trading colony from the Mombasa base', as Fergusson, the Parliamentary Under-Secretary of the Foreign Office, described Hutton's project on 20 November.[6] Hutton was at first not even prepared to subscribe to a mere relief expedition—he eventually gave £250—but wanted to form a syndicate with very wide aims indeed. It planned, more precisely,

To open a direct and safe route to Victoria Nyanza, to obtain further concessions and establish British stations and commerce in other districts in Equatorial Africa.

To administer by Charter or otherwise those districts and countries in Equatorial Africa, relating to which treaties and concessions have been obtained.

[1] *FO84/1796*, De Winton to F.O., 30 Dec. 1886.
[2] Stanley, *Darkest Africa*, I, 35. Hird, op. cit., 221.
[3] *FO84/1795*, Mackinnon to Stanley, 11 Dec. 1886, Telegram, Copy. Stanley, *Darkest Africa*, I, 34.
[4] *FO84/1794*, Fergusson, Memo., 20 Nov. 1886.
[5] *M.P.*, Kirk to Mackinnon, 23 Mar. 1887. *FO84/1860*, Mackinnon to Sultan, 14 Mar. 1887, Copy, forwarded to F.O. by Mackinnon, 18 Mar. 1887. *FO84/1863*, Pauncefote, Memo., 18 May, 1887. Hird, op. cit., 265.
[6] *FO84/1794*, Fergusson, Memo., 20 Nov. 1886. *M.P.*, Hutton to Mackinnon, 21 Dec. 1886.

The relief expedition should be used 'to further the objects of the syndicate as far as possible' without interfering with its own objects, and on this basis the syndicate would subscribe up to £3,000 to the relief expedition itself. Its own initial capital would amount to £60,000.[1]

If Mackinnon was not prepared for such an ambitious scheme it can be argued that his ultimate aims were no less ambitious and that he certainly intended to use the expedition to further those aims. That by January 1887 he had decided to go ahead with the foundation of a large East African commercial company is strongly suggested by a commission which Stanley executed for Mackinnon when he called at Zanzibar in February 1887 to recruit porters for the relief expedition. He got the Sultan to agree to the opening of negotiations for the concessions which were the necessary basis of an East African scheme.[2] (Moreover, the Sultan's favourable response to Stanley's approach was immediately followed by the opening of formal negotiations by Mackinnon[3] and the initiation of steps to form a company—the British East Africa Company.[4]) Certainly, Stanley could have received the instructions to approach the Sultan on this matter by cable on his journey to, or arrival at, Zanzibar, but there is no reason to suppose that they were not given him before he left England in January. Indeed, Mackinnon's letter of introduction which Stanley presented to the Sultan, and its dating, suggest the latter.[5] In short, the decision to go ahead with a large East African concession scheme was almost certainly integrally bound up with the decision to send relief to Emin Pasha and not, as has been suggested, a subsequent and independent decision in the implementation of which it was then decided to make use of the relief expedition.[6] The two projects were conceived in

---

[1] *M.P.*, Hutton to Mackinnon, 27 Nov. and 21 Dec. 1886. Memo., 'Scheme of Syndicate for the Development of British Commerce and to establish British Stations and Administration in Equatorial Africa', Dec. 1886.
[2] Stanley, *Darkest Africa*, I, 62, 68–69.
[3] *FO84/1860*, Mackinnon to Sultan, 14 Mar. 1887, Copy, forwarded to F.O. by Mackinnon.
[4] De Kiewiet, op. cit., 83.
[5] Dated 28 Jan. 1887, the letter besought the Sultan 'to communicate freely with Mr. Stanley on all points—as freely as if I had the honour of being there to receive the communications myself' (quoted in Stanley, *Darkest Africa*, I, 61–62). It is difficult to conceive of any other subject of discussion between Stanley and the Sultan which would warrant language of this sort.
[6] De Kiewiet, op. cit., 83.

conjunction with each other, the decision to embark on the concession scheme being a consequence of the events of the end of October 1886 only less immediate than the decision to send relief to Emin. Is not this interpretation, whose proof is admittedly less than absolute, also inherently probable? Mackinnon could use the relief expedition to open a route to the Lakes and Upper Nile, and to enable Emin to hold on in Equatoria. He would in this way be able to establish a lien on the region—Emin had offered it to Britain anyway[1]— as a future sphere of operations for the company which, as a result of the boundary agreement, now had a secure basis for its operations, and which he would simultaneously take steps to set on foot. The difference between Hutton and Mackinnon would appear to be, in short, that Hutton, with his eyes firmly fixed on Equatorial Africa, the rapid obtaining of a charter and the securing of further concessions wished a syndicate to start working for these objects straight away. Mackinnon, quite simply, was more cautious.

Looked at in a different perspective, Mackinnon's decision of November 1886 to go ahead in East Africa may appear to be related to the frustration of his Congo hopes, in the failure of the Congo Railway Syndicate, in September. This, in turn, suggests a not unexciting theory about the whole course and timing of Britain's East African expansion. It is reasonably clear that Mackinnon's turning to Leopold and the Congo in 1879–80 was caused by a disillusionment with his own prospects in East Africa. Is it not, then, also the case that he only turned back to East Africa when the Congo hope died on him, and that, since Mackinnon was the only conceivable agent of British expansion in East Africa in the early 1880's, nothing less than the whole timing of the Imperial penetration of East Africa was determined by the Congo hope, the Congo mirage?

In its purity and starkness the theory cannot stand. Notably, it ignores the consideration that even before the failure of the Congo railway scheme, Mackinnon seems to have been

---

[1] Stanley, *Darkest Africa*, II, 420. *Scottish Geographical Magazine*, Dec, 1886, quoted in De Kiewiet, op. cit., 79. The Relief Committee also probably knew of an even more forthright offer which Emin made through Mackay, the Uganda missionary, in a letter of 6 July 1886: 'To your question, am I prepared to aid in the annexation of this country by England, I reply frankly, Yes.' (Emin to Mackay, 6 July 1886, quoted in De Kiewiet, op. cit., 79–80.)

dissuaded from action in East Africa by fear of Germany, and that it was the release from this fear, the belief that the Anglo-German agreement gave both security and a golden opportunity, that led to the decision to go ahead with a considerable East African scheme and to use the relief expedition to further its purposes. But on the other hand, it may very well be that the failure of his Congo hopes predisposed Mackinnon, as a man still anxious to play a part in the development of Africa, to take the first opportunity of fulfilling this role that presented itself. It is also arguable, though in a highly speculative way, that, if Mackinnon's Congo hopes had been realized in the grant of the railway and associated concessions, their working out would have involved such a drain on his energies that he might well have been discouraged from ever taking significant action in East Africa. In these senses the theory is valid.

The Relief Committee was not left undisturbed to make the arrangements necessary to carry out its purposes. Early in January 1887 Leopold II intervened. Stanley was still in the employ of the Congo Free State and Leopold intended to use his control over him to ensure that the expedition should perform certain services for the Free State. To this end Leopold wrote to Mackinnon on 3 January and told him he was anxious that the expedition should take the Congo route to Emin's province as he was unwilling, Mackinnon reported to Stanley, 'to allow a break in the continuity of your connexion with the Congo State'.[1] Admittedly Stanley had himself originally advised in favour of the Congo route,[2] but it has been seen that the Committee had chosen an eastern route. On the 7th, however, the Comte de Borchgrave wrote to Stanley in stronger terms than Leopold in his letter to Mackinnon, saying that it would be impossible for the king to release him if the expedition proceeded by the eastern route. On the other hand the use of the Free State's river flotilla was offered as a positive inducement to take the Congo route.[3] Since the Committee was anxious to retain Stanley, since Stanley favoured the Congo route anyway and since, as will appear, the use of the west coast route in the outward direction would

---

[1] Stanley, *Darkest Africa*, I, 44.   [2] Stanley *Darkest, Africa*, I, 33.
[3] De Borchgrave to Stanley, 7 Jan. 1887, quoted in Stanley, *Darkest Africa*, I, 43–44.

not in itself prejudice the Committee's aims, the Committee deferred to Leopold. Further negotiation was now necessary in order that the aims of the Relief Committee might be reconciled with the use of Stanley's services which Leopold proposed to make. Following the decision, taken on 12 January, to take the Congo route, Stanley, and possibly Mackinnon also, crossed to Brussels and had discussions with Leopold.[1] The outcome of these discussions was, firstly, that Stanley undertook to take the opportunity of his call at Zanzibar to recruit porters to conclude an agreement with the renowned Arab slave and ivory trader, Tipoo-Tib. Tipoo-Tib had recently caused a good deal of alarm to the Free State authorities by his depredations in the Stanley Falls region culminating in his capture of the Free State's station at that place. Tipoo-Tib was to be placated, for the moment at least, by being appointed Free State Governor of the Stanley Falls district.[2] The (perfectly legitimate) advantage which Leopold derived by virtue of his claim on Stanley was not only that he could get Stanley to make the agreement with Tipoo-Tib, but also that Stanley was to use the steamer chartered for the relief expedition to carry Tipoo-Tib and his entourage round the Cape to the Congo-mouth. They would then accompany the expedition up the Congo itself, and, in the event, were escorted to Stanley Falls by a detached party. Thus the restoration of the Free State's position in the Stanley Falls area could begin without delay.

The alternatives which Stanley was to offer to Emin must also have involved some discussion in Brussels. In order that the Egyptian Government could discharge its obligation to Emin, Stanley had first to propose that Emin obey the wishes of the Egyptian Government, that is, evacuate his province and return to Egypt. But if Emin refused to leave, Stanley was empowered to make him an alternative offer on behalf of the Free State Government, namely that he should enter the Free State's service. His duties would be to maintain law and order in the Equatorial Provinces and to keep open the route between the Congo and the Nile. The offer was conditional on the provinces yielding a reasonable revenue, and on annual

---

[1] *FO84/1830*, Vivian to F.O., 16 Jan. 1887, Africa No. 5. Stanley, *Darkest Africa*, I, 46–47. Masoin, op. cit., II, 233–4. P. Daye, *Stanley* (Paris, 1936), 200.
[2] Stanley, *Darkest Africa*, I, 386–8.

expenditure not exceeding £10,000 or £12,000. When in May 1888 he eventually met Emin, Stanley, as a third alternative, made him an offer on behalf of the British East Africa Company. It was that he, Stanley, should conduct Emin and his people to the Kavirondo region on the north-east shore of Lake Victoria Nyanza where Emin would establish stations and exercise all his influence on behalf of the Company. To assist him, he would be sent two small prefabricated steamers. According to one account, these would make it possible for him to seize Buganda and Bunyoro, found there a new province and eventually extend it northwards *'jusqu'à son ancien territoire'*. This last offer was not as clear-cut as Leopold's in that Stanley was not authorized to commit the East Africa Company as regards the terms on which Emin would enter its service. But Stanley's published claim that he had no authority to make the proposition itself, is misleading, for there seems no reason to doubt Consul Euan-Smith's report of the offer as it was relayed to him by Emin.

Mr. Stanley informed him . . . that he was empowered by Sir William Mackinnon to settle him and his followers at some place upon the eastern shores of the Victoria Nyanza where he should work and use all his influence in the interests of the Imperial British East Africa Company.

(Stanley's published version was probably inspired by a concern to avoid any charge of duplicity towards Leopold, and by a wish to avoid giving any occasion of protest to Germany.)[1] This last offer, however, may have been authorized by cable or letter sometime *after* Stanley had left Europe—and with much,

[1] Stanley, *Darkest Africa*, I, 386–93, contains the published account of Stanley's transmission of proposals to Emin. This should, however, be read in conjunction with Emin's account of the matter as reported by Euan-Smith (*FO 84/2060*, Euan-Smith to F.O., 14 Mar. 1890, No. 113, Secret), with a letter of Emin to the German Consul-General at Zanzibar (Emin Pasha to German Consul-General, Zanzibar, 31 Mar. 1890, printed in Sir J. M. Gray, 'Another Letter of Emin Pasha', *Uganda Journal*, Vol. XIV, No. 2, 1950, 219–20), and with Emin's account as given to the head of the German East Africa Co. at Zanzibar, and reported, at fourth-hand, by the Belgian minister in Berlin to his chiefs (*M. des A.E., A. 641/390*, Greindl to Ministère des Affaires Etrangères, 12 Apr. 1890). It is the last of these sources which speaks of the seizure of Buganda and Bunyoro and a subsequent push northwards 'jusqu'à son ancien territoire'. Emin's letter to the German Consul-General and the account he gave to the representative of the German East Africa Co. date from after Emin's entry into the German service, following, in part from opprobious remarks made about him by Stanley. *M.P.*, Stanley to Mackinnon, 3 Sept. 1888 and Hird, op. cit., 228–9 throw further light on the question of the authorization of the British East Africa Co.'s offer to Emin.

including, perhaps, the very putting of it, left to Stanley's discretion—for Stanley noted in his diary on 2 February 1887 that 'the English subscribers to the fund hope he will not [abandon the province], but express nothing; they leave it to Emin to decide.'[1] On the other hand it may all along have been intended as a second best way of making use of Emin's services if he did not wish to remain in his province in Leopold's service.

It may appear that Leopold's intervention in the plans of the Relief Committee had resulted in the expedition being made to serve the interests of the Congo Free State rather than those of Mackinnon and the Committee. Certainly the price which Leopold was able to exact as the cost of Stanley's services was the grant of various important advantages. One was the carriage of Tipoo-Tib to Stanley Falls so that he could without delay begin to reassert the authority of the Free State there. Another was the possibility of obtaining Emin's services. Most important of all, if the expedition took the Congo route it would pioneer the route from the Upper Congo, along the Aruwimi, to Lake Albert and the Upper Nile. Fundamentally Leopold's insistence on the relief expedition taking the Congo route seems to have stemmed from his passionate interest in extending the borders of the Free State northwards from the Upper Congo to the Upper Nile, and even the Sudan, which at that time was, of course, not under the control of a European power but of a native potentate, albeit the Mahdi.[2]

But wide though Leopold's hopes were, he was not asking the Relief Committee to do more towards their fulfilment than could naturally follow from taking the Congo route, and he was not asking the Relief Committee to subordinate any of its vital aims to his own. Mackinnon's intention that Stanley should open up a trade route between the east coast and the Lakes and Equatoria on his return journey was not affected, as it was never

[1] Quoted in Stanley, *Darkest Africa*, I, 58.
[2] This is not the place for a full examination of the development and significance of Leopold's interest in the Nile, but reference may be made to the fascination exercised by Egypt as attested by a number of visits to that country before he ascended the throne; to the hope he expressed as early as September 1884 that the International Association would eventually be able to occupy the Bahr el Gazal and Sudan (*Strauch MSS.*, *No. 306*, Leopold to Strauch, 4 Sept. 1884); to his initiation in May 1888 of measures which were to culminate in the occupation in force of several points on the Nile (*Strauch MSS.*, *Nos. 736, 751*, Leopold to Strauch, 6 and 29 May 1888).

proposed that the expedition should return other than via the east coast. The use of the Congo route would involve, it must have been realized, the carriage of Tipoo-Tib to Stanley Falls. But this was not an excessively burdensome obligation and did not involve the main expedition in any detour from its route, for Tipoo was escorted to the Falls by a detached party. In any case it was compensated for by the prospect of obtaining through Tipoo-Tib's good offices the porters necessary to evacuate Emin's store of ivory, the sale of which was expected to recoup the expenses of the expedition. Moreover the use of the Congo route would bring with it the loan of the Free State's river flotilla whilst, viewed in a purely geographical light, the Congo route was thought to be the easier. Again, Emin might accept the invitation to enter Leopold's service: but if he did, Mackinnon's hope that the trade of Equatoria would be open to the company he proposed to form would still have the sanction of his continuing friendship with Leopold and of the Free Trade Zone created by the Berlin Act. Indeed, Mackinnon may positively have hoped that Emin would enter Leopold's service, for this would preserve the province in friendly hands at a time when, with his company barely established, he was scarcely in a position to suggest that he himself should take responsibility for an Emin who remained in Equatoria. The most that Stanley, on behalf of Mackinnon, could hold out to Emin was the rather general offer that he become his representative in the Victoria Nyanza area. Whether Mackinnon would have preferred that Emin should stay in his province as Leopold's governor, or evacuate to Victoria Nyanza as his own agent, is impossible to say. Mackinnon may well have been undecided and have been quite ready to leave the matter in Stanley's hands. On Stanley's loyalty Mackinnon could completely rely—'I considered myself only as your agent'—Stanley testified when the expedition was over.[1] That he could speak thus was, of course, a consequence of the deterioration in his relations with Leopold, and may well have been a factor in persuading Mackinnon to accept the Congo route. Stanley would never subordinate Mackinnon's interests to Leopold's, should an unforeseen clash arise.

On this basis co-operation between Mackinnon and the

[1] *M.P.*, Stanley to Mackinnon, 19 Jan. 1890.

Relief Committee, and Leopold is explicable. Each saw in the relief expedition a means to the attainment of differing but compatible ends.

The fulfilment of the agreed co-operation rested with Stanley. When in April 1888, after a terrible march through the rain forest, Stanley reached Emin, Emin considered and, as definitely as he ever did anything, rejected the Egyptian Government's wish that he evacuate his province. Stanley then conveyed to Emin Leopold's proposal. According to the confidential account of Emin himself, as reported by Colonel Euan-Smith, the consul-general at Zanzibar, he discussed Leopold's offer with Stanley over the course of several days, and before Stanley had told him the nature of Mackinnon's proposal or anything but the bald fact that he had a second proposal to transmit. Eventually, and according to Euan-Smith's report, 'with Mr. Stanley's concurrence', Emin rejected the first proposal. He had little faith in the Congo Free State generally, and in the practicability of reliable communications with it, doubts which Stanley, after his own terrible experience of the rain forest, could scarcely have refrained from underlining. Nor need it be supposed that Leopold would have wished Stanley to press the Free State offer, had he known of Stanley's desperate march—clearly that route to the Upper Nile was not practicable. Mackinnon's proposal was then put to Emin, and after consideration he accepted it, prompted, on his own account, by gratitude, but also, it would seem, by the opportunity which it gave him of remaining in Africa.[1] But in the end nothing came of this scheme, for mutiny amongst Emin's followers left no alternative but the evacuation of Emin, and those who wished to accompany him, to the coast. Stanley was not even able to pioneer a route to the coast which would be useful to Mackinnon's East Africa Company. With his own forces depleted and with many non-combatants in the ranks of Emin's followers, Stanley felt the risk of passage through the powerful Kingdom of Buganda, leading to the crossing of Lake Victoria Nyanza and a march to the sea through the British sphere, to be too great.[2] He was thus

---

[1] *FO84/2060*, Euan-Smith to F.O., 14 Mar. 1890, No. 113, Secret. Stanley, *Darkest Africa*, I, 386–93.
[2] Stanley, *Darkest Africa*, II, 330–2.

obliged to march to the coast through the German sphere. From the point of view of Mackinnon's wider aims the expedition was a failure save in the negative sense that it laid bare the obstacles to be overcome before any commerce could be opened up with the Lakes region and the Upper Nile.

The co-operation of Leopold and Mackinnon over the Emin Pasha Relief Expedition took place because each saw advantages in that co-operation. A similar motive led to the next, and last notable act of co-operation between the two, the so-called Mackinnon Treaty of 1890. Each gained from it— Leopold because it furthered his Nile ambitions, Mackinnon because it served a new enthusiasm. Leopold's main ambition had remained constant: Mackinnon's ambitions, since the time when the Emin relief expedition was set on foot, had broadened.

With scant regard for the Von Plessen agreement of July 1887, by which the British and German Goverments undertook to discourage annexations behind the other nation's sphere of influence,[1] Peters, in the early summer of 1889, encouraged by rumours of the death, or defeat by the Mahdists of Stanley, had led into the interior an expedition whose aim was to make a similar use for Germany of Emin's position as Stanley was seeking to make for Britain.

With Emin's withdrawal, however, all plans based on the Equatorial province fell to the ground, and Anglo-German rivalry in the interior, from the end of 1889 onwards, was focused on the control of the kingdom of Buganda. The seriousness of the national rivalries there, which became involved with domestic politics and religious disputes, made a settlement of the issue between governments imperative.

By 1889–90 Salisbury was prepared for more positive action in the Uganda–Equatoria area than he had been ready to undertake in 1886–7. To say that the decision to remain in Egypt had been taken is to explain this change–the control of the sources of the Nile had become a vital question—and the immediate way in which it was necessary to safeguard Egyptian security was to assert British paramountcy in Uganda. Thus in the spring of 1890 the Foreign Office encouraged the British East Africa Co. to strengthen its influence in Uganda, whilst in the negotiations for the settlement with Germany—

[1] De Kiewiet, op. cit., 129–30. Hertslet, op. cit., II, 625–7, No. 126.

the outcome of which was the Heligoland treaty—Salisbury saw his principal objective as a German admission that Uganda lay in the British sphere of influence. This would be obtained through some continuation westward of the 1886 partition line or, in other words, the translation into more precise terms of the Von Plessen agreement.[1]

On commercial grounds alone, Mackinnon would have been wise to display a similar singleness of purpose. Uganda, economically speaking, was generally believed to be the pearl without price. Moreover, Mackinnon failed to see that there was a limit to what could be demanded of Germany, and pressed ardently that the settlement with Germany should also serve what for him had become a somewhat intemperate enthusiasm—the project for an all-British Cape to Cairo route.

Harry Johnston, the explorer-empire builder, who originated the idea, appears to have won Mackinnon to the Cape to Cairo scheme[2] as he had earlier won Rhodes. By 1890, Anderson wrote, Mackinnon's 'ruling idea' was 'to join hands with Rhodes so as to realize the project of a continuous British sphere from the Cape to the Nile'.[3] The main territorial obstacle to the completion of this link was the Von Plessen agreement of 1887 which, it could be argued, had the effect of bringing the German sphere up to the boundary of the Congo Free State.

Mackinnon nevertheless sought to gain the requisite strip of territory, and he was doubtless rendered more ready to do so by the attempt of Peters to establish German influence in Uganda behind (in the British view) the British sphere. Certainly he was strongly anti-German by 1890—in Salisbury's view, Mackinnon had 'no energy for anything except quarrelling with the Germans'.[4] When, therefore, in March 1890 Salisbury began to negotiate the settlement with Germany Mackinnon urged on the Foreign Office that Britain must not only insist on her claim to Uganda, of greatest importance to England and the

---

[1] This section on the development of Anglo-German rivalry in the interior is based on De Kiewiet, op. cit., 178–206.
[2] *M.P.*, Johnston to Mackinnon, 26 Sept. 1888.
[3] *FO84/2263*, Anderson, Memo., 17 Nov. 1892, quoted in De Kiewiet, op. cit., 199.
[4] Lady G. Cecil, *Life of Lord Salisbury*, IV, 281.

British East Africa Company, and which could be justified in terms of the Von Plessen agreement, but also lay claim to all the territory between Lake Victoria and the Congo Free State, which could not be justified, since most of it was at the back of the German sphere. In his representations to the Foreign Office, Mackinnon was aided by a series of public speeches made by Stanley who had by this time returned to England.[1] Now it was as an insurance against a possible refusal by Salisbury (and such was eventually the case) to press for this block of territory that Mackinnon conceived the idea of fulfilling his purpose—the obtaining of a vital link in the all-red route— by acquiring a strip of Congo State territory by arrangement with Leopold. Such an arrangement was possible because the British East Africa Company for its part had something to offer, namely, the renunciation of aspirations to territory on the left bank of the Upper Nile in favour of the Free State.

Negotiations appear to have begun during May and were no doubt facilitated by the presence in London, on a visit, of Leopold.[2] The result was the signature of a 'treaty' between the British East Africa Company and the Free State Government on 24 May 1890. The first step in this agreement was to modify the boundary of the spheres of influence of the Congo Free State and the British East Africa Company in accordance with a general understanding reached by Stanley and Leopold in Brussels a week or two earlier.[3] The line was now to run three miles out from the western shore of Lake Albert down to the mouth of the Semliki River, thence along the line of that river to Lake Albert Edward, thence, roughly, down the centre of that lake to the mid-point of the southern shore and thereafter in a straight line to the northern end of Lake Tanganyika. The bargain was then made. The British East Africa Company agreed to recognize the sovereign rights of the Congo Free State over the territories lying on the west bank of the Nile between the south end of Lake Albert and Lado. In return for this the Congo Free State recognized the sovereign rights of the British East Africa Company over a five-mile-wide strip of Free State territory, on or close to the agreed frontier line,

[1] W. L. Langer, *The Diplomacy of Imperialism* (2nd ed., New York, 1951), 118. De Kiewiet, op. cit., 198–200.
[2] Langer, *Imperialism*, 119.
[3] *Autobiography of Henry M. Stanley* (London, 1909), 413–14.

between the southern end of Lake Albert Edward and the northern extremity of Lake Tanganyika.[1]

Thus Leopold and Mackinnon had each gained something which they believed to be of great potential value (though, in the event, neither was permitted to pluck the fruits of the bargain). As in the case of the Emin Pasha Expedition, they had dealt with each other not as the intimate collaborators of the decade before 1886, but as independent powers who could each best serve their distinct interest by a limited and defined co-operation.

* * *

This 'limited and defined co-operation' is, of course, a poor thing when contrasted with the intimate collaboration of the decade before 1886. That decade witnessed the flowering of a unique hope, the expectation of a trio of Englishmen—Mackinnon, Hutton and Kirk—together, in a qualified sense, with Stanley, that the economic development of the Congo basin, of the very heart of Africa, might fall largely to British enterprise working through Leopold II of Belgium. Such a hope explains, notably, the strenuous exertions made by Leopold's British supporters against the Anglo-Portuguese treaty, which they conceived to be a threat to their hope's realization, and in favour of British recognition of the *Association Internationale du Congo*, which would bring nearer their hope's fulfilment. The scale and compass of the hope itself is shown in the ambitious plans of the Congo Railway Syndicate, whilst the hope's very existence may also have affected the course and timing of British expansion in East Africa.

Whilst Mackinnon and his friends worked through Leopold for the opening up of the Congo basin, the British Government, when forced to action by French penetration of the Upper Congo, pursued the more limited object of keeping the doorway open by an agreement with Portugal. In this it was unsuccessful—in that failure, the agitation aroused by Leopold's British sympathizers was of more consequence than might at first sight appear—and it was more by good luck than by good management that Britain, in the Berlin Act and related agreements, was able to secure her interests in the Congo basin as

[1] The text of the Mackinnon Treaty is printed in *FO84/2082* and in *Aus den Archiven*, III, 142.

AFTERMATH AND CONCLUSIONS

well as she did. The real opportunity for an agreement with Portugal had come, and had been lost, in 1879–81. An agreement such as Morier had then urged would have had more far-reaching implications than that abortively negotiated in 1882–4 for it would have been a part of a 'grand design' for the opening up of Portuguese Africa, present and future, and for a new era of Anglo-Portuguese colonial co-operation possessing possibilities of the most fruitful kind.

Both the plans of Morier in 1876–81 and the actions of the British Foreign Office in 1882–4 involved a *volte face* in a well-tried policy of resistance to Portugal's Congo claim. But in another sense they were but a reversion to a traditional harmony—the Portuguese alliance—and to a traditional technique—the use of a client state to serve the interests of Great Britain and of Free Trade. Until this time Britain's policy towards the Portuguese Congo claim, if of arguable legality, had served her purposes adequately. In conjunction with treaty-making with native chiefs, and with the anti-slavery and anti-piratical activity of the Royal Navy, it had enabled British trade with the Congo region to reach a level whose importance seems hitherto to have been underrated.

The most direct expression of official British interest was the Tuckey expedition of 1816. Not primarily inspired by an interest in the River Congo as such, but conceived as a part of the Niger quest, it commands interest as a notable example of the officially sponsored expeditions of African discovery and penetration of the earlier nineteenth century. British expansion in the Congo region did not, as has been seen, thereafter take such a direct form but was, rather, of an informal kind. In this, it reflected, in a variety of interesting forms, the most favoured technique of British expansion in the nineteenth century.

BIBLIOGRAPHY

Documentary Sources

For the Tuckey expedition the source of most value is the file on the expedition contained in *Ad.1/2617*, whilst much material on the condition of the Congo before the 'Scramble', and on the form and extent of British influence in the region in that period is to be found in the correspondence of the Foreign Office with the Admiralty, the Loanda Commissioners and the Loanda Consul. More obviously rich (because concentrated) are the sources which relate to the Portuguese Congo claim and the British response thereto in the period up to 1881 (*FO63/1112–17*), and to the Anglo-Portuguese treaty negotiations (*FO84/1801–11*). These two collections comprise documents drawn from a number of series of correspondence, and thus save the historian, as they were originally designed to save the officials of the Foreign Office, much labour. There are, however, gaps and omissions which I was sometimes able to make good by reference to this or that series of official correspondence.

Of major importance in another category of documentary source are the *Mackinnon Papers*. It is pre-eminently the study of the letters which Mackinnon received from his British associates and his various Brussels correspondents, together with such drafts and copies of his own letters as the collection contains, that reveals at least something of Mackinnon's hopes and plans and of the nature and significance of his relationship with Leopold II. On the Belgian side the *Strauch MSS.* are of particular value, indicating, as they do indicate, something of Leopold's attitude to his British sympathizers, of the collaboration between them, and, indeed, of the Belgian king's African designs generally.

These and other relevant documentary sources are fully listed below.

I. IN THE PUBLIC RECORD OFFICE, LONDON

Material relating to Tuckey's expedition:
Ad.1/2616–17, 4234; Ad.3/186.

BIBLIOGRAPHY

Reports of Commanders-in-Chief, Cape of Good Hope Station, 1816–39:
 Ad.1/67–86.
Letters from Commanders-in-Chief, West Africa Station, 1840–44:
 Ad.1/5495, 5505, 5512, 5529, 5538.
Correspondence between the Foreign Office and Admiralty, 1818–75:
 Relevant volumes in the Slave Trade series of the Foreign Office Papers:
 (a) as listed under 'Domestic Various', which sub-series included F.O.–Admiralty correspondence between 1818 and 1838, FO84/7–FO84/265.
 (b) as listed under 'Admiralty' and 'Admiralty Drafts', FO84/301 (1839)–FO84/1420 (1875).
Correspondence between the Foreign Office and Loanda Commissioners, 1843–70:
 Relevant volumes of the Foreign Office Slave Trade series as listed under 'Loanda Commissioners', 'Loanda Commissioners, Drafts', etc., FO84/461 (1843)–FO84/1334 (1870).
Correspondence between the Foreign Office and the Loanda Consul, 1844–84:
 (a) in F.O. Slave Trade series under 'Loanda Consul', 'Loanda Consul, Drafts', etc., FO84/630 (1846)–FO84/1670 (1884).
 (b) In F.O. Portugal series under same heads, FO63/590 (1844)–FO63/1153 (1884).
Correspondence relating to the Portuguese territorial claim in the Congo region, 1845–81:
 Six volumes in F.O. Portugal series, FO63/1112–17.
Correspondence relating to the Congo, Jan. 1877–June 1884:
 Eleven volumes in F.O. Slave Trade series, FO84/1801–11.
Correspondence relating to the Congo and Berlin West Africa Conference, June 1884–Feb. 1885:
 Eleven volumes in F.O. Slave Trade series, FO84/1812–22.
Correspondence relating to the Lourenço Marques treaty:
 Eight volumes in F.O. Portugal series, FO63/1100–3, 1129–32.
 Individual volumes in F.O. Portugal, and F.O. Slave Trade (especially Domestic Various) series, as adjudged relevant.

Granville Papers:
PRO30/29/156: Correspondence, Belgium and Holland, 1880–5.
PRO30/29/183: Correspondence, Portugal, 1880–4.
PRO30/29/198: Correspondence, Belgium, etc., 1880–5.

II. IN THE ARCHIVES OF THE *MINISTÈRE DES AFFAIRES ETRANGÈRES*, BRUSSELS

Lambermont MSS. (1876–88); Strauch MSS.; *Correspondance et Documents, Afrique*, A.I.C., 1883, 1884; Report of Proceedings of 1876 Geographical Conference.

III. PRIVATE PAPERS

Mackinnon MSS. (in School of Oriental and African Studies): principally letters from Stanley, Kirk, Hutton, Austin Lee, Gerald Waller, Horace Waller, Sanford, Lambert, Strauch and Devaux.

Dilke MSS. (in the British Museum): Letters from Morier in General Political Correspondence, 1876–82, Dilke MSS. 43884–91.

Waller MSS. (in Rhodes House): Letters from Gordon to H. Waller, 1880.

Johnston MSS. (Central African Archives—The Royal Commonwealth Society has a portion of the MSS. on microfilm).

Kirk MSS. (a portion), in possession of Col. J. W. C. Kirk.

Anti-Slavery Society MSS. (in the Bodleian): Various.

Manchester Chamber of Commerce Records: Annual Reports, 1881–5.

IV. PUBLISHED DOCUMENTARY SOURCES

Reports by Consul Hopkins on (I) The Trade, Commerce, Navigation, etc. of the Provinces of Angola and its dependencies for the year 1874, and (II) The Trade, Commerce, Navigation, etc. of the Districts comprised within the northern limits of Angola and Black Point, including the River Congo: Accounts and Papers, 1875, C1132, LXXV.

Votes and Proceedings of the House of Commons, 1883 and 1884, Parliamentary Papers, 1883 and 1884.

Minutes of the House of Lords, 1883 and 1884, PP 1883 and 1884.

Correspondence respecting the Territory on the West Coast of Africa lying between 5° 12′ and 8° of south latitude, 1845–77 A.&P., 1883, C3531, XLVIII.

Correspondence relating to Negotiations between the Governments of Great Britain and Portugal for the Conclusion of the Congo Treaty, 1882–4: A.&P., 1884, C3885, LVI.

Dispatch to Her Majesty's Minister at Lisbon, enclosing the Congo Treaty, signed 26 February 1884, . . .: A.&P., 1884, C3886, LVI.

Further Papers connected with the Negotiations with Portugal for a Treaty respecting the Congo River and the adjacent Coast: A.&P., 1884, C4205, LVI.

Hansard.

Aus den Archiven des belgischen Kolonialministeriums, Parts II and III (Berlin, 1918). This material from the Belgian archives was first published by the Germans in *Deutsches Kolonialblatt*, from 1916 onwards.

Documents Diplomatiques Français, 1871–1914 (D.D.F.), First Series, Vol. v.

V. CONTEMPORARY NEWSPAPERS AND PERIODICALS

The Times — 1 Nov. 1877–31 Dec. 1878.
Manchester Guardian — 1 Jan. 1883–31 Dec. 1886.
Manchester Examiner

Anti-Slavery Reporter (The journal of the Anti-Slavery Society) 1883 and 1884.

BOOKS

The new, later eighteenth-century form of Britain's imperial activity, the background of Tuckey's expedition, is seen in a work of major importance, Professor Vincent T. Harlow's *The Founding of the Second British Empire, 1763–1793* (London, 1952), of which the first volume has so far appeared. A mine of information on the expedition itself and its immediate background is the *Narrative of the Expedition to explore the River Zaire, usually called the Congo* . . . (London, 1818), which was apparently edited by Sir John Barrow himself, whilst there are some important titbits in E. Smith, *The Life of Sir Joseph Banks* (London, 1911).

Traders' accounts, with the possible exception of J. Monteiro, *Angola and the River Congo*, 2 vols. (London, 1875), are disappointing as sources for the history of the region. An appreciable amount of valuable information can be culled from Barrow's *Narrative*, from two of H. M. Stanley's works—*Through the Dark Continent* (cheap edition, London, 1890), and *The Congo and the Founding of its Free State* (London, 1885), from Miss Ruth Slade's *English-speaking Missions in the Congo Independent State* (Brussels, 1959), and, in a more general way, from J.-H. Pirenne, 'Les Eléments fondamentaux de l'ancienne structure territoriale et politique du Bas-Congo', *Bulletin des Séances de l'Académie Royale des Sciences Coloniales*, Brussels, v–1959–3. Miss Slade's work on English-speaking missions and an article by her—'L'Attitude des Missions Protestantes vis-à-vis des Puissances Européenes au Congo avant 1884', *Bulletin des Séances de l'Institut Royal Colonial Belge*, xxv–1954–2, together with W. Holman Bentley, *Pioneering on the Congo*, 2 vols. (London, 1900), and H. H. Johnston, *George Grenfell and the Congo*, 2 vols. (London, 1908), are authoritative on the activities of British missionary societies.

There is little published work in English on Portuguese history and the history of Portuguese expansion, but the background to Portugal's Congo claim is well and conveniently traced in J. Duffy, *Portuguese Africa* (Harvard, 1959), and the bones of nineteenth-century Portuguese domestic history can be found in H. V. Livermore, *History of Portugal*, (Cambridge, 1947). No student of British expansion in the nineteenth century can neglect John Gallagher and Ronald Robinson, 'The Imperialism of Free Trade', *Economic History Review*, 2nd Series, Vol. vi, No. 1, 1953, whilst the African policy of Palmerston, one of the most notable architects of that expansion, and the ideas that lay behind that policy, are most ably presented in R. J. Gavin, *Palmerston's Policy towards East and West Africa, 1830–1865* (Cambridge, Ph.D. thesis, 1958). Dr. Gavin does not, however, deal in any detail with his subject's policy towards West Central Africa. C. Lloyd, *The Navy and the Slave Trade* (London, 1949), is important for the British suppression of the Congo slave trade.

The diplomacy of the Anglo-Portuguese treaty and immediately subsequent periods is contained in W. L. Langer, *European Alliances and Alignments* (2nd ed., New York, 1950), and in A. J. P. Taylor, *The Struggle for Mastery in Europe, 1848–1918* (Oxford, 1954). The same author's *Germany's First Bid for Colonies* (London, 1938) has a more particular relevance as has also Mrs. Joan P. Schwitzer, *The British Attitude to French Colonization, 1875–1887* (London, Ph.D. 1954), whilst I have relied heavily on Miss S. E. Crowe, *The Berlin West Africa Conference, 1884–1885* (London, 1942). A specific study of British policy towards Portugal's Congo claim is Miss I. Bains, *British Policy in relation to Portuguese Claims in West Africa, 1876–1884* (London, M.A. thesis, 1940). Miss Bains' treatment of the subject is to a limited extent similar to my own, but a number of my conclusions differ from hers. She has much of value to say on Morier's 'grand design', a matter which also receives useful consideration in A. J. Hanna, *History of Nyasaland and North-Eastern Rhodesia, 1875–1895* (London, Ph.D., 1948), and in the same writer's *The Beginnings of Nyasaland and North-Eastern Rhodesia, 1859–1895* (Oxford, 1956).

The collaboration between Leopold and his British supporters receives only incidental attention in published works. There are references to aspects of it in *The Autobiography of Sir Henry Morton Stanley* (Ed. Lady Dorothy Stanley, London, 1909), and in Stanley's *The Congo and the Founding of its Free State* (already mentioned), and *In Darkest Africa*, 2 vols. (London, 1890), and in F. Hird, *H. M. Stanley, the Authorised Life* (London, 1935). Certain aspects of this collaboration have, however, been more fully treated in articles, mostly in recent years. These are R. S. Thomson, 'Léopold II et la Conférence de Berlin', *Congo*, 1931, II; J. Stengers, 'Rapport sur le Dossier "Correspondance Léopold II–Strauch"', *Bulletin des Seances de l'Institut Royal Colonial Belge*, Brussels, XXIV–1953–4; Miss R. Slade, 'L'Attitude des Missions Protestantes vis-à-vis des Puissances Européenes au Congo avant 1884' (already detailed); and P. Ceulemans, 'Les Tentatives de Léopold II pour engager le Colonel Charles Gordon au service de l'Association Internationale Africaine, 1880', *Zaire*, XII–3–1958. A notable contribution to the consideration of the partly distinct question of Stanley's relations with Leopold is an article by J. Stengers—

'Stanley, Léopold II et l'Angleterre' (extract from the review *Le Flambeau*, No. 4, 1954). It is a pity that Hird's biography of Stanley has no footnotes and there is a strong case for a new biography of Stanley which would take account of material which has become available since the mid-1930's. There are no biographies of Mackinnon, Hutton and Kirk, but their East African activities are treated in R. Coupland, *The Exploitation of East Africa, 1856–1890* (London, 1939), and Miss M. J. de Kiewiet, *History of the Imperial British East Africa Company, 1876–1895* (Univ. of London, Ph.D. thesis, 1955). The latter—a most illuminating work—draws to a considerable extent on the *Mackinnon Papers*, and necessarily gives to Mackinnon a central position. The only published source of information on British financial involvement in the Congo Free State appears to be the very rare book by H. Waltz, *Das Konzessionwesen in Belgischen Congo*, 2 vols. (Jena, 1917).

R. S. Thomson, *La Fondation de l'Etat Indépendant du Congo* (Brussels, 1933), remains the best overall study of the work of the *A.I.A.*, the *Comité* and the *A.I.C.*, but in more recent years Father A. Roeykens has gathered together much valuable information about Leopold and his African hopes and schemes in the period up to 1880, though not all his conclusions command agreement. His work to date is summarized in *Léopold II et l'Afrique* (Brussels, 1958).

A number of other books of note whose relevance either needs no comment or is quantitatively more restricted are listed below.

J. N. L. Baker, *A History of Geographical Discovery and Exploration* (2nd ed., London, 1948).
E. Banning, *Mémoires* (Paris–Brussels, 1927).
H. C. F. Bell, *Lord Palmerston*, 2 vols. (London, 1936).
Biographie Coloniale Belge, 4 vols. (Brussels, 1948–1956).
Cambridge History of the British Empire, Vol. ii (1940), Vol. iii (1959).
V. L. Cameron, *Across Africa*, 2 vols. (London, 1876).
J. Macmaster Campbell, *Sir William Mackinnon, Bart.* (reprinted from the *Campbeltown Courier*), undated.
G. Casati, *Ten Years in Equatoria*, 2 vols. (London, 1891).
Lady G. Cecil, *Life of Lord Salisbury* (London, 1931), Vol. iv.
R. J. Cornet, *La Bataille du Rail* (Brussels, 1947).

BIBLIOGRAPHY

J. Cuvelier and L. Jadin, *L'Ancien Congo d'après les Archives Romaines* (Brussels, 1954).
J. Cuvelier, *L'Ancien Royaume de Congo* (Bruges, 1946).
P. Daye, *Léopold II* (Paris, 1934).
P. Daye, *Stanley* (Paris, 1936).
Dictionary of National Biography.
K. O. Dike, *Trade and Politics in the Niger Delta 1830–1885* (Oxford, 1956).
Document Notte, *Stanley au Congo, 1879–1884* (Ministère du Congo Belge et du Ruanda-Urundi, Private Circulation, n.d.).
Emin Pasha in Central Africa, Ed. G. Schweinfurth, F. Ratzel, R. W. Felkin, G. Hartlaub (London, 1888).
R. C. K. Ensor, *England, 1870–1914* (Oxford, 1936).
Lord E. Fitzmaurice, *The Life of Lord Granville, 1815–1891*, Vol. ii (London, 1905).
H. R. Fox-Bourne, *Civilization on the Congo* (London, 1903).
S. Gwynn and G. Tuckwell, *Life of Sir Charles Dilke*, 2 vols. (London, 1917).
E. Hertslet, *The Map of Africa by Treaty* (London, 1894).
J. A. and P. C. Hutton, *Hutton Families* (Privately Published, 1939).
H. H. Johnston, *The Story of My Life* (London, 1923).
A. B. Keith, *The Belgian Congo and the Berlin Act* (Oxford, 1919).
J. S. Keltie, *The Partition of Africa* (2nd ed., London, 1895).
W. L. Langer, *The Diplomacy of Imperialism* (2nd ed., New York, 1950).
F. Masoin, *Histoire de l'Etat Indépendant du Congo* (Namur, 1912–13).
A. Maurice, *Stanley, Lettres Inédites* (Brussels, 1955).
Lord Mayo, *De Rebus Africanis, The Claims of Portugal to the Congo and adjacent Littoral, with remarks on the French annexation* (London, 1883).
J. Morley, *The Life of William Ewart Gladstone* (London, 1907 edition).
Roland Oliver, *Sir Harry Johnston and the Scramble for Africa* (London, 1957).
K. Peters, *New Light on Dark Africa* (London, 1891).
A. Redford, *Manchester Merchants and Foreign Trade, Vol. ii, 1850–1939* (Manchester, 1956).

A. Roeykens, *Léopold II et la Conférence Géographique de Bruxelles, 1876* (Brussels, 1956).
—— *Les Débuts de l'Œuvre africaine de Léopold II (1875–1879)*, (Brussels, 1955).
J. Stengers, *Textes Inédits d'Emile Banning* (Brussels, 1955).
P. Van Zuylen, *L'Echiquier Congolais* . . . (Brussels, 1959).
A. J. Wauters, *Stanley's Emin Pasha Expedition* (London, 1890).
—— *L'Etat Indépendant du Congo* (Brussels, 1899).
Sir Charles Webster, *The Foreign Policy of Palmerston, 1830–1841*, 2 vols. (London, 1951).
R. Wemyss, *Memoirs and Letters of Sir Robert Morier*, 2 vols. (London, 1911).

APPENDIX A

THE ANGLO-PORTUGUESE TREATY,
signed 26 February 1884[1]

ARTICLE I

SUBJECT to the conditions of the present Treaty, Her Britannic Majesty agrees to recognise the sovereignty of His Most Faithful Majesty the King of Portugal and the Algarves over that part of the West Coast of Africa situated between 8° and 5° 12' of south latitude; and inland as far as follows:

On the River Congo the limit shall be Nokki.

On the coast situated between 8° and 5° 12' of south latitude the inland eastern frontier shall coincide with the boundaries of the present possessions of the coast and riparian tribes. This frontier shall be defined, and the definition shall be communicated with the least possible delay by His Most Faithful Majesty to Her Britannic Majesty.

The definition, when approved by the High Contracting Parties, shall be recorded in a Protocol to be annexed to the present Treaty.

ARTICLE II

The territory specified in Article I shall be open to all nations, and foreigners of all nationalities whatever, conforming themselves to the laws of the country, shall enjoy within the said territory the same benefits, advantages, and treatment, in every respect, as the subjects of Portugal.

They shall have full liberty to enter, travel, or reside, with their families, in any part of the said territory.

They shall be permitted to establish factories or trading stations; to possess, purchase, rent, or lease land, houses, manufactories, warehouses, shops, and premises, and all other kinds of property.

They shall be allowed to carry on commerce by wholesale or retail either in person or by any agents whom they may think fit to employ and in accordance with the existing local usages and customs of trade.

ARTICLE III

The High Contracting Parties recognise the entire freedom in respect to commerce and navigation of the Rivers Congo and Zambesi and their affluents for the subjects and flags of all nations.

The claims of Portugal on the Shiré shall not extend beyond the confluence of the River Ruo with that river.

ARTICLE IV

The trade and navigation of all rivers and waterways within the territory specified in Article I, and along the sea-coast thereof, shall be

[1] *FO93/77/41. A.&P., 1884, C3886*, LVI, 45.

open to the flags of all nations, and shall not be subject to any monopoly, exclusive concession, or other impediment, nor to any customs duties, tolls, charges, fees, fines, or other imposts whatever not expressly provided for in the present Treaty, or hereafter agreed upon by the High Contracting Parties.

A mixed Commission, composed of delegates of Great Britain and Portugal, shall be appointed to draw up Regulations for the navigation, police, and supervision of the Congo and other waterways within the territory specified in Article I and to watch over their execution.

The Regulations may impose such tolls as may be sufficient to defray the cost of works necessary to facilitate trade and navigation and the expenses of the Commission.

The Commission shall come to an arrangement with the Portuguese authorities for the erection and maintenance of lighthouses, beacons, and marks to denote channels.

ARTICLE V

No transit or other duties, direct or indirect, of whatever denomination, shall be levied on goods in transit by water through the territory specified in Article I. This freedom from duties shall apply to goods transhipped in course of transit, or landed in bond for further conveyance by water. The transhipment or landing in bond of such goods will be effected under the supervision of the Portuguese authorities, in order to prevent any fraud, and the expenses of such supervision will be chargeable to the traders or their agents. The scale of such charges will be fixed by the Mixed Commission. No such duties shall be levied on goods in transit by land through that territory, which shall have been legally imported and which shall have paid the duties imposed by the Tariff approved by the present Treaty.

ARTICLE VI

All roads in the territory specified in Article I now open, or which may hereafter be opened, shall be kept free and open to all travellers and caravans, and for the passage of goods.

ARTICLE VII

Complete protection shall be afforded to missionaries or other ministers of religion of any Christian denomination, of whatever nation or country, in the exercise of their vocation, within the territory specified in Article I.

They shall not be hindered or molested in their endeavours to teach the doctrines of Christianity to all persons willing or desirous to be taught; nor shall any natives who may embrace any form of the Christian faith be on that account, or on account of the teaching or exercise thereof, molested or troubled in any manner whatsoever.

It is further agreed that the local authorities shall set apart a piece of land within a convenient distance of each of the principal towns, to be used as a burial ground for persons of whatever religious denomination.

All forms of religious worship and religious ordinances shall be tolerated, and no hindrance whatever shall be offered thereto by the Portuguese authorities.

Missionaries of religion, whether natives or foreigners, and religious bodies, shall have a perfect right to erect churches, chapels, schools, and other buildings, which shall be protected by the Portuguese authorities.

All religious establishments, of whatever denomination shall be on a footing of perfect equality as regards taxation and local charges.

ARTICLE VIII

Her Britannic Majesty engages to communicate to His Most Faithful Majesty immediately after the ratification of the present Treaty, all Treaties or Engagements subsisting between Great Britain and native chiefs in the territory specified in Article I.

His Most Faithful Majesty engages to communicate to Her Britannic Majesty all Treaties or Engagements subsisting between Portugal and native chiefs in the said territory.

His Most Faithful Majesty engages to respect and confirm all the rights of the native chiefs and of the inhabitants of the said territory under any of the Treaties and Engagements above mentioned, so far as is compatible with the sovereignty of Portugal; and undertakes to protect and maintain the said Chiefs and inhabitants in the free possession and enjoyment of the lands and other property now held by them, and not to allow them to suffer on account of anything which has happened in the past.

ARTICLE IX

The Customs Tariff in the territory specified in Article I shall not, for the term of ten years from the date of the exchange of ratifications of the present Treaty, exceed that which was adopted in the Province of Mozambique in the year 1877. At the end of that term the Tariff may be revised, with the consent of the two High Contracting Parties, but no alteration shall be made therein pending such revision.

Provided always that, in the territory specified in Article I of the present Treaty, British ships shall not at any time hereafter be liable to the payment of any higher or other duties and charges, or be subject to any other restrictions, than are there payable or imposed on Portuguese ships; and goods, whether the property of British subjects, or imported in British vessels, or of British origin or manufacture, shall not at any time hereafter be subject to any differential treatment whatsoever, but shall be on the same footing in every respect as goods the property of Portuguese subjects, or imported in Portuguese vessels, or the produce or manufacture of Portugal.

Such equality of treatment shall apply to British vessels and goods, from whatever port or place arriving, and whatever may be their place of destination.

In all the African possessions of Portugal the present Customs Tariff shall not be raised for the term of ten years from the date of the exchange of the ratifications of the present Treaty.

No bill of health or other quarantine formality shall be required in any Portuguese port from British ships bound direct for British ports.

ARTICLE X

His Most Faithful Majesty guarantees to British subjects and their commerce in all the African possessions of Portugal, in addition to any rights which they may already possess in the Portuguese Colonies, the treatment of the most favoured third nation:

1. As regards residence, whether temporary or permanent; the exercise of any calling or profession; the payment of taxes or other imposts; and the enjoyment of all legal rights and privileges, including the acquiring, holding, and power of disposing of property.

2. As regards commerce; in respect of import and export duties and all other charges on or in respect of goods of whatever description, and whatever may be their place of origin or manufacture, and whether intended for consumption, warehousing, or re-exportation. Also with respect to the transit of goods, prohibition of importation, exportation, or transit; samples, Customs formalities, and all other matters connected with commerce and trade.

3. As regards navigation; in respect of vessels, whether steam or sailing, from whatever place arriving, and whatever may be their place of origin or destination of their cargoes. Also in respect of all charges or dues on or in respect of the said vessels and cargoes, and all formalities and regulations relative to them.

4. Any favour, privilege or immunity in regard to subjects, commerce or navigation, as well as any reduction of customs duties or other charges on or in respect of goods or vessels which may hereafter be conceded by Portugal to any third Power, shall be extended immediately and unconditionally to Great Britain.

5. British Consular officers, as regards appointments, residence, functions, and privileges, shall be placed on the footing of the most favoured nation.

ARTICLE XI

Every assistance shall be given by the local authorities in all the African possessions of Portugal to vessels wrecked on the coasts or in the rivers, or forced into the ports on the entrance of rivers by the stress of weather.

Such vessels and their cargoes shall be exempt from all customs duties, charges, fees, fines, and other imposts whatever, except as regards any goods landed therefrom for purposes of sale or barter.

Information of such wrecks shall be given, without delay, to the nearest British Consular officer, who shall be authorized to interpose for the protection of the ship, its merchandise, and effects.

ARTICLE XII

The Portuguese legislation for the complete extinction of slavery and the Treaties for the suppression of the Slave Trade shall, from the date of the exchange of the ratifications of the present Treaty, be effectively applied to the territory specified in Article I.

The High Contracting Parties bind themselves to use all possible means for the purpose of finally extinguishing slavery and the Slave Trade on the eastern and western coasts of Africa.

His Most Faithful Majesty agrees to grant, from the date of the ratification of the present Treaty, permission to Her Britannic Majesty's ships employed in suppressing the Slave Trade to enter the bays, ports, creeks, rivers, and other places in the eastern African Colonies or possessions of Portugal where no Portuguese authorities shall be established, and to prevent the Slave Trade from being carried on in such places. British vessels employed in this service shall exercise all the powers conferred on Her Majesty's vessels by the Slave Trade Treaty between Great Britain and Portugal of the 3rd July, 1842.

Similar powers shall be given, if required, for similar purposes to Portuguese vessels in Her Britannic Majesty's South African dominions.

Whenever the Commander of a cruiser of one of the High Contracting Parties shall have occasion to act under the provisions of this Article in the territorial waters of the other High Contracting Party, such Commander shall, whenever practicable, having regard to the circumstances of the case, invite a naval or other officer of the other High Contracting Party to accompany the expedition, in order to represent the national flag in such territorial waters.

The provisions of this Article shall come into force immediately on the exchange of the ratification of the present Treaty, except as regards any provision which may be found to require legislative sanction in either country, and as regards such provision, it shall come into force from the date when such legislative sanction shall have been obtained and duly notified by the High Contracting Party requiring the same to the other High Contracting Party.

ARTICLE XIII

The provisions of the present Treaty, affecting the territory specified in Article I, shall be fully applied to all territories adjoining the same in Africa that may hereafter be brought under the sovereignty of His Most Faithful Majesty the King of Portugal and the Algarves.

ARTICLE XIV

His Most Faithful Majesty the King of Portugal and the Algarves engages for himself, his heirs and successors, that if at any time it shall be the intention of Portugal to withdraw from the fort of St. John the Baptist of Ajuda, on the coast of Mina, due notification of such intention shall be given to Great Britain, to whom the cession of the fort, and of all rights appertaining to its possession, shall be offered; and no arrangement shall be made for the cession of the fort to any other Power without the previous consent of Great Britain.

This engagement shall apply in all its terms to the abandonment or cession by Portugal of any rights which may be claimed by her between 5° east and 5° west longitude on the same coast.

ARTICLE XV

(Concerning ratifications, which were to be exchanged as soon as possible).

APPENDIX B

MEMORANDUM FOR PRIVATE CIRCULATION ONLY

THE CONGO RAILWAY SYNDICATE, LIMITED

Estimated Capital required for Railway, Steamers, and Plant

£1,000,000

THE CONGO RAILWAY SYNDICATE, LIMITED, propose to form a Company, and obtain a concession in favour of such Company, as follows:

The objects in view in founding the Company are to establish direct and regular communication between the Upper and Lower Congo, by the construction of a railway and placing light-draught steamers on the river. It is proposed to construct a 2-foot gauge light railway, on the plan of the Festiniog line, and which it is estimated can be constructed on the Congo at about £3,000 per mile, inclusive of plant. The line to run in the first instance from Vivi to Isangila, about 50 miles, whence steamers could run to Manyanga, a distance of about 88 miles, and thence to Stanley Pool, 100 miles.

Accompanying is rough estimate of the necessary outlay.

The Company to take full powers to carry out the concession and to develop the land acquired, to acquire the assets of any trading concern, to open trading stations and to carry on trade at any place within the territories of the State or elsewhere, and to carry on mining, banking, or any industrial enterprise, including transport by road, rail, or water, and any other commercial undertaking which might be of advantage to the enterprise, and all such other powers as they may be advised, for which it is estimated that a capital of £1,000,000 would be required in addition to the £1,000,000 for railway and flotilla capital.

The Company to be registered as a British Company.

ORIGINAL ESTIMATES OF MR. H. M. STANLEY for the Congo Railway and Flotilla, MADE OCTOBER, 1885

Banana—Plant etc. at Banana or mouth	£30,000	
River steamers and barges for traffic from mouth to Vivi	30,000	
Vivi—Landing place, stores and stations	30,000	
		£90,000
50 miles Rail to Isangila, 50 miles at £3,000		150,000
Station and stores at Isangila		7,000
Three river steamers for traffic from Isangila to Manyanga		24,000
Station and stores at Manyanga		7,000
Complete in one and a half to two years		£278,000

100 miles Rail from Manyanga to Stanley Pool, 100 miles at £3,000		300,000
Station and depot at Kinshasha		20,000
Four river steamers for traffic above Stanley Pool, £8,000		32,000
	Complete in three to four years	£630,000
85 miles Isangila line to Manyanga when required, 85 miles at £3,000		255,000
	Complete in probably five to six years	£885,000
Contingencies		115,000
235 miles		£1,000,000

Proposed Terms of Concessions

1. The Congo State to concede to the Company in perpetuity, free of all payments, taxes, and tolls, all the lands necessary for the railway, for its stations and depots, and also the river banks at and around any station, terminus, or crossing of the river or rivers.

2. In case of any land already occupied which may be required by the Company, the State to procure for, and engage to grant in perpetuity to the Company, free from all payments, taxes, and charges at each of the stations, and at any port or landing places as may be required for stations, depots or other purposes, at least 300 acres of land, in either one or more blocks as may be required by the Company.

3. Also to concede the whole of the land up to a mile in depth belonging to the State, and not now occupied, on the south bank of the river, from a mile below the falls at or opposite to Leopoldville up to the upper end of Stanley Pool.

4. Also at any trading place, station, or depot, established at any time either along the railway or on the River Congo, or on any of its affluents, either at, above, or below Stanley Pool, such quantity of land as may be required by the Company at any future time, the total not to be less than 10,000 acres, for ever free from all taxes, for each mile of railway completed and opened for traffic. The whole of the lands thus ceded to include all minerals, and the Company to be freed from liability for royalty, taxes or dues. This land to be in as many blocks of land, large or small, as the Company may require, and the Company to have the right to select for the above-named 10,000 acres per mile, 3,000 acres on either or both sides of the line of railway, and the remaining quantity at any place which they may select within the territories of the Congo State.

5. The State to reserve for its own requirements such land and places as may be requisite for the security and defence of the country.

6. The State to give the Company the first option of acquiring or undertaking any railway, canal, or road projected or to be made within

MEMORANDUM OF CONGO RAILWAY SYNDICATE

the said State, other than those now proposed by the Company, also of purchasing or occupying any additional land before ceding it to any other person or company.

7. The State to empower the Company and its agents to collect all the customs revenues at such ports or places as may be necessary, either at the mouth at Vivi or other port or place, at Stanley Falls, or other place or places above Stanley Pool, on condition that the Company shall recoup itself the expenses of collection, and retain for its own revenue fifty per cent. of all such net revenue, and pay the remaining fifty per cent. of net revenue to the Congo State.

8. The State to determine the rates of customs to be collected.

9. The State to guarantee that the Company shall be allowed to carry the whole of their goods and passenger traffic on their railway or steamers between Vivi or the terminus on the Lower Congo and Stanley Pool. The tariff to be agreed hereafter, but the State to guarantee that during ten years after the completion of the railway and river flotilla open for traffic to Stanley Pool, the minimum amount to be paid annually for such traffic either on any part of the railway or river opened for traffic above Vivi, shall not be less than £10,000 to commence on the day any part of the line is opened for traffic from Vivi.

10. The Congo State to engage to give to the Company and its Agents the utmost assistance and protection, and to protect the lives of those in the employ, and also the lands and property of the Company, and to give immediate redress of any neglect or maladministration affecting the Company, by the officials of the Congo State or any person over whom the State shall have jurisdiction. Also to exercise its best influence to secure the co-operation and assistance of the native chiefs of the lands and territories at the stations, and along the line of the railway, and along its water communications and traffic.

11. But if at any future time the authority and power of the Congo State shall not be adequately maintained, the Company or its agents shall have the right and power to exercise authority and jurisdiction in its own territories, and for securing its communications, and for the maintenance of order and peace in said territories, but always in the name of the Sovereign of the State.

12. His Majesty the King to be Hon. President.

13. For every £10,000 of Capital subscribed, one-twentieth of £500 of fully paid-up shares to be allotted to the King; such shares to be deferred shares, and not to rank for dividends until the ordinary shares receive 6 per cent., and thereafter to rank pro rata with ordinary shares but for the purpose of dividend so much only shall be treated as paid up on such shares as shall be equal to the average amount per share paid up on the other ordinary shares.

14. The King, or his heirs and successors, to have power of nominating one director to represent his or their interests.

It is proposed that this agreement should form the subject of an understanding between the Sovereign of the Independent Congo State and of H.B.M.'s Government, whereby the latter should have a right to intervene for the protection of the Company's rights in the event of any interference therewith by any other Power.

APPENDIX C

EXTRACTS FROM STANLEY TO JOHNSTON, LEOPOLDVILLE, 23 JULY 1883

... You have aroused me by your remarks on the Portuguese. ... I hope you will not be tempted by the self-interested hospitality of the Portuguese to give your vote that the Congo shall be given to them. If England but waits a little she will see sufficient cause to judge that she has as much right as any other nation which only seeks to exclude British trade from this outlet to Central African trade. Despite every prognostication to the contrary, this river will yet redeem the lost Continent. By itself it forms a sufficient prospect, but when you consider its magnificent tributaries which flow on each side of it giving access to civilisation to what appeared hopelessly impenetrable a few years ago, the reality of the general utility and benefit to these dark tribes and nations fills the sense with admiration. Every step I take increases my enthusiasm for my work and confirms my first impression. ... Such an ample basin ... with its unmeasured resources would you bestow on the Portuguese, who would but seal it to the silence of the coming centuries? Would you rob the natural birthright of the millions of Englishmen yet to issue, seeking homes similar to those which their forefathers built in the Americas and the Indies? For what? Is the robust Empire called the British on its wane that you will put a limit to its growth? Such an idea is simply self-murder, and a present confession of impotence. Follow the dictates of Nature. As with man as with nations that is the best guide. Statistics tell us that Englishmen are increasing fast, that ships are building more and more each year, that trade is extending, that the revenue is augmenting, that colonies are forming, that wealth incessantly flows from all lands to England, that education creates thousands daily of men fit to cope with life's best work viz. to thrive and multiply, and we are well aware that the present Government is not less able than its predecessors to direct, and maintain the force of the nation. Then why lock the gates of a promising field against yourselves? Let it be. Keep the gates open. Let him who seeks to enter do so without let or hindrance and leave it to Time. Time will teach the British Government where its interest lies. Meantime observe your treaties with the native chiefs of the Lower Congo. Protect them as you promised to the chiefs as far back as 1845 through your naval chiefs. If you deliver these people into the hands of the Portuguese, the past as well as the present teaches us what to expect. You deliver them—soul and body—to Hell and slavery. To avoid the imputation of being false and faithless, proclaim a Protectorate over the Congo, and rescue these poor people from their present impending fate.

You can write and that well. Set to work—the very fact that you are fresh from our work will give what you say an importance. Lend one hand to the present movement so that neither French nor Portuguese nor any other particular nation shall defraud England of her rights and privileges in Africa in broad daylight.

It was Livingstone, an Englishman, who discovered this river, it was Anglo-American money which explored it and made it known. It was international money, part of which is English, which began the task of making it useful to the world. They are English goods, products, manufactures, which enable us to move on and win the love of the Congo nations. Will you still vote that we shall sacrifice all this in honour of Diego Cam whose countrymen allowed the pearl of African rivers to lie idle for nearly four centuries? Bah! the very thought sickens me.[1]

[1] *Johnston MSS.*

INDEX

Aberdeen, Lord, 13-14; and admission of Portuguese Congo claim, 43
'Aberdeen Act' (1845), 38
Adamson, Daniel, 191
Admiralty, 1, 5, 15, 36, 132
Afonso I, 41
African Association, 2-5
African Exploration Fund, 63
African Steam Ship Co., 28, 30, 119, 179
Afrikaansche Handelsvereeniging, 30-32
Afrikaansche Venootschap, 32 n.
Albert, Lake, 222, 227
Albert Edward, Lake, 227-8
Alcock, Sir Rutherford, 58-61, 63
Alecto, steam sloop, 11-12
Ambriz, 13, 16, 20-23, 46, 133
Ambrizette, 23; treaty with, 39; Portuguese claims at, 91
Amelia, frigate, 7
Anderson, H. P., 121, 147, 152, 157 n., 162, 172-3, 180, 211, 226; reappraisal of Anglo-Portuguese negotiations, 110-12, 139, 142, 167; and Leopold, 143, 157-8, 171
Anglo-Belgian India Rubber Co., 209 n.
Anglo-German boundary agreement (1886), 214, 219
Anglo-Portuguese slave trade treaty, 43
Anglo-Portuguese Treaty (1884), 19, 31, 65, 68, 106 ff., 139 ff., 173, 186, 187 n., 228; opposition to, 106, 112 ff., 139, 142-3, 145 ff. 168, 183, 202.
Angola, 18, 19, 20, 37, 41, 96, 97, 179
Angra Pequena, 163-4
d'Antas, 93, 109, 110, 139, 162
Anti-Slavery Reporter, 124
Anti-Slavery Society: support of Leopold, 64; and Anglo-Portuguese Treaty, 123-4, 154; and *A.I.C.*, 178
Arrogant, H.M.S., 17
Arthington, Robert, 34-35
Aruwimi, River, 222
Association Internationale Africaine (*A.I.A.*), 65, 68, 70, 74-76 and n., 77-78, 168-9, 203; creation, 60; British National Committee and, 61-64, 72
Association Internationale du Congo (*A.I.C.*), 81, 83, 105, 106 and n., 117-18, 120-1, 123-4, 127-34, 137, 143, 145-6, 148-51, 155-61, 165, 167 ff., 186-8, 196, 202, 204 and n., 205, 222 n., 228
Aston, C. H., 118
d'Athoguia, Viscount, 46-47

Bagamoyo, 59, 73
Bahr el Gazal, 222 n.
Baker, Samuel, 58
Bakongo, 29
Banana Point, 28, 31, 192
Bandeira, Viscount de, 51
Bandinel, James, 38
Banks, Sir Joseph, 5
Banning, Emile, 129, 196 and n.
Baptist Missionary Society, 34-35, 113, 120-2; support of Leopold, 64; reports to F.O. on De Brazza, 100-1; against establishment of Portugal and France on Congo, 122-3; and *A.I.C.*, 35, 123, 178-9; and Anglo-Portuguese Treaty, 123, 125, 134, 154
Baptists, 154-5
Barclay, Thomas, 198, 200
Barnsley, 154
Barrow, Sir John, 1-2, 5
Bateke, 30
Bathurst, Lord, 1
Bayanzi, 30
Baynes, Rev. Alfred, 121-2, 179
Bazombo, 29-30
Belmore, Earl of, 152
Benin, Bight of, 11, 33
Bentley, Rev. W. Holman, 34, 155, 179, 184
Berlin Act, 188, 194, 198, 200, 223, 228
Berlin West Africa Conference, 19, 106, 170, 176-80, 183-5, 188-9, 194, 205
Biafra, Bight of, 20, 33
Bibbens & Blagden, 21
Birmingham, 154; Chamber of Commerce, 119 and n., 154-5; Fair Trade Union, 153
Bismarck, 163-4, 184, 213; and Anglo-Portuguese Treaty, 156, 162, 165; support of Leopold, 183
Black Point, 18
Board of Trade, 33 n., 44-45
Boma, 7-8, 22, 26-29, 35, 82, 128, 129 n., 148-51
Boma, Chief of, 7-8
Bond, F. W., 179

INDEX

Bonny, 27–28
Borchgrave, Comte de, 189, 219
Boulton & Watt, 5–6
Bourke, R., M.P., 130, 133, 136, 152, 172
Braamcamp, Senor, 91 n., 92–94, 96
Bradford, 134
Bradshaw, James, 175
Brazil: slave trade, 11, 22, 37–38; importance to Portugal, 41
Brazza, Lieutenant S. de, 55, 100–1, 115, 118, 126–7, 134, 138, 168, 184, 195
Bright, Jacob, M.P., 122, 125 n., 138, 172; supporter of Leopold, 64; and campaign against Anglo-Portuguese Treaty, 130–6, 151–2, 155; urges recognition of *A.I.C.*, 174, 179; director of Congo railway syndicate, 191
Bristol, 119, 134, 154; Chamber of Commerce, 119 and n., 154–5
British and African Steam Navigation Co., 28, 32–33, 118–19, 179
British India Steam Navigation Company, 67, 70, 210
Brussels Geographical Conference, 57–60, 70–71; actions of British delegation on return from, 60–64
Buganda, 224–5
Burdett-Coutts, Baroness, 58, 70, 202
Burton, Richard, 26 n.
Buxton, Sir T. Fowell, 125, 172; attends Brussels Geographical Conference, 58; doubts about British committee, 62; road building, 72; Anglo-Portuguese treaty, 123–4

Cabinda, 13, 26, 45; treaty with, 39; Portuguese claim to, 41 ff.
'Cacimbo', 160
Cam, Diego, 7, 40
Cameron, Commander, V.L., R.N., 34, 58, 82; declaration of protectorate over Congo basin, and British Government's reaction, 54–55
Campbell, Lieutenant, 3
Canning, George, 42
Cape to Cairo Scheme, 226–8
Capper, John, & Co., 29, 155
Capper, Robert, 155
Cardiff, 118, 154; Chamber of Commerce, 119
Challemel-Lacour, M., 165–6
Chamberlain, Joseph, 137, 160
Charles et Georges, 52–53
Charybdis, H.M.S., 21
China and China trade, 2–3

Chincoxo, 26
Clapton, 154
Clara B. Williams, 12
Clarendon, Lord, 45–48, 134
Cochin China, 2
Colonial Office, 54, 88–90
Comber, Rev. Thomas, 34
Comité d'études du haut Congo, 68, 74, 81, 114, 151, 169–70, 203, 208; foundation and aims, 66; capital and reconstitution, 79–81
Company of African Merchants, 26
Congo, sloop, 6–8
Congo District Defence Association, 179 ff.
Congo Free State, 19, 66, 185, 189, 192 ff., 216, 219, 220, 222–4, 226, 227
Congo, kingdom of the, 30, 34, 40–41
Congo, railway, 80, 170, 187–9, 191–201, 205–9, 218–19, 228
Congo, River Commission, 135, 140–7, 154
Congo & Central African Co. Ltd., 29, 179
Cook, Captain, 2
Cookson, E. H., 179
Corvo, Senor, 85–87, 90, 92
Cotton goods, 21, 31
Cotton, raw, 7, 20
Cranch, Mr., 5
Crudgington, Rev. Henry, 34
Cuba, 22–24
Currie, Donald, 66

Dahomey, 14, 104
Daily News, 155
Dar-es-Salaam, 72, 73, 75, 214
Derby, Lord, 54–55, 61, 85
Devaux, J., 68, 129-31, 136, 148–50
Dewsbury, 119, 154
Dilke, Sir Charles, 96, 99, 114, 116, 120, 122, 131, 136, 160
Dorothy, troopship, 6–8
Dundee, 154

East India Company, 3
Edmonstone, Commodore, R.N., 16, 25
Edward, Prince of Wales, 58, 61–62, 130
Edwards Bros, 179
Egerton of Tatton, Lord, 191
Egypt, 86, 137, 162-4, 166, 212–13, 220, 222 n., 225
Elgin, 154
Emin Pasha, 212 ff.
Emin Pasha Relief Expedition, 209, 214 ff., 225, 228; committee formed, 216; negotiations with Leopold, 219–24

INDEX

Equatoria, Equatorial Province, 212–14, 216, 218, 220, 222–3, 225
Euan-Smith, Consul-General, 221 and n., 224

Falkland Islands, 2
Farsley, 154
Fergusson, Sir James, M.P., 191, 216
Ferry, Jules, 158, 161
Ffestiniog Railway, 192
Firefly, H.M.S., 16
Fitzgerald, William R.S.V., 52
FitzMaurice, Lord E., 106 n., 136, 138, 149, 156, 157 n., 172, 181; defends Congo policy, 135; and River Commission, 143; wants stiff treaty, 145; advises change of tactics, 159–60
Forster, W. E., M.P., 125 n., 172; supporter of Leopold, 64; subscriber to Anti-Slavery Society, 125; and campaign against Anglo-Portuguese treaty, 130–3, 136, 152, 155–6
Fortnightly Review, 172
France, 116, 118, 120, 122, 126–8, 163, 168, 171–2, 176–7, 180 ff., 186, 205; treaty-making in western Africa, 39; 'emigration' scheme, 25, 51; Makoko Treaty, 101, 104, 117; Stanley Pool and Upper Congo, 106, 134–5; protectionism, 117; threat to British interests, 138; and Portugal, 144, 147; and Anglo-Portuguese treaty, 156, 161, 165–6; and Congo railway, 187–8
Freeman, 179
Frere, Sir Bartle, 58, 60, 61, 63

Gaboon, River, 21, 102
Gambia, 102
Germany, 85–86, 161–5, 183–5, 205; and E. Africa, 210 ff.
Gladstone, W. E., 129, 131, 135–6, 151
Glasgow, 118, 134, 154; Chamber of Commerce, 118, 153–4, 178
Goa, 86–88, 90, 96, 103
Goldsmid, Sir Frederick, 82–83, 114, 148–9, 155, 157 n., 172
Gordon, 'Chinese', 168, 212; Mackinnon and Leopold, 71, 76–78, 81
Goulburn, Henry, 1, 3
Grant, Colonel J. A., 58
Granville, Lord, 95, 99, 100, 104, 108–10, 112, 123–4, 128, 146, 148, 156–7, 159–60, 162, 172, 177; forbids opening of Congo negotiations, 98; Niger more important than Congo, 105; and Leopold, 106 n., 149–50, 158; and *A.I.C.*, 174, 183
Great Britain, policy towards the Congo region: treaty-making on Congo, 15–16; official representation in Congo region, 18–19; role of diplomacy in establishment of British paramountcy, 37 ff.; new Congo policy, 83, 101–9, 122, 131, 138; stiffens attitude towards Portugal, 109–12; Government bends before parliamentary opposition, 135–7; revised draft treaty and further negotiations, 139–50; signs treaty, 150; policy in regard to ratification, 157–62; abandons treaty, 162; bearing of Anglo-German relations, 163–4; bearing of Anglo-French relations, 166; hostility to Leopold, 171–2; and *A.I.C.*, 176, 182–5; summary of Congo policy, 228–9. *See also* Tuckey: Congo expedition, Royal Navy, Palmerston, Clarendon, Derby, Morier, Salisbury, Granville, Anderson, Fitzmaurice.
Great Britain, policy towards East Africa: establishment of *A.I.A.* in E. Africa, 78; negative policy in face of German irruption, 211; more positive policy under Salisbury, 211; and Emin Pasha, 212–13, 215; timing of E. African expansion, 218–19; and Von Plessen agreement, 225; relevance of decision to stay in Egypt, 225; encouragement of I.B.E.A., 225; negotiations with Germany, 225–6
Greenock, Chamber of Commerce, 119
Grenfell, Rev. George, 34
Greindl, Baron, 203
Groundnuts, 23
Groundnut oil, 26
Guinea, Gulf of, 1
Guinness, Mrs. Fanny, 122
Guinness, Henry, 35

Halifax, 154; Chamber of Commerce, 154–5
Hallamshire, 154; Company of Cutlers, 155
Hamburg, 33 n., 156, 164
Handsworth, 154
Hartington, Lord, 127, 137
Hartley, Consul, 18, 28
Hatton & Cookson, 16–17, 21, 23–25, 32, 51, 118–19, 179, 186–7
Havre, 33 n.
Heath, Admiral Sir Leopold, 58

INDEX

Heligoland Treaty, 226
Helm, Elijah, 177
Herslet, Sir Edward, 55, 139
Hewett, Commodore, R.N., 18, 53
Hickley, Commander, R.N., 51
Hill, Clement, 127
Holland, 31; and Anglo-Portuguese Treaty, 161, 165
Holmwood, Vice-Consul, 72–73, 76 n., 117, 210
Holt, John, 29, 118 179
Hopkins, Consul, 18
Hornby, Commodore, R.N., 26–27
Horsfall & Son, 10, 21 and n., 23–24
Houldsworth, W. H., M.P., 152, 179, 191
Howard, Mr., 47–48, 50
Howard de Walden, Lord, 44
Huddersfield, 154; Chamber of Commerce, 119 and n.
Hull, 154; Chamber of Commerce, 154–5
Hunt, Commander, R.N., 11, 13
Hutton, James F.: career, 65–66; and *Comité*, 66–67, 79–80; and opposition to Anglo-Portuguese Treaty, 114–27, 130, 132, 137, 148, 152 ff.; and Congo hopes, 167–8, 202, 228; and *A.I.C.* 168 ff., 173 ff.; relations with Leopold, 169–71, 207–9; weakening of his influence, 179 ff.; and early attempts at Congo economic development, 186–7; and Congo railway, 189 ff.; and East Africa, 187 ff., 210–12; Emin Pasha, and East African commercial project, 213 ff.

Imperial British East Africa Company, 66, 69, 217, 221 and n., 224, 227
International Arbitration and Peace Association, 178
Irebu, 30
Irvine, James, & Co., 29, 118–19
Isangila, 191
Italy, 85–86; and Anglo-Portuguese Treaty, 161, 165
Ivory, 21

Johnston, H. H., 68–69, 204 and n., 205, 211; informs F.O. of exclusive treaties of *A.I.C.*, 106, 157; and Cape to Cairo scheme, 226
Jones, A. L., 179
Jones, Commander, R.N., 27
Joubert, M., 187

Kavirondo, 221
Kemball, General Sir Arnold, 66, 82

Kennaway, Sir John, 58, 172
Kennedy, C. M., 156
Kerdyk & Pincoffs, 25. *See also Afrikaansche Handelsvereeniging* and *Afrikaansche Venootschap*
Kilimanjaro, Mt., 210–12, 214
Kimberley, Lord, 95, 98, 160
Kinnaird, Lord, 129
Kinsembo, 23, 26, 28, 51; treaty with, 39
Kirk, John, 62, 68–69, 73, 125, 213; explains objects of *A.I.A.* to Sultan, 63; early career and support of Leopold, 65; and 1877 concession scheme, 70; on 1879 concession, 72, 76 n.; and *A.I.C.*, 105–6, 169–70; and Anglo-Portuguese Treaty, 127 ff., 139 and n., 146–7; and Katanga Co., 209; and Anglo-German boundary agreement (1886), 214–15; nature and implications of Congo hopes, 228

Ladies' Negroes Friend Society, 154
Lado, 227
Lagos, 14
Lambermont, Baron, 194 n., 196 and n., 199 n., 201
Lambert, M., 68, 75, 130, 186, 208
Landana, 26, 28, 133
Lander, Richard, 9
Lavradio, Count, 45–47
Law, E. F., 114–15, 172
Law officers, 47
Lee, Austin, 136, 149, 177
Lee, Sir Joseph, 21, 152, 159–60, 180
Leopold II, King, 64, 70–71, 73–75, 81–83, 106 n., 114, 124–31, 143, 146–7, 165, 168 ff., 202, 209 n., 210, 218, 228; and British Congo missions, 35, 122–3; early extra-European projects, 57; Brussels Geographical Conference, 57–58; president of *A.I.A.*, 60; and *Comité*, 55, 66, 79–80; foothold in E. Africa and negotiations with Gordon, 76–79; and opposition to Anglo-Portuguese treaty, 114–15, 127, 130–1, 136–7, 148–50, 156–7 and n.; and recognition of *A.I.C.*, 146-7, 172, 174; negotiations with France and U.S., 158–9, 168; and Congo economic development, 185 ff.; fears of British predominance, 187 and n.; and Congo railway, 187 ff.; relations with Stanley, 202–7; and Emin relief expedition, 219 ff.; and Mackinnon treaty, 225, 227–8

Leopold II, King, British sympathizers and supporters, 56, 64, 83, 114, 138, 145, 148, 157, 167, 172, 182, 184-5, 187, 206, 209, 228
Leopoldville, 168, 192
N. G. Lewis, barque, 12
Liberal Party, 137
Likona, River, 185
Lister, T. V., 187; resists all Portuguese African encroachments, 54; explains new Congo Policy to C.O., 101; and new treaty draft, 139; awareness of public opinion, 143
Liverpool, 187; and Congo trade, 7, 20, 22; African Association on Congo trade figures, 32; alarm at occupation of Ambriz, 49; African Association makes representations to Foreign Office, 49-50; and French African trade, 117; and Anglo-Portuguese treaty, 118-19, 125, 131, 134, 153-4, 160; protests at Portuguese occupation of Landana, 148; African Association against Treaty, 154-5; and recognition of *A.I.C.*, 175 and n., 178; and Congo District Defence Association, 179; indifference to Stanley in 1878, 203
Livingstone, David, 65, 68, 82, 123
Livingstone Inland Mission, 35, 121-2
Loanda, 13, 29, 133
Loanda Commissioners, 18, 43
Loango, 21
London, and French African trade, 117; and Anglo-Portuguese treaty, 134, 154; and Congo railway, 191, 194-5
  Chamber of Commerce, and Anglo-Portuguese treaty, 119-20, 153; and *A.I.C.*, 174, 178
Long, Rev. James, 172; directs Anti-Slavery Society's campaign against Anglo-Portuguese treaty, 124-5, 130
Lourenço Marques, 86, 88; treaty, 87, 104, 109, 111
Lualabɔ, 34
Luculla, treaty with, 39
Lumley, Sir Saville, 130
Lyons, Lord, 101, 165-6
Lytton, Lord, 87

McFarlane, J., 29
Mackenzie, Robert, 67
Mackinnon, William, 76 n., 117-18, 124-5, 206-7; attends Brussels Geographical Conference, 58; and *A.I.A.*, 62, 75-78; East African projects in the seventies, 64, 70-73; career, character, African interest, 67-70; and Leopold, 70, 73-75, 169-71, 208-9, 225, 227-8; and *Comité*, 79-81; and *A.I.C.*, 81-82, 168-72, 177-8, 184; and opposition to Anglo-Portuguese treaty, 114, 126-32, 136-7, 146-53, 157 and n., 162, 167; Congo hopes and aims, 167-8, 202, 228; and abortive attempts at Congo economic development, 186-9; and Congo railway, 80, 189-201; *C.C.F.C.* and Katanga Co., 209; and East Africa (1879-85), 210-11; negotiations with Peters, 211-12; and Emin Pasha, 212 ff.; and E. African commercial projects, 213 ff.; and timing of British E. African expansion, 218-19; and Mackinnon treaty, 225-8; Germany and Cape to Cairo route, 226-8
Mackinnon & Mackenzie, 67
Mackinnon treaty, 209, 225-8
McLesh, Wylie & Co., 29
Mahdi, the, 212, 222
Majuba, 98, 137
Makoko treaty, 101, 117, 184
Malachite, 21, 23
Malet, E., 149, 183, 184
Malmesbury, Lord, considers Congo settlement, 52
Manchester, 152-3, 160, 175-6, 178, 181, 187, 191; and Congo trade, 22-23; estimates of Congo trade, 31-32; and French African trade, 117; and Anglo-Portuguese treaty, 118, 134, 154; protests at Portuguese occupation of Landana, 148; group of merchants support recognition of *A.I.C.*, 176; indifference to Stanley in 1878, 203
Manchester Chamber of Commerce, 66, 114, 123, 125, 132, 154, 156, 159, 173-4, 179, 181, 191; on extent of Congo trade, 23, 32; support of Leopold, 64; representations on Congo, 115-16, 119-21, 152; and *A.I.C.*, 175-8; doubts about Hutton, 180-1
Manchester Cotton Spinners' Association, 159
Manchester Examiner, 126, 136, 138, 155, 182
Manchester Guardian, 125-6, 136, 138, 155, 181-2, 203 n.
Manyanga, 29, 185, 191
Marmagao, 87
Massabé, 178, 184
Matadi, 35

Matson, Commander, R.N., 13
Maxwell, Captain, 7
Maxwell, Sir Herbert, M.P., 152
Mayo, Lord, *De Rebus Africanis*, 147
Medora Creek, 12
Mellalla, treaty with, 39
Mercer, Lieutenant, R.N., 20
Missionary Herald, 179
Molembo, 39, 41 ff.
Mombasa, 214, 216
Moncorvo, Baron, 43
Morier, Sir Robert, 51, 229; conception of new Anglo-Portuguese relationship and advocacy of informal imperialism, 85–86; friendship with Corvo, 87; Goa treaty, 87-88; Lourenço Marques treaty negotiations and signature, 88–90; and Congo question, 55, 84–85, 90 ff.; failure of his 'Grand Design', 98-99; complaints at his treatment, 99-100; influence on later negotiations, 104-5
Morley Chamber of Commerce, 153
Mossilongi, 17
Mount Temple, Lord, 133
Mountain Ash, 154
Mozambique, 85, 144
Mozambique tariff, 85, 108–10, 134, 140, 142, 144–5, 153, 159–60
Münster, Count, 161-2

Nantwich, 154
Napoleon I, 11
National African Co., 33
National Review, 155
Niari-Kwilu, River, 178
Niger, delta, 20, 105; city-states, 19, 22, 28
Niger, Expeditions, 3, 9, 14
Niger, River, 1–3, 9, 183, 229; British trade on, 20, 33
Nile, River, 1, 60, 211, 215, 218, 220, 222 and n., 224–5, 227
Nokki, 8, 115, 145, 148–51, 158, 177, 185
Nokki, Chief of, 8
North, Colonel, 209 n.
Nyangwe, 34, 60
Nyasa, Lake, 61, 72–73, 75, 141

Oldham Chamber of Commerce, 178

Padron, Point, 12–13
Pakenham, Sir Richard, 45–46
Pall Mall Gazette, 155
Palm oil, 23–24, 29
Palmerston, Lord, 13, 15; and Portuguese slave trade, 38–43; reinvigorates treaty-making policy, 38–39; and Portuguese territorial claims in Congo region, 43–49; conception of African policy, 48
Park, Mungo, 1–2, 3 n.
Parliament, 143, 153, 156, 160, 179; campaign against Anglo-Portuguese treaty, 130 ff., 151-2, 154; Commons, 38, 119, 147, 154, 157, 160; Congo debate in, 126, 132–9, 142, 145; Lords, 119, 133, 155
Pauncefote, Julian, 94, 98
Peddie, Captain, 3
Peile, Commander, R.N., 26
Pelly, General Sir Lewis, 82
Peters, Dr. Karl, 211-12, 225–6
Petre, Sir George, 165
Piracy in Congo region, 17–18, 24 ff., 53
Portugal, 66, 171, 180–6, 204, 228–9; early Congo exploration, 7; and slave trade, 11, 37–38, 134; Congo territorial claim, 19, 40 ff.; occupies Ambriz, 23–24; tariff reduction and Goa treaty, 86–88; Lourenço Marques treaty negotiations and signature, 88–90; and Congo negotiations with Britain, 93 ff., 139–62 *passim;* seeks agreement with France, 144, 147; occupation of Landana, 147-8; and Congo railway, 188
Protestant Dissenters, 154
Punta da Lenha, 12, 17, 24–26, 28, 51, 145
Purchas, Samuel, 1

Rabaud, M., 75
Rattray, Messrs., 29
Rawlinson, Sir Henry, 58, 61
Redhill, 154
Reed, Sir J., M.P., 118
Rennie, George, 5
Rennie, John, 5
Rhodes, Cecil J., 226
Rhos, 154
Ribeiro, Count Casal, 88, 92
Richards, R. C., 181
Rosebery, Lord, 130
Rothschild, Baron Ferdinand de, 202
Rovuma, River, 214
Royal Belgian Elephant Expedition, 73
Royal Geographical Society, 1, 58, 61, 63–64, 70
Royal Navy, 229; suppression of slave trade in Congo region, 10–15; encouragement of legitimate trade and action against piracy, 16–18, 27–28; active north of Line, 20; changing importance of naval

INDEX 259

Royal Navy—*Cont.*
 support of merchants, 24–27;
 naval squadron reduced, 27; summary of role in promoting British influence, 35–36. *See also* Tuckey: Congo expedition
Royal Niger Company, 66
Rubber, 26
Russell, Lord John, 14, 16

Saint Antonio, treaty with, 39
St. Helena, 11, 13
San Salvador, 30, 34, 40, 113, 122
San Thomé, 41, 133
Salisbury, Lord, 214; opinion of Mackinnon, 69, 226; and Congo, 91, 93–95; and East Africa and Equatoria, 211, 213, 225–6
Sanford, General H. S., 68, 151, 161 n., 165, 168, 170, 188–9, 199, 201, 208
Second British Empire, 2
Semliki, River, 227
Senegal, 20
Seppings, Mr., 6
Serpa, Senor, 108–9, 112, 114, 121, 142–3
Shark's Point, 12, 17, 25
Sheffield, 154; Chamber of Commerce, 154–5
Shiré, River, 141, 144–5
Sierra Leone, 4
Slagg, J., M.P., 132
Slave trade, 4, 7–11, 20, 22–24, 28, 37, 41, 51, 85, 90–91, 97, 103, 108–11, 113, 133; (Arab), 59, 62, 77
Smith, Professor, 5
Smith, Dr. Towers, 199
Solvyns, Baron, 120, 149, 156
Spain: slave trade, 11, 37–38; Anglo-Portuguese treaty, 161, 165
Stafford House, 66, 88, 90, 96
Stanley, H. M., 29, 34–35, 64–65, 68, 74, 79, 178, 181, 187 n., 188, 214; follows course of Congo to sea, 55; and *Comité*, 66; and Mackinnon, 72, 76 n., 81, 217 and n.; character and achievement, 82–83; help to B.M.S., 123; recognition and boundaries of *A.I.C.*, 168, 171, 174–7, 184; and Congo commercial prospects, 174–6; and Congo railway, 189 ff.; and Leopold, 196–7, 202–7; Congo hopes, 82, 202–7, 228; and Emin Relief Expedition, 213 and n., 216 ff.; F.O. and Mackinnon treaty, 227
Stanley Falls, 83, 147, 220, 222–3
Stanley Pool, 29–30, 34–35, 100–1, 104, 106, 123, 127, 147, 166, 178, 184, 189, 190–3, 205

Stead, W. T., 155
Steinthal, H. M., 191
Strauch, General, 68, 74, 76–77, 80–82, 123, 125, 127, 146–7, 157, 171–2, 174, 186–7, 190, 195–6, 204 n., 208
Stuart & Douglas, 29, 179
Sunderland Chamber of Commerce, 119
Sutherland, Duke of, 66, 90, 202
Sverige, 17
Swansea Chamber of Commerce, 153

Tana, River, 214
Tanga, 210
Tanganyika, Lake, 59–61, 65, 227–8
Taylor, Laughland & Co., 26, 179
Tenterden, Lord, 61, 93–94
Terra Australis Incognita, 2
Thais, frigate, 7
Thring, Sir Henry, 61–62
Thys, Captain, 199, 201–2
Times, The, 126, 136, 138, 147, 155, 160, 171–3, 182, 198–9, 203 n.
Tipoo-Tib, 220, 222–3
Tobin & Son, 16–17, 20, 21 n., 23–24
Trade, Congo, 118, 120 n., 140, 185; organization, 22, 29–30; importance, 52; growth, 55; threatened, 116; allegedly paralysed, 151–2; glowing prospects, 175
Trade, American, 21, 22
Trade, British, 117, 121, 126–7, 132, 135, 138, 204–5, 229; advancement of in late 18th and early 19th centuries, 2–4, 8; development of in Congo region, 19 ff.; element of monopoly in, 52 and n.; threatened by France, 101; nature of, 113; need of protection, 116; and French African trade, 117; value of, 134, 160; and Mozambique tariff, 153
Trade goods, 21–22, 26, 31
Transvaal, 57, 88, 90, 137
Triple alliance, 163
Tritton, Joseph, 120, 154
Tuckey, Captain James K.: Congo expedition, 3–9, 10, 20, 229
Tudor, Mr., 5
Tudor, Commander, R.N., 16
Tungwa, 30
Twiss, Sir Travers, 197, 200

Uganda, 213, 221 and n., 225–6
Ujiji, 59–60
United States, 116, 120 n., 158 n., 165, 168, 170, 183, 204 n., 205; 'Emigration' scheme, 51; recognizes *A.I.C.* flag, 159–61; and Anglo-Portuguese Treaty, 165

Unyoro, 221 and n.
Upoto, 30

Vacca, Manuel, 17, 27–28
Van Eetvelde, M., 190, 194 n., 199
Vanga, 214
Verney, Sir Harry, 58, 172
Victoria, Lake, 60, 71, 214–16, 221, 223–4, 227
Victoria, Queen, 130, 161 n.
Vivi, 35, 127–8, 145–7, 189–93
Vivian, Sir H. C., 199
Von Plessen agreement, 225–7

Waddington, M., 156
Waller, Gerald, 73
Waller, Rev. H., 68, 70–71, 148 n.
Ward, Mr., 46
Warrington Chamber of Commerce, 119
Washington, Treaty of (1862), 15, 26
Whitley, E., M.P., 131, 135

Whydah, 104, 108, 141, 144
Wilmot, Commodore, R.N., 15, 17–18, 26, 45
Windward, brigantine, 12
Winton, Colonel Francis de, 83
Wodehouse, E. R., M.P., 134–5
Wolverhampton Chamber of Commerce, 153
Worms, Baron Henry de, M.P., 130, 133
Wrangler, H.M.S., 17
Wylde, W. H., 27, 110; and Portuguese Congo claim, 51–53, 91

Yellala Falls, 8

Zambesi, River, 60, 65, 85, 89, 104, 141–2
Zanzibar, 4, 59, 62, 70, 72, 79, 86, 147, 210 ff.; Sultan of, 63, 65, 70–72, 76–78, 210, 213–14, 217

CPSIA information can be obtained at www.ICGtesting.com
Printed in the USA
LVOW011441011211

257271LV00007B/4/P

9 780313 233661